THE ACADIANS

THE ACADIANS

A PEOPLE'S STORY OF EXILE AND TRIUMPH

DEAN JOBB

John Wiley & Sons Canada, Ltd.

Library and Archives Canada Cataloguing in Publication

Jobb, Dean, 1958-
   The Acadians : a people's story of exile and triumph / Dean Jobb.

Includes bibliographical references and index.
ISBN-13 978-0-470-83610-5
ISBN-10 0-470-83610-5

1. Acadians—Expulsion, 1755.   2. Acadians—History.
3. Cajuns—History.   I. Title.

FC2041.J62 2005   971.01'87   C2005-901757-0

Production Credits:
Cover design: Ian Koo
Interior text design: Adrian So R.G.D.
Printer: Tri-Graphic Printing Ltd.

John Wiley & Sons Canada, Ltd.
6045 Freemont Blvd.
Mississauga, Ontario
L5R 4J3

Printed in Canada
10 9 8 7 6 5 4 3 2 1

~ To Kerry, for making me believe anything is possible ~

CONTENTS

INTRODUCTION

This is the story of one of the great crimes of history, a brutal act of genocide committed two and a half centuries ago. More than 10,000 men, women, and children were removed from their homeland at gunpoint and sent into exile. They were stripped of the farms that had nurtured and sustained their families for four generations. Their homes and most of their possessions were destroyed. Five thousand of these unfortunate people, maybe more, died of disease and deprivation or perished in shipwrecks. The destitute survivors were scattered along the East Coast of North America or wound up in the port cities of England and France; some sought refuge in the jungles of South America or as far away as the windswept barrens of the Falkland Islands. Most were sent to live among people who spoke a different language, detested their religion, and considered them an enemy. Family and friends were separated, never to be reunited. Children were taken from their parents to work as servants or apprentices. An entire generation knew nothing but the squalor of refugee camps, the humiliation of enslavement, or the upheaval of a nomadic life.

This crime was committed in Canada, a country built on the principles of democracy and the rule of law. The perpetrators were agents of a British government with a far longer tradition of upholding these ideals. The scene of the crime was the northeastern corner of North America, now the Canadian provinces of Nova Scotia, New Brunswick, and Prince Edward Island. In 1755, when the deportations began, this area was known as Acadie and had been since 1604, when France founded the first European colony north of Florida. The victims of this horrible crime were the descendants of these early French settlers, a people that had prospered in the New World for more than a century.

They established a string of coastal settlements and built dikes to reclaim fertile marshland for their farms. Their population exploded, from a few hundred in the mid-1600s to more than 15,000 a century later. The frontier molded them into a new, distinct people. Their homeland was Acadie and they called themselves Acadians. They were proud, stubborn, self-reliant, and bound together by blood and marriage. They were progressive, electing deputies to represent their communities and asserting a sense of independence that exasperated a succession of governors. They asked only to keep their Catholic faith and to be allowed to remain neutral in time of war, but geography and history conspired to trap the Acadians in the crossfire as France and Britain fought for supremacy over North America.

Time and again Acadie changed hands, finally falling under British rule for good in 1710. In 1755, with Europe's superpowers on the verge of fighting yet another war, Acting Governor Charles Lawrence demanded that the Acadians swear allegiance to the British. He would accept nothing less than complete loyalty. When the Acadians refused to promise to fight their old masters to defend their new ones, Lawrence had the pretext he needed to banish them from their homeland.

And so the entire population of Acadie was convicted without trial and condemned to exile. It was, to modern eyes, clearly an act of genocide and ethnic cleansing. A United Nations convention adopted in 1948, after the horrors of the Holocaust defines genocide as an act designed to destroy a national, ethnic, religious, or racial group. The definition encompasses mass murder, of course, but also acts of serious physical or mental abuse, the forcible removal of children from their families, and deliberately subjecting a group to "conditions of life calculated to bring about its physical destruction in whole or in part." Lawrence's cruel and cavalier treatment of the Acadians falls within this broad definition; he set the wheels in motion, organized every facet of the expulsion in minute detail, and displayed a callous disregard for whether his victims lived or died. Were he to face a modern-day war crimes trial, the only mitigating factor in his defence would be that he stopped short of ordering Acadians to be lined up and shot.

The deportation was a human catastrophe on a scale unprecedented in Canada and perhaps the darkest chapter in the nation's history. It sends a warning to our own troubled times about the depths of human hatred, the vulnerability of minorities, and the scourge of intolerance and prejudice. In September 1755, as the Acadians were being rounded up, a news item appeared in the *Pennsylvania Gazette* touting the deportation as "a great and noble scheme" to protect British interests in North America. It was neither. The deportation was a deliberate attempt to destroy a people and wipe out a distinct culture. It failed. The Acadians were too tough and too resilient. Their ordeal became the catalyst for a cultural revival and a resurgence of national pride. Today, there are an estimated 3 million Acadian descendants worldwide. Acadians who escaped deportation and those who returned established new communities in Atlantic Canada, where they now number close to 300,000. Thousands of deportees made their way to Louisiana, where "Acadian" was transmuted to "Cajun" and the new surroundings forged a distinct culture although true to its northern roots. More than a half-million Americans, most of them in Louisiana and eastern Texas, are descendants of these refugees.

This year, 2005, marks the 250th anniversary of Lawrence's order to deport the Acadians. It is as good a time as any to take stock, to examine what we know about this pivotal event in the development of North America and what the Acadians can teach us about survival and belonging. The Acadians and the deportation have been the subject of hundreds of books and articles; despite this avalanche of words, misconceptions abound. The deportation was not a single event. The largest single expulsion occurred in 1755, but the war on the Acadians continued for eight years as escapees and refugees were hunted down and sent into exile. Not a single Acadian was deported to Louisiana. Lawrence deliberately scattered them among other British colonies to ensure they would not strengthen the enemy. Louisiana was a French colony and most of the Acadians who sought refuge there did not arrive until 1785, by way of France. There is also a lingering impression that the Acadians brought the deportation on themselves. Their defiance and obstinacy, so the thinking goes, painted the British into a corner and left them no choice but to rid themselves of an unruly band of potential fifth columnists in a time of war; had the Acadians simply faced facts and done as they were told, they would have been spared all this misery and enjoyed the benefits of enlightened British rule. But this version of events is at odds with historical evidence and common sense. It ignores the ruthlessness of Charles Lawrence, a bully and a tyrant and a master of the art of manipulating people and events. It glosses over the paranoia, desperation and hatred of the French that motivated Lawrence and the other British commanders and officials. behind the decision to deport. And it ignores the Acadians' sense of themselves as a distinct, self-made people, the proud citizens of the nation of Acadie. It is my hope that this book will help put to rest, once and for all, any notion that the deportation was inevitable, or that the Acadians deserved their fate.

As I write this, the setting sun is bathing the ice-bound Bay of Fundy and the snowy cliffs of Cape Blomidon in a warm, golden glow. From my office window overlooking the town of Wolfville, I can pick out the dikes that snake along the edge of the Minas Basin. They are successors to dikes the Acadians built to hold back the sea three centuries ago, when this idyllic scene was the hub of Acadie. The Acadians were torn from this place, but deportation and exile did not destroy the Acadians as a people. They survived against incredible odds. They preserved a vibrant culture, a zest for life, and a deep respect for their heritage. This is a story of the triumph of the human spirit in the face of cruelty and unimaginable hardship. This is the story of the Acadians.

Many people helped make this book a reality, and I am grateful to everyone who took the time to guide me through the twists and turns of Acadian history. Alan Melanson, an interpreter at Fort Anne National Historic Site and president of the Historical Society of Annapolis Royal, showed me around the picture-perfect town he has done so much to preserve. His brother, Wayne Melanson, introduced me to the Port-Royal Habitation and its significance to Acadian history. Sara Beanlands and her mother, Hope, braved a rainy morning in order to show me around the Shaw farm near Windsor,

Nova Scotia, the former site of Village Thibodeau. Thanks, too, to Donna Doucet, executive director of the Société Promotion Grand-Pré, and her staff for their assistance during my numerous visits to the Grand-Pré National Historic Site.

My review of the historical debate over the deportation was completed as part of a graduate research course in the Atlantic Canada Studies program at Saint Mary's University in Halifax. Dr. John Reid, an authority on Acadie before the deportation, oversaw this research and our discussions shaped some of my views about the causes of the expulsion. Jonathan Fowler, who teaches history and archeology at Saint Mary's, introduced me to the history of Grand-Pré and other Acadian archeological sites; I wish him well in his quest to unearth more traces of Acadie and its people. I would also like to thank Rob Ferguson of Parks Canada and Flannery Surette, Mike Gibson, and other members of Fowler's field team for showing me around their excavations at Grand-Pré. Dr. Naomi Griffiths, the leading authority on all aspects of Acadian history, set aside time during a visit to Halifax to share her insights into the expulsion and its impact. Special thanks to Dr. Bill Godfrey, an historian at New Brunswick's Mount Allison University and my thesis adviser when I was a student there. More than twenty-five years ago he assigned me to write a paper on the Acadians in exile that neither of us could have imagined would sow the seeds for this book.

Isabelle Dussault, communications assistant for Congrès mondial acadien 2004, arranged for a media pass to *congrès* events on short notice. Janette Gallant of Parks Canada, a descendant of one of Prince Edward Island's first Acadian settlers, Michel Haché-Gallant, took me on a guided tour of the Port-la-Joye-Fort Amherst National Historic Site. I would also like to thank Theresa Bunbury and Kimberlee Trainor of Parks Canada, who helped to arrange visits, and interpreters at the Acadian Museum of Prince Edward Island in Miscouche, La Maison Doucet in Rustico, P.E.I., and at Fort Anne and the Port-Royal Habitation. Thanks to Jocelyne Marchand, proprietor of the antique and used book store Marchandise in Grand-Pré, for devoting the better part of an afternoon to a discussion of Acadian history. I am also indebted to Peggy Eldershaw of Morell for her hospitality during my research trip to P.E.I.

Thanks are also due to the Acadian descendants who journeyed to Nova Scotia from Louisiana and other parts of the United States for the *congrès* and took time to speak to me—Jeanette and Glynn Romero, Patricia and Mark Sporl, Loubert Trahan, Don Thibodeaux, Dick Thibodeau, Page Thibodeaux, and Dale Broussard. Ron Thibodeaux, chief of the St. Tammany bureau of the New Orleans *Times-Picayune*, furnished copies of his articles on the future of Cajun culture and his coverage of the *congrès*. Genealogist Shirley Thibodeaux LeBlanc of Lafayette, who has traced the thousands of descendants of Pierre Thibodeau, introduced me to her family's history. Author and genealogist William Gerrior's presentation during the *congrès*, discussing some of his family's deportation experiences, was also helpful.

In Louisiana, curator Brenda Comeaux Trahan introduced me to the Acadian Memorial, and guide James Akers showed me around and shared his insider's stories about St. Martinville's history. Dr. Carl Brasseaux, director of the Center for Louisiana Studies at the University of Louisiana Lafayette, set aside his many duties for a long discussion of the transformation of Louisiana's Acadian refugees into today's Cajuns. Shane Bernard, historian and archivist for the McIlhenny Company in Avery Island, helped me to understand the prospects for the survival of Cajun culture. Jim Bradshaw, regional editor of the Lafayette *Daily Advertiser*, offered his stories and insights as well as copies of his columns on Acadian and Cajun history. Thanks as well to Warren Perrin, the Lafayette lawyer who took on the queen and won recognition of the wrongs done to the Acadians, for making time in his busy schedule for interviews during his visit to Grand-Pré and my visit to the Acadian Museum in Erath.

Colleagues at the University of King's College School of Journalism also deserve thanks. I am indebted to the director, Kim Kierans, for her support and her confidence in my work as a writer and teacher. Author and journalist Stephen Kimber allowed me to audit one of his courses to learn more about the art of bringing people and events to life on the page. Elaine MacInnis of the King's College library arranged for wider borrowing privileges as I combed libraries for books and articles.

Literary agent Linda McKnight of Westwood Creative Artists guided me through the complexities of book contracts, and I am grateful for her advice and support. Editor Don Loney of John Wiley & Sons Canada was convinced the Acadian story deserved to be retold with drama and insight. I thank him for his guidance and encouragement, and for giving me the chance to tackle this project.

My sons, Matthew, Ben, and Evan, help keep me grounded and I appreciated their company on some of my research trips. Most of all I want to thank my wife, Kerry Oliver, for the advice and encouragement she has provided every step of the way.

Wolfville, Nova Scotia, January 2005

1 Paradise Lost

In the Acadian land, on the shores of the Basin of Minas,
Distant, secluded, still, the little village of Grand-Pré
Lay in the fruitful valley. Vast meadows stretched to the eastward,
Giving the village its name, and pasture to flocks without number.

—Henry Wadsworth Longfellow, *Evangeline: A Tale of Acadie*

The plan was bold, perhaps even foolhardy. It was certainly fraught with risk, but in Charles Belliveau's mind, the choice was clear. Mutiny or exile. Hope or despair. They must make a dash for freedom or remain penned like animals, awaiting an uncertain fate on an unknown shore.

They had been cooped up in the hold of the *Pembroke* for days, huddled together in their floating prison to ward off the winter cold. There was no fresh air to relieve the stench and only foul-tasting water to wash down their meager ration of bread and meat. If Belliveau had done a head count, he would have come up with the figure 232—37 women, 32 other men, 162 sons and daughters, many of them children. Nearly all were related by blood or marriage. They were French-speaking Acadians, inhabitants of a corner of North America their people had called Acadie—and had called home—for more than a century.

Their British rulers called it Nova Scotia, and for the past forty-five years they had called the shots. In the fall of 1755 soldiers fanned out over the countryside, rounding up thousands of people as hundreds more fled into the woods. Columns of smoke and flame rose skyward as homes and barns were put to the torch. Cattle were slaughtered or confiscated. The season's precious harvest of grain and hay was burned. Possessions the Acadians could not carry with them were looted or went up in flames. Young and old, healthy and infirm, they were herded onto the ships that would carry them into exile. Their only offense was a stubborn refusal to promise to fight for the king of Britain. Their only crime had been to insist on the right to live in peace as England and France rushed headlong into another war.

The *Pembroke* was a small square-rigger, its capacity a modest 139 tons. It had been dispatched, along with six other ships, to the Annapolis River to pick up a human cargo—1,664 people uprooted from villages that had lined the river for generations. On December 8, with the ships loaded and the winter chill setting in, the convoy slipped into the Bay of Fundy and turned south. A British warship, the *Baltimore*, served as escort. One vessel was bound for Boston, two for Connecticut, and another for New York. The *Pembroke* and the rest were to continue to South Carolina. Charles Belliveau was fifty-eight, a widower who had raised ten children. As he scanned those taking their places in the hold, Belliveau saw plenty of familiar faces: his eighty-year-old uncle, Charles Melanson; his aunt Marguerite, a widow in her sixties who was accompanied by at least two of her seven children; another uncle, seventy-year-old Ambroise Melanson, and his wife, Marguerite. There were Grangers, Dugas, and Boudreaus as well.

Belliveau had no love for their British captors. His father, Jean, had helped the French garrison defend Acadie's capital, Port-Royal, against an attack in 1707. The British were repulsed, but his father was mortally wounded in a skirmish. Jean Belliveau was in his early thirties and left a wife and four children under the age of fourteen. Charles was only ten. The family's home was burned in the raid, compounding their misery. Three years later, in 1710, the British finally captured Port-Royal and renamed it Annapolis Royal. The colony had been under British rule ever since. Belliveau inherited his father's farm, but became best known in the area as a sailor and shipwright. Those skills had been pressed into service barely two weeks ago when the *Pembroke* limped into port after taking a battering in a storm. The main mast had snapped and Belliveau was hired to build a replacement. When the work was finished, though, the captain refused to pay. Belliveau calmly picked up his ax and took aim at the new mast, and the captain coughed up the money. By a cruel twist of fate, Belliveau found himself imprisoned in the stinking hold of the very ship he had made seaworthy.

There was a chance he could still have the last laugh. When the remnants of the convoy reached the waters off New York, the *Baltimore* veered off to tackle its next assignment. Before sailing away, the warship's captain hailed the master of the *Pembroke* and reminded him to be on his guard—he was carrying a number of able-bodied men who could handle a ship. The *Pembroke's* eight-man crew, well aware of the risk, had been taking precautions to prevent an uprising. Each deportee had been checked for guns and knives before boarding. And despite the poor ventilation in the *Pembroke's* hold, only six Acadians were allowed on deck at a time for a precious thirty minutes of fresh air.

With the escort gone and the convoy scattered, Belliveau knew this was his chance. He recruited the five strongest men he could find. When the hatch was opened to make the exchange, Belliveau and his group stormed onto the deck. With fists as their only weapons, they quickly overpowered the crew. Belliveau took the wheel and made a sharp turn back the way they had come. The captain, now a prisoner, projected that the mast would snap under the strain. "You lie," Belliveau shot back, relishing this sudden reversal of fortune. "I made this mast and I know it will not break." The crew was put ashore somewhere along the coast of Maine, roughed up but otherwise unharmed.

Acadians call it *le grand dérangement*, the great upheaval. Today, some refer to it as an act of attempted genocide, the Acadians' holocaust. The *Pembroke* was among dozens of ships that sailed from Acadie in 1755, bound for ports along the eastern seaboard, from Massachusetts to Georgia. More than 6,000 men, women, and children were sent into exile during 1755. Conditions on the ships were appalling—the cramped quarters, poor ventilation, and bad food and water on the *Pembroke* were typical. Disease took its toll: half of the 417 people crowded aboard one ship died before reaching South Carolina. Other deportees arrived sick or destitute, at the whim of local authorities who had no warning of their arrival. Proud, self-sufficient farmers were thrust into misery and poverty. Families were torn apart as children were taken from their parents to become servants or apprentices. More deportations, deaths, and hardships lay ahead as Britain and France fought for supremacy in North America. Amid this tide of human suffering, the passengers on the *Pembroke* were among the few who found the will and the leadership to fight back.

The lives of 231 people were in Belliveau's hands as he took the wheel. What now? More shiploads of deportees were likely headed their way as the British pursued their ruthless campaign against the Acadians. A warship or convoy might spot them at any time. And where were they headed? Was there any safe haven in this world gone mad, where people could be stripped of everything they held dear—their homes, their livelihoods, even their loved ones—without provocation or warning? Belliveau hugged the coast and steered a course toward the mouth of the Saint John River, just across the Bay of Fundy from Annapolis Royal. With any luck, the area was still in French hands. With any luck, they would find help there.

Acadie, pronounced *ack-ah-dee*. There are two theories about the origin of the name. The more romantic version credits Italian explorer Giovanni da Verrazzano, who cruised the Atlantic coast of North America in the 1520s and gave the name *Archadia* to an area that became Delaware. He must have regarded this untouched land as a paradise; Arcadia is a mountainous area of southern Greece and, in Greek myth, the home of the god Pan, a rural Eden where shepherds passed their days making music. The name stuck, but drifted northward. Maps drawn in the latter half of the 1500s indicate a region known as *Larcadie* or *Arcadie* closer to what is now Quebec. A map published in 1586 clearly applied the name *Arcadie* to the Nova Scotia peninsula. Later maps, however, labeled the region as *La Cadie*, *Acadie* or *La Cadye*, which may have been derived from *cadie*, a word the Indigenous people, the Mi'kmaq, used for place or piece of land. Shubenacadie, a farming area in central Nova Scotia, for instance, roughly translates from Mi'kmaq as "the place where potatoes grow." The French explorer Samuel de Champlain used the word *Arcadie* in a book published in 1603, but the commission for the first French settlement in North America, issued the same year, used the word *La Cadie*. In any event, it became Acadie, or Acadia, in English. Since the words *arcadia* and *cadie* are so similar, and both theories are plausible, Verrazzano may have chosen a name that, by coincidence, was almost identical to one the natives were already using to describe their homeland.

It was—and remains—a land of stunning beauty and stark contrasts, worthy of being christened a new Arcadia. The wave-battered granite rocks along the southern coast, best captured in the iconic images of the lighthouse at Peggy's Cove, are only 50 miles as the crow flies from the muddy tidal flats of the Bay of Fundy. A four-hour drive by car whisks a traveler from the prairie-like marshes along the New Brunswick border to Cape Breton's mountainous Cabot Trail, where sheer cliffs drop hundreds of feet into the sea. Tethered to the rest of North America by a narrow strip of land, the Isthmus of Chignecto, Nova Scotia is almost an island, and the ever-present ocean has shaped its climate, its history, and its people. The province juts into the Atlantic Ocean and lies parallel to the Gulf Stream, a relentless tropical current that fights a see-saw battle with icy winds and waters moving south from the Arctic. Depending on which force of nature has the upper hand, much of Nova Scotia can have a mild, rainy winter or endure a battering of blizzards and heavy snow. Summers can be bathed in sunshine or a roller coaster ride of unsettled weather and thick blankets of coastal fog. Nova Scotia is also an inviting target for the remnants of the fall lineup of hurricanes and tropical storms, and sometimes takes a direct hit. Despite the unpredictable weather, Nova Scotia has attracted visitors for centuries. The Vikings likely took a look around 1,000 years ago after establishing their Newfoundland outpost. Five centuries later John Cabot, Jacques Cartier, and other explorers dropped by. By the 1500s Basque, French, and English fishermen were spending their summers on the cod-rich grounds and European merchants were trading for furs with the Aboriginal inhabitants.

Unlike the Arcadia of myth, Acadie was not a peaceful land. From the first permanent European settlement in 1604 to the mid-1700s, this was hotly contested territory, a no-man's land between rival superpowers. The boundaries of Acadie shifted at the whim of kings who granted lands they had never seen and diplomats who swapped territory as one war ended and plans were laid for a new one. At its greatest extent, Acadie included the present-day Canadian provinces of Nova Scotia and New Brunswick, as well as chunks of Quebec's

Gaspé Peninsula and northeastern Maine. The real Acadie, the area French pioneers settled after 1630, was more compact, focused on the shores of the Bay of Fundy. No more than 50 miles across, the bay separates the western end of Nova Scotia from the New Brunswick mainland. It is a huge funnel, open at the southwestern end and stretching more than 100 miles to the northeast before splitting into a network of basins and river valleys. Seawater forced into the confines of this narrow waterway produces the highest tides recorded anywhere on the planet—a rise and fall of more than 50 feet in some areas. Within the space of a few hours, a boat stranded on an expanse of mud will be found bobbing in chocolate-colored water; a few hours later, the boat will again be high and dry as the sea recedes and regroups for another onslaught.

This land where earth and sea collide became central to the Acadian identity. The land created the Acadians, forging a distinct society and culture over the course of four generations as they developed a network of tightly knit communities along the Fundy shore. And they created the land, building dikes to tame the surging tides and reclaim the rich marshland for their farms. The name of the most famous Acadian community, Grand-Pré, translates as "great meadow" and draws its name from an expanse of human-made prairie wrested from the ocean. The Acadians prospered and flourished and their numbers exploded, from a few hundred in 1650 to at least 15,000 a century later. Yet while Acadians regarded Acadie as their homeland, France and England saw it as a strategic prize in an endless round of colonial wars. The English made a habit of raiding or capturing Acadie's capital, Port-Royal, and treaty negotiators promptly returned it to France. In 1713 most of Acadie—what is now the Nova Scotia mainland—was finally ceded to Britain and the Acadians became a French-speaking majority under British rule, but they were still caught in the middle. The French pressured them to rise up and fight for France. Their new masters demanded allegiance to Britain and a promise to fight the enemies of the British king. The Acadians, for their part, asserted the right to remain neutral. By 1755 Britain and France were on the brink of a new war and the Acadians, like so many civilian populations in time of conflict, found themselves in the wrong place at the wrong time.

In June 1755 the British attacked a French stronghold at Beauséjour, in disputed territory that now marks the Nova Scotia–New Brunswick border. When the fort fell after a brief siege, Nova Scotia's acting governor, Lieutenant-Colonel Charles Lawrence, seized the chance to end what he saw as a French menace within his borders. Soldiers and ships amassed for war were re-deployed in a campaign to round up and expel civilians. Villages were cleared and burned in a scorched-earth campaign. But the events of 1755 were only the beginning of the suffering. Some families escaped to the woods or sought refuge in nearby French territories, only to be captured and deported in a reign of terror that continued until 1763. Those who escaped faced starvation in the wilderness or harrowing journeys on foot to safer ground in Quebec. Almost 1,000 refugees wound up in England, where they were held as prison-ers of war for seven years. Exiles were scattered as far afield as the Caribbean, Guiana, and the Falkland Islands. At least 700 Acadians perished when ships carrying them to France were lost at sea. Refugees in the American colonies and most of those repatriated to France gathered in southern Louisiana. Southern drawls soon shortened Acadian to 'Cadien and, over time, to Cajun, as exiles and their descendants adapted to life in a steamy climate half a conti-nent away from their lost homeland.

More than 10,000 people were deported between 1755 and 1763. At least half died in exile. Acadie was destroyed, but the Acadian people survived. Separation, loss, and distance strained the strong ties of family and community, but could not break them. The ordeal of exile sowed the seeds of a revived Acadian community on Canada's East Coast and created a new Cajun culture in Louisiana. An estimated 3 million people worldwide can trace their roots to the Acadians of 1755. Some are household names. The leading Acadian geneal-ogist, Stephen White, followed pop star Madonna's family tree back six generations and discovered that one of her ancestors married into the Orillons, an Acadian family. The grandmother of another diva, Quebec-born Celine Dion, was a Barriault of Acadian descent. Former Canadian prime minister Jean Chrétien is related, through his mother's family, to the Melansons who settled in Port-Royal and Grand-Pré before the deportation. Other Melanson descendants include Jean Béliveau, the Montreal Canadiens' hockey star of the 1950s and 1960s, Oscar-nominated Canadian actress Geneviève Bujold, and Nova Scotia–born singer Anne Murray. Quebec's former premier, Bernard Landry, is among the more than 1 million Québécois of Acadian ancestry. The forces of assimilation have left many Doucets, LeBlancs, and Arsenaults only vaguely aware of their Acadian heritage and no longer able to speak French. Surnames have been anglicized over the years, in a bid to fit into the mainstream of North American life: LeBlancs have become Whites, while some Aucoins have opted for a literal but rather inelegant translation of their name, to Wedge. Yet Acadians and Cajuns have drawn on the tragedy of their shared past to preserve their vibrant and distinct cultures. Theirs is a story of survival in the face of incredible adversity, of the resilience of a people subjected to oppression and genocide. The story of the Acadians is a story of triumph.

The Acadian tragedy was immortalized in verse in *Evangeline: A Tale of Acadie*, the epic, sometimes ponderous and widely read poem by the great American writer Henry Wadsworth Longfellow. Rendered in unrhymed hexameter—an old-fashioned style with a rigid pattern of six beats per line—the poem appeared in 1847 and tells the story of two young lovers cruelly separated during the deportation. Evangeline Bellefontaine, just seventeen, and Gabriel Lajeunesse are about to be married when British soldiers descend on Grand-Pré in the summer of 1755. Gabriel and his father, Basil, the village blacksmith, are carried away on a ship while Evangeline and her elderly father, Benedict, remain on shore to await their turn. That night soldiers begin putting farmhouses and barns to the torch and Benedict dies, apparently from a stroke brought on by the shock and stress of it all. Gabriel and his father, like many deportees, eventually make their way to Louisiana to start again. Longfellow never reveals the destination of Evangeline's ship, but she spends years wandering the continent in search of Gabriel. Heartbroken over the loss of her true love, she becomes a nun who cares for the victims of an epidemic in Philadelphia, the destination for hundreds of deportees. In the melodramatic final scene, Evangeline enters a poorhouse and recognizes a dying old man as her beloved Gabriel. They share a kiss as he dies in her arms and Evangeline thanks God for reuniting them at last.

Evangeline was an instant success. Over the next century more than 270 editions were published and the poem was translated into a staggering 130 languages. The introduction to the Macmillan Pocket Classics edition of 1907 declared it "the most read poem in American literature." For generations it was a staple on high school and college reading lists in Canada and the United States and, while its appeal has waned, multiple editions remain in print. Modern students and readers can be forgiven if they balk at Longfellow's flowery descriptions, his archaic language—kine for cattle, wains for wagons—and his penchant for beating around the bush. But the story's universal themes of loss and hope continue to resonate. To quote Dr. Lewis B. Semple's introduction to the 1907 edition, "It is a story of love, ideal love, so simply told that the least imaginative can understand." Everyone, imaginative or not, is searching for something—love, riches, fame, knowledge, spiritual fulfillment, or perhaps simply the meaning of life—in the same way the faithful Evangeline pursues her life-long quest to find Gabriel.

How an American writing in English came to capture the tragedy of the French-speaking Acadians is a story in itself. Born in Portland, Maine, in 1807, Longfellow was the son of a lawyer who grew up immersed in books and determined to carve out a literary career at a time when no one in the United States was making a living by writing alone. He attended nearby Bowdoin College and studied classics and languages in Europe for several years before taking up a professorship at the school. After scoring some success with his poems and recovering from the sudden death of his first wife, he moved on to teach at Harvard and publish ballads based on stories from New England's past. The Acadian saga came his way through a rather circuitous route. The details have become blurred with time, but a minister in the Boston area, Rev. Horace Conolly, is said to have heard a story from one of his parishioners about a young couple separated during the deportation.

Conolly recounted the tale in 1838 to one of his friends, novelist Nathaniel Hawthorne of *The Scarlet Letter* fame. Hawthorne jotted down an outline of the story in his notebook, and it is the basic plot of *Evangeline*—the deportation separates a young couple on the eve of their wedding and, after a lifetime of searching, she finds her lost fiancé on his deathbed. In this version, as Hawthorne recorded it, the shock of finally finding her betrothed "was so great that it killed her likewise." Hawthorne and Longfellow were classmates at Bowdoin and during the winter of 1840–1841, Longfellow invited

Hawthorne and Conolly over for dinner. The minister retold the story, which struck Longfellow as "the best illustration of faithfulness and the constancy of woman" he had ever heard. Hawthorne was toying with the idea of turning the story into a novel, but agreed to give Longfellow a crack at using it as the basis for a poem. Longfellow considered christening the heroine "Gabrielle" or "Celestine" before settling on a combination of "Eve"—the first woman—and "angel." He did not put quill to paper until the fall of 1845 and completed the poem fifteen months later.

Longfellow's descriptions of Grand-Pré's vast marshes and Cape Blomidon, the fog-shrouded mountain that serves as a backdrop to the deportation, are remarkably accurate, considering the poet never visited Nova Scotia. He relied for the most part on two published sources, both of which portrayed the Acadians as hapless victims. One was French historian L'Abbé Guillaume Thomas Raynal's account of Acadian life and the deportation, the other Thomas Chandler Haliburton's two-volume history of Nova Scotia, which appeared in 1829. Haliburton, a renowned satirist and judge, considered the Acadians a "deluded people" betrayed by the French, but described the deportation as a stain on the province's reputation. All of Longfellow's characters are fictional, save one—René Le Blanc, Grand-Pré's notary, who in real life was separated from his large brood of children during the deportation and died in Pennsylvania. *Evangeline* conveys a sanitized, almost bloodless version of the events of 1755 and beyond. In his telling, the Acadians watched "in dismay" the destruction of their homes, then "cried aloud in anguish, 'We shall behold no more our homes in the village of Grand-Pré,'" a passage that barely begins to capture the horror and desperation of the moment. The human tragedy, too, is soft-pedaled: Benedict Bellefontaine dies in the midst of the chaos and Gabriel many decades later, but they are the only victims mentioned. The true scale of the disaster—thousands of deaths, disease, and the hardships that awaited the Acadians in exile—is lost as Evangeline undertakes the fruitless search for her lover. Likewise, the poet ignores the complex chain of events that culminated in the expulsion.

For all its faults, *Evangeline* brought widespread attention to the deportation for the first time. The plight of the Acadians had been a footnote to the long struggle between France and England for hegemony over North

America. Longfellow's sympathetic portrayal of peaceful peasant farmers mistreated at the hands of their British rulers put Acadie and Grand-Pré on the map. People soon began referring to Nova Scotia's Annapolis Valley as Evangeline Country. Tourists descended on Grand-Pré, poem in hand, to survey the vast marshlands and red cliffs of Blomidon that Longfellow had described. The Nova Scotia government, stung by the unwelcome attention, published a thick volume of Acadian-related archival documents in 1869 in an effort to show "the necessity for their [Acadians] removal." Sir Adams G. Archibald, a retired politician revered as one of Canada's Fathers of Confederation, stood before a meeting of the Nova Scotia Historical Society on a cold winter night in 1886 and blasted Longfellow for portraying the deportation as "an act of absolute barbarity" and "indefensible cruelty." The poem, Archibald complained, was a "perversion of historical fact" and lacked "a single allusion to the grounds of the expulsion, not a hint of any justification or excuse or even palliation for it."

In the 1920s, the chairman of the board of governors of the University of Toronto tried to have *Evangeline* banned from Canadian schools, arguing it created "a wrong impression of British justice, chivalry and administration." Unwittingly, Longfellow also helped fuel an Acadian renaissance. The first French translation was published in Canada in 1865, just as the descendants of Acadians who returned to Atlantic Canada were beginning to assert their identity as a people. In Evangeline, a heroine sprung from the imagination of an American writer, they found a tangible symbol of the injustices and hardships their ancestors endured. Parents began naming their daughters Evangeline, even though the name was unknown in Acadie at the time of the deportation. Nowadays no Acadian festival in the Maritime provinces is complete without the selection of a Gabriel and an Evangeline to reign over the celebration as king and queen.

Evangeline has been burned into the popular imagination like few other fictional characters, perhaps with the exception of Lucy Maud Montgomery's unruly young redhead, Anne of Green Gables. The poem was the basis of the first Canadian feature film, which hit theaters in 1914; Hollywood produced two movie versions in the 1920s. The adaptations continue—in the fall of 2004 an amateur theater troupe in Baton Rouge, Louisiana, staged *Evangeline*, *the Musical*, scored by the band director of a local high school. Evangeline's name and wholesome image have been used to hawk everything from sliced bread and chocolates to pancake syrup and hot sauce. As early as the 1930s a visitor to Grand-Pré noted that everything seemed to be named after Evangeline, and expressed dismay that commercialism was rampant "in such a remote part of the dominion." There was a time when Nova Scotians could sip Evangeline soft drinks from a distinctive bottle bearing the image of an Acadian lass in a bonnet.

Her name remains synonymous with the Annapolis Valley. Today's tourists are invited to drive the scenic Evangeline Trail through the heart of what was once Acadie. Along the way you can chow down on sandwiches and thick slices of homemade pie at the Evangeline Café in Grand-Pré, where the menu bears an image of you-know-who. Stay the night at the adjacent Evangeline Inn & Motel or pitch your tent at the Land of Evangeline Family Campground across the wide marsh at Evangeline Beach. A flat tire or leaky radiator can be repaired a little farther along the trail at Evangeline Motors. While you wait, flag down an Evangeline Taxi and head into Kentville for a coffee and muffin at another café named for Longfellow's heroine. Dozens of other Nova Scotia businesses have adopted the name, from Evangeline Plumbing & Heating to the Evangeline Allergy Clinic. The good folks at Evangeline Excavators may even know a thing or two about building a decent dike.

Like the Evangeline of fiction, the Evangeline statue at the Grand-Pré National Historic Site stands on a pedestal. She is portrayed in blackened bronze in a flowing dress, frozen in mid-step as she gazes wistfully into the distance in search of her lost Gabriel and her lost homeland. The sculptor used his sister as a model and some say her face appears to age as the viewer circles the base of the statue. The historic site, a 14-acre park, sits on the northern edge of modern-day Grand-Pré, but in 1755 this was the heart of the village. The church of Saint-Charles-des-Mines, where soldiers imprisoned the area's men and boys during the deportation, stood on a low ridge just behind Evangeline's statue. In its place is a chapel known as the Memorial

Church, with walls of dappled brown stone and French-style flared eaves trimmed in vibrant red paint. Gravel pathways enclose the neatly trimmed hedges that crisscross the grounds. If Evangeline could turn around, she could gaze upon massive willows that stand guard over a chain of ponds, home to a citizenry of swans and ducks. To the north, across an expanse of marshland, the rust-colored cliffs of Cape Blomidon hold court over the tides of the Bay of Fundy, just as Longfellow said they would. Each year about 100,000 people visit this site to pay homage to their ancestors, to learn about the deportation, to add names to the family tree, or simply to enjoy the park's natural beauty. Few leave without having their photograph taken at the foot of Evangeline's statue.

This peaceful scene exists due to the efforts of one man. John Frederic Herbin was a Victorian gentleman with a dapper handlebar mustache who combined the business of selling jewelry with the art of writing poetry. Herbin's father was a goldsmith and immigrant from France, his mother was a Robichaud whose Acadian ancestors had re-established at Meteghan in southwestern Nova Scotia. Herbin established a jewelry store that's still a main-street fixture in Wolfville, just up the road from Grand-Pré, and served a term as the town's mayor in the early 1900s. In his off-hours, he immersed himself in Acadian history and churned out maudlin poems about Grand-Pré and the heartbreak of the deportation. In one offering, "The Returned Acadian," he lamented:

> Neglected long and shunned our dead have lain,
> Here where a people's dearest hope had died.
> Alone of all their children scattered wide,
> I scan the sad memorials that remain.

The neglected dead were the Acadians buried in the parish cemetery of Saint-Charles-des-Mines. By the time Herbin came along, generations of English settlers had planted crops and pastured cattle on the site. The sad memorials were a few remnants of the Acadian era—a pile of rocks believed to mark the foundation of the church, a stone-lined well filled with discarded iron implements, and a line of gnarled, lichen-crusted willows reputed to have been planted by the Acadians. The cemetery was discovered in the 1880s when two youths looking for buried Acadian gold dug up the area and located a coffin. No trace of its occupant remained, but for years the dirt-encrusted box was an object of morbid curiosity at Grand-Pré's railroad station. One nineteenth-century travel writer recounted how a "gallant conductor, with an air of mystery" led her to a storage room at the station, chopped fragments from a clay-covered plank, and presented her with "pieces of the coffin of one of the Acadians" as a souvenir. The coffin itself disappeared long ago—reduced to souvenir fragments, presumably—as has a second that was unearthed and put on display at the American House, a local inn.

Herbin, determined to prevent further destruction and desecration, bought the land in 1907 in hopes of establishing a permanent memorial. The following year the Nova Scotia legislature passed an act to protect the site and, in 1909, Herbin used the foundation stones to erect a large cross to mark the cemetery. After trying for years to convince the Acadian community to take over the site, he sold it in 1917 to the Dominion Atlantic Railway, which ran through the middle of the Annapolis Valley and along one edge of Herbin's land. The DAR's owners were already cashing in on the Longfellow craze—two of their locomotives were christened "Evangeline" and "Gabriel"—and recognized the tourism potential of developing the site into a park. Gone were the days of employees giving away pieces of exhumed coffins. The railroad commissioned the Evangeline statue, unveiled in 1920, and offered a parcel of land—as Herbin had stipulated in the deed—to the Société nationale l'Assomption, the leading Acadian organization of the time, to build a memorial. This time there was no hesitation. Money raised from Acadian descendants in Canada and the United States was used to build the Memorial Church. The centerpiece of the site, it was completed in 1922. Herbin died the following year and a plaque honoring his efforts (but misspelling his middle name as Frederick) was added to the cemetery's stone cross. In 1924 an iron cross was erected on the marsh at Horton Landing, about a mile and a half to the east, the approximate point where Grand-Pré's deportees were ferried to the waiting ships.

All the pieces were in place. Visitors alighting from DAR trains were treated to a picture-perfect vista—Evangeline's statue in the foreground, framed by the church rising behind her and, off to the right, the line of hardy Acadian willows. George Nestler Tricoche, a French writer who stopped by in those early days, noted that the site was already a must-see for visitors and, thanks to Longfellow, "the goal of all pilgrims to the land of Evangeline." Ceremonies marking the 175th anniversary of the deportation in 1930 drew more than 5,000 people, including a senator from Louisiana, who brought along a bevy of young women dressed as Evangeline. In 1955 Grand-Pré was again the focus of a ceremony and mass to coincide with the 200th anniversary of the deportation, with an estimated 10,000 in attendance. As train travel declined in the late 1950s, the railroad lost interest and sold the park to the Canadian government, which designated it a national historic site in 1961.

Grand-Pré has become the symbol of the deportation, the Acadians' Ground Zero. The park has been shortlisted for designation as a United Nations world heritage site. Not all this attention is Longfellow's doing. The Minas region was the largest Acadian community in 1755 and Grand-Pré was the scene of the largest of that year's deportations. About 2,000 people were shipped into exile from this area, so hundreds of thousands of Acadian descendants around the world can trace their family tree to this spot. For the rest, Grand-Pré is a stand-in for the other communities obliterated in 1755 and in the years that followed. It is a place to pause and reflect on the pastoral life of the Acadians before a nightmare engulfed their world. Parks Canada, the federal agency responsible for historic sites, and a non-profit Acadian group, the Société Promotion Grand-Pré, jointly manage the park. In 2003 an interpretation center opened beside the park, on a site a developer once hoped to use for a garish Acadian theme park. The center offers exhibits and artifacts that document Acadian life and history, with an emphasis on events surrounding the deportation. A highlight for visitors is a twenty-minute video that re-creates the horror of the Acadians' removal and exile, screened in a theater with walls framed in curved timbers to resemble the hold of an eighteenth-century ship. At the end of the film, the surnames of the families deported in 1755 are projected onto the walls of the theater. Some visitors whip out their cameras and try to photograph this fleeting link to their ancestors before the houselights come up and the names fade away.

~ ⚓ ~

Grand-Pré and its rebuilt church were a magnet for the thousands of Acadian descendants who converged on Nova Scotia for the 2004 installment of the Congrès mondial acadien, the World Acadian Congress. Every five years since 1994, Acadians and Cajuns have gathered for family reunions and to celebrate their history and culture. The first *congrès* was held in Moncton, New Brunswick, the second in Louisiana. This one, staged amid the historic sites and monuments of Old Acadie, coincided with the 400th anniversary of the founding of the first French settlement in North America. The two-week event culminated in an outdoor mass adjacent to the Grand-Pré site that drew some 10,000 people. "Here, we connect with our ancestors," said Loubert Trahan, a Korean War vet from Louisiana who was making his fourth pilgrimage to Grand-Pré. "It's a return to our roots." Before the deportation, his branch of the Trahan family lived about 15 miles to the east, an area known in Acadian times as Piziquid and renamed Windsor by the British. As far as he can tell from checking old maps, the site of his ancestral home is buried beneath the main highway that links Halifax to the Annapolis Valley. Grand-Pré is the only tangible link to his past. Shirley Thibodeaux LeBlanc, a retired Realtor from Lafayette, Louisiana, who has assembled a massive genealogy of the Thibodeau family, describes a visit to Grand-Pré as an emotional experience. "Anybody you talk to from Louisiana, you ask them their first experience up here, what were their feelings, they'll tell you the same thing. 'I'm home. This is home.'"

At the midpoint of the *congrès*, Grand-Pré hosted a Louisiana Day, in honor of the thousands of Cajuns who headed north to attend *congrès* events and family reunions. The rollicking sound of fiddles and accordions straight from the bayous spilled from a circus-sized tent as chefs served up gumbo and spicy jambalaya. Louisiana T-shirts outnumbered Acadian tricolor flags and pins as visitors toured the grounds or paused to compare family trees with strangers who turned out to be distant cousins. Loubert Trahan was struck, as he always is, by how much the Acadians he meets in Nova Scotia resemble the Cajuns he knows back home. "It's like we have a bond," he said, switching from English to French with ease, "the facial features, the walk, the talk, are so close." Before the official welcomes and speeches, a sixty-four-year-old U.S. Department of

Agriculture manager from Abbeville named Dale Broussard was coaxed on stage to show these long-lost northern cousins how to do a proper Cajun yell. "You can't become an honorary Cajun until you do it well," he shouted, his eyes twinkling with mischief under the brim of a black cowboy hat. "Eye-YEEEEE!" he bellowed into a microphone as the Louisiana contingent chimed in and the rest of the crowd did its best. Later in the day a Louisiana visitor paused in front of an oversized photograph of northern New Brunswick's frozen landscape in the dead of winter, part of an outdoor display of images capturing the spirit of Acadie and its people. "You know, y'all," he drawled, "I'm kinda glad they deported us. I couldn't take that kinda cold."

The climate is not a problem on this August afternoon as the sun beats down on Grand-Pré. Jeanette Romero and her friend Pat Sporl spent the better part of a year planning a trip from Louisiana to Nova Scotia for the *congrès*, and this was the place they wanted to see the most. They are here with their husbands and about thirty-five other couples who belong to the Baton Rouge–based Cruisin' Cajuns RV Club. The motor homes are nowhere in sight, but club members are easy to spot. Most have their names engraved on large red pins molded in the shape of a map of Louisiana. Members spend a lot of time on the road, "running from that four-letter word, work," says Pat's husband, Mark, a retired serviceman for a New Orleans gas company. The club's membership rules and mission are simple. "It's a group of people who have motor homes, and they party," Pat explains, her enthusiasm riding the steady pulse of the Cajun band. "Once a month we have a rally and we get together—good food, good music, and partying."

Jeanette's maiden name is Richard (or *Ree*-shard, as it comes out in her Gulf Coast accent). Pat's mother was a Boudreaux and both women have traced their ancestors to the Grand-Pré area. Jeanette's grandmother was a Boudreaux as well, and after meeting through the RV club, they realized they are distant cousins. That was not the only surprise for Jeanette, who began to dig into her family's past when she and her husband, Glynn Romero, retired after running a supermarket in a small town near Lafayette. While Glynn is descended from Louisiana's Spanish settlers, he has Richards in his family tree. The couple was startled to discover, after being married for forty-three years, that they are seventh cousins.

Pat was here in 1989, but Jeanette visited Grand-Pré for the first time a couple of weeks ago. Her past hit home when she saw the video depicting the hardships of the deportation. "I had tears in my eyes because I really didn't realize what our forefathers went through—so many people and being so sick and dying along the way," she says, a lobster earring the color of her bright-red lipstick clinging to each earlobe. "Once we came here, and realized what they went through, it just meant so much more. I had goosebumps." She and Glynn are heading to the Richard reunion in Halifax later in the week, where she hopes to uncover more family history. "I want to find out about my Richard ancestry, my Boudreaux ancestry. Where were they deported to first? And from there, how did they get to Louisiana?" She's determined to find the answers, "so our children's children will understand where we come from. Growing up, we were not taught that we were deported. It was like a shame ... no one wanted to talk about it."

For Jeannette and Pat and thousands of others, the search for roots begins at the Memorial Church. The absence of pews surprises most visitors as they enter. This is a museum and a shrine, not a place of worship. The walls and vaulted ceiling are painted in tones of muted rose. Benches line either side, offering a vantage point to study a half-dozen paintings that depict key events in Acadian history. Above the oak doors of the main entrance, a spectacular semi-circular stained-glass window depicts boatloads of people being ferried to ships against the backdrop of Cape Blomidon. The image is rendered in somber shades of purple and deep blue, but narrow panes of bright red and orange fracture the scene, a reminder of how the deportation shattered the Acadian people. Toward the back of the church, two brass tablets polished to a mirror finish bear the names of the families who called Acadie home at the time of the deportation. Visitors pause to scan the lists in search of the surname that will link them to this peaceful valley where land and ocean meet.

When Jeanette toured the church two weeks ago, she found the name of her Richard ancestor. The name has already slipped her mind. Was it Michel? Pierre? No, maybe it was Jean-Pierre. Later in the afternoon she and Pat walk over to double-check. In an alcove at the back of the church, in front of life-sized cutouts of grim-faced soldiers herding shocked deportees into exile, a knot of people surrounds an oversized black binder. It holds a facsimile of a list, compiled in November 1755, of the families deported from the Minas area. The heads of 446 families are accounted for, along with the number of wives and children—1,923 people in all. The officer in charge of the operation, Lieutenant-Colonel John Winslow, kept a meticulous record of their livestock, all of it forfeited to the British Crown. The well-thumbed list has long been a starting point for Acadians tracing their roots.

It takes Pat less than a minute to find her ancestor. Etienne Boudro, number 89, had two sons and three daughters at the time of the deportation, four oxen and seventeen cattle, plus a herd of fifty sheep, more than twenty hogs, and three horses. When Jeanette's turn comes, she runs her finger down the left-hand side, passing over Landrys, LeBlancs, Trahans, and Comeaus. None of the names are in alphabetical order and she scans page after page, until she reaches number 310.

"There he is," she reports. The name is Joseph Richard, but she's certain this is her ancestor, and the Richards on the lines directly below, Jacques and Jean, were his brothers. She runs her finger across the columns opposite his name, and reads each number aloud. Joseph had five sons and three daughters. He owned six oxen, twenty-two head of cattle, ten sheep, and fifteen hogs. She has trouble making out the notation above the last column, but it turns out he also had a horse. "And two mistresses," Glynn pipes up. Jeanette chuckles along with other visitors who have overheard the joke, but she's also forming a mental picture of this prosperous farmer who supported a family of ten. Livestock was a measure of wealth for the Acadians, making Joseph Richard one of the richest farmers around. "He was pretty well off," she says. It's a lot to absorb—a snapshot of long-lost family members, their world reduced to statistics as their lives were being torn apart.

Jeanette steps back, removes her glasses, and wipes away the tears welling up in her eyes. It has suddenly become too hot in the crowded church, she tells Pat. She heads outside, past the gleaming brass tablets bearing the surnames of Acadian settlers, past the paintings and the stained-glass window that chronicle the destruction of Grand-Pré and the Acadie of her ancestors, past the knots of people from far-flung places who, like her, have come to Nova Scotia to trace roots that run four centuries deep.

2 THE LIFE AND TIMES OF ACADIE

... it was a Fine Country and Full of Inhabitants, a Butifull Church & abundance of ye Goods of the world. Provisions of all Kinds in great Plenty.

—Lieutenant-Colonel John Winslow, *Journal*, September 3, 1755

The Melanson brothers were born half an hour apart, but they work in different eras. Each workday Wayne Melanson dons the uniform of a French gentleman roughing it in the bush—linen shirt, woolen breeches, wooden shoes—and steps into the seventeenth century. He is a Parks Canada interpreter at the Port-Royal Habitation, a faithful reconstruction of the French outpost built on the shores of the Annapolis River in 1605, the first permanent European settlement north of Florida. A few miles upriver, the earthen ramparts of the Fort Anne National Historic Site stand guard over the picturesque town of Annapolis Royal. There, Alan Melanson helps visitors understand the history of the Acadians and the succession of battles France and England fought, in the century after 1650, for bragging rights to this corner of Canada.

Tourists who visit both sites can be forgiven for thinking the man who showed them around Fort Anne has changed clothes, jumped into a car, and sped out to the Habitation in time to greet them. The differences between the forty-seven-year-old twins are subtle. One is right-handed, the other is a southpaw. Alan, the younger of the two, has a bit more flecks of gray in his dark hair and beard. Wayne sports a goatee, wears his hair in a Beatles mop, and has a slighter build. But both are stocky and about 5'10", with dark complexions and darker eyes. "If someone wanted to cast a stereotypical Acadian," Wayne concedes with a chuckle, "we might not be a bad choice." When they were younger, both profess to have been far more interested in girls and sports than in history. But ask either one a question about their historic site or their heritage—both are descendants of the Ambroise Melanson who was aboard the *Pembroke* when it was commandeered—and it soon becomes clear they share a passion for the past.

Some visitors who do a doubletake when they encounter the Melanson twins are just as surprised to discover that Acadian history did not begin at the Port-Royal Habitation. "This site represents one of the earliest attempts by the French to settle on the continent, [to] bring their French culture, their way of life, their methods, their society," Wayne explains as he stands before the habitation's modest palisade on a blustery September afternoon. "It also laid the groundwork for others to follow, who would become the Acadian community, but this was not an Acadian community. They were Frenchmen living in Acadia."

This compound of buildings, with its wooden clapboards and shingles weathered to a dull gray, is actually France's second stab at establishing a permanent settlement in North America. The mastermind behind both colonizing efforts was Pierre du Gua, sieur de Monts, a nobleman who had the good fortune of fighting alongside King Henry IV in the wars between Catholics and Protestant Huguenots that convulsed France before the signing of the Edict of Nantes in 1598. When de Monts put forward his vision of creating a New France in the New World, the king obliged in 1603 with a ten-year monopoly on the fur trade in a swath of eastern North American that stretched from modern-day Philadelphia to Cape Breton Island. It was a grand gesture that ignored the enterprising Frenchmen who were already spending the summers bartering with the Native peoples for furs, not to mention English and Dutch claims to much of the area. Beaver pelts were prized for a soft layer of fur close to the hide, which was processed to make the felt hats that were the rage among fashionable Europeans. Tribes along the coast were eager to swap pelts for knives, kettles, and trinkets. But de Monts's mission was to give France a year-round presence, not simply trading posts. He pledged to recruit 100 colonists each year, convert the Native peoples to Christianity, and explore for gold and silver. King Henry was generous with land he would never see, but not with his treasury—this venture, while state-sanctioned, was financed by the private sector. On the strength of his monopoly, de Monts was able to convince merchants in the port cities of western France to ante up money for ships and supplies.

De Monts recruited 120 men to establish his North American beachhead. It was "a turbulent lot, insubordinate, dangerous," one historian has claimed, but it does not appear that de Monts was forced to take advantage of his power to seize vagrants and exiles to fill his roster. On the contrary, he had some high-class companions, including Samuel de Champlain, a young cartographer who had already crossed the Atlantic twice, and Jean de Biencourt, sieur de Poutrincourt, another of the king's old war buddies. Carpenters, masons, artisans, surgeons, a priest, and a group of Swiss mercenaries also signed on. Subsequent events would suggest they had at least one thing in common—a death wish.

The expedition set out from Le Havre in two ships in March 1604. After a stormy crossing, they made landfall two months later in Nova Scotia, between the future sites of Lunenburg and Liverpool. This was not unknown territory—Basque and French ships had been frequenting these shores for decades, fishing for cod on the Grand Banks or trading for furs. De Monts promptly enforced his monopoly by seizing a French ship he found laden with furs. After setting up a temporary base on shore, they spent several weeks scouting the coast for a suitable site for a settlement. Finding a narrow channel through the cliffs that line the southern shore of the Bay of Fundy, they sailed into an expansive harbor ringed by mountains, known today as the Annapolis Basin. Champlain was so impressed, he christened it Port-Royal. "He remarked in his journal that up to that point in his journey, he had not seen as beautiful a port, and that the 2,000 vessels of the French fleet back home could safely anchor in the shelter that it offered," Wayne Melanson says, gesturing toward the stretch of water in front of the habitation. Poutrincourt was equally impressed and asked de Monts to grant him the area, so he could settle his family there on a future voyage. De Monts, who had the right to grant land and could be as magnanimous as his king, agreed.

The expedition probed farther into the bay, then doubled back along its northern shore, the south coast of present-day New Brunswick. At Passamaquoddy Bay they followed a river—now the boundary between Canada and the United States—northward to a point where tributaries merged in the shape of a cross. De Monts named it the Sainte Croix and chose a small, football-shaped island in its midst as the site for their winter camp. In the heat of midsummer, the choice made sense. An island was easily defended and the central location of this one—akin to setting up shop at a busy intersection—should attract Native peoples in canoes brimming with furs. It was to prove a tragic mistake. De Monts's men built about a dozen buildings connected by a palisade and planted some grain. They chopped down most of the trees—mistake number two—in the belief they could skip over to the mainland during the winter to gather firewood. Poutrincourt took the ships back to France to fetch supplies for the following year. Then on October 6, far earlier than usual for the area, snowflakes began to fall.

The winter was long and bleak, with 3 to 4 feet of snow still lying on the ground at the end of April. It was so cold their supply of cider froze, and had to be cut into blocks and issued by the pound. Renowned Acadian novelist Antonine Maillet has joked that the colony's name may have emerged from that bitter winter—"Arcadia" came out as "Acadia" when spoken through frozen lips. Fundy's tides churned up the ice in the river, making it impossible to walk or row the half-mile to shore. "So they became prisoners of the island that was supposed to defend them," Wayne Melanson notes with a shrug. With little firewood for cooking, they subsisted on salted meat and frozen vegetables. Thirty-five of the seventy-nine men who stayed for the winter died of scurvy, and twenty more nearly succumbed. Champlain was spared and offered a vivid description of the ravages of the disease—swollen limbs, abdominal pain, a hacking cough, shortness of breath, and gums so rotten that teeth could be extracted with the fingers. Victims "had almost no strength, and suffered intolerable pains," he wrote. "In brief, they were in such a state that the majority of the sick could neither get up nor move, nor could they even be held upright without fainting away ...."

Natives with fresh meat to trade kept the survivors going until the spring thaw. Once supply ships arrived from France in June 1605, de Monts and

Champlain set out in search of a new site. They cruised the Maine coast—an area Champlain had explored in a small boat the previous summer—and ventured as far south as Cape Cod. They entered what is now Boston Harbor and Champlain named the Charles River the Rivière du Gua in a transparent attempt to curry favor with the boss. The climate was better, but thoughts of establishing a settlement vanished after a party sent ashore to fetch water was accosted by Native peoples who wanted their kettles. One of de Monts's men was killed in the skirmish and the expedition turned back. But for that incident—the first violent death of a European recorded in the region—New France might have been founded in the heart of what was to become New England, and history would have taken a dramatic turn.

It was early August by the time they made it back to Sainte Croix. De Monts was running out of time and Port-Royal looked like the safest bet for the coming winter. Most of the buildings on the island were dismantled and shipped across the Bay of Fundy to a site tucked under a mountain that blocked the north wind. This time all the buildings—living quarters, trading house, kitchen, dining hall, and forge—were joined to form a compact rectangle that enclosed a courtyard, with a well at its center. It was a better defense against the elements and two palisaded platforms, extending from the corners facing the ocean, offered protection against unwanted visitors. Champlain's detailed drawing of the Habitation, as it became known, was used as the basis for the reconstructed version that greets visitors today, complete with European-style high-pitched roofs and leaded-glass windows.

De Monts, who had investors to reassure and rival merchants to keep at bay, returned to France with a cargo of furs and most of the survivors of the disastrous first winter. Champlain and two others stayed on with about forty newcomers. Despite better accommodations and milder weather, scurvy claimed a dozen more lives over the winter. The victims included a priest and a Huguenot minister—de Monts recruited without regard to denomination—who had been locked in bitter quarrels over religion. They died the same day and were reputedly buried in the same grave to see if they would get along better in death than they had in life. Poutrincourt arrived in the summer of 1606 with a relief ship and a batch of new recruits that included Marc Lescarbot, a Parisian lawyer with literary ambitions who became the colony's writer-in-residence. Crops were sown and furs were collected. The local Mi'kmaq—led by a towering chief named Membertou, who claimed to be more than 100 years old—became friends and allies. Poutrincourt and Champlain once again ventured south in search of greener pastures, but four of their crewmen were ambushed and killed by a Cape Cod tribe, reinforcing the wisdom of staying put at Port-Royal.

Despite the hardship and hazards, the Habitation developed into something of an oasis of European civilization. If the reconstructed buildings are any indication—and they have been furnished and outfitted to reflect the lifestyle of better-off Europeans of the time—the colonists lived in relative comfort. "The colony was composed of gentlemen used to a certain standard of living," Melanson explains, "who tried to bring a bit of that sophistication and culture here to Acadia." In the fall of 1606, while Shakespeare was putting the finishing touches on *King Lear*, the men of the Habitation were practising lines and sewing costumes for a water-borne pageant to celebrate the imminent return of Poutrincourt and Champlain. When the explorers dropped anchor in the basin in November, they were treated to the world premiere of *Le Théâtre de Neptune*, a play Lescarbot wrote in their honor. In what must have resembled a scene from a Monty Python skit, the god of the sea, clad in blue robes and brandishing a trident, greeted them with a speech dripping in flowery prose. Cannons fired, trumpets sounded, and other Frenchmen, dressed as Native peoples, rowed alongside to offer furs for trade. Champlain, perhaps inspired by this burst of backwoods creativity, established the Order of Good Cheer to boost morale and improve the colonists' diet during the winter that followed. Each day one of the men was assigned to plan and provide the evening meal, and they tried to outdo each other by parading into the dining hall with exotic delicacies like boiled moose nose and smoked beaver tail. Thanks, perhaps, to these culinary experiments, only seven men died of scurvy that winter.

This impressive string of North American firsts—the first permanent European settlement north of Florida, the first theatrical production, the first social club—came to an abrupt end in 1607. News arrived that de Monts's monopoly had been revoked in response to rising prices and the lobbying of rival traders, and the post would be abandoned. Once the harvest was in and the season's furs were packed for shipment, the colonists left the Habitation in Membertou's care and returned to France. De Monts, who never returned to Acadie, managed to have his monopoly reinstated for a year and dispatched Champlain to the St. Lawrence River to found Quebec in 1608. Once again, history took a dramatic turn—had the monopoly remained in force, Acadie might well have remained the focus of French colonization efforts. Champlain, who went on to lay the foundations of France's expansion into the heart of North America, has eclipsed his mentor in fame. A bronze bust of de Monts, in a feathered hat that makes him a dead ringer for one of the Three Musketeers, sits atop a stone column at Annapolis Royal. The inscription proclaims him "the pioneer of civilization in North America." Most visitors assume it is a memorial to Champlain.

Poutrincourt managed to have his claim to Port-Royal recognized, but was unable to finance a renewed effort to colonize the area until 1610, and only after agreeing to bring along Jesuit missionaries to convert the Native peoples. Even though three years had passed, the Habitation was in good shape and in need of nothing more than some roof repairs. Farming and fur trading resumed, but there was a falling-out with the zealous Jesuits, who left in 1613 to found a new colony on Mount Desert Island, off Maine. By now, however, the French had new neighbors to worry about. The English had founded Jamestown, Virginia, in 1607 and a raider named Captain Samuel Argall sailed from there in the fall of 1613. He plundered the Jesuit settlement, then crossed over to Port-Royal and cleaned out the Habitation before burning it to the ground. About two dozen French colonists were left to fend for themselves until help arrived in the spring. They survived only because the Mi'kmaq took them in for the winter.

Leaning against the counter that spans the trading room of the reborn Habitation, and surrounded by an array of pots, kettles, and tools, Wayne Melanson ponders the significance of this site. Completed at the start of the Second World War, it showcases the craftsmanship of the retired Nova Scotia shipbuilders who built it, and represents the Canadian government's first effort at historical reconstruction. It is also a gesture of reconciliation—the driving force behind the restoration was Harriette Taber Richardson, a New Englander who summered in the area and raised the seed money used to undo Argall's destruction. Thanks to her efforts, each summer Melanson and his fellow interpreters are able to take 45,000 visitors on a trip back in time.

The original Habitation stood for just eight years, Melanson points out, but in many ways it set the tone for the history of Acadie. The French government offered lukewarm and unreliable support for the struggling colony, expecting it to pay its own way. What the French settlers built, their English neighbors promptly showed up to destroy, a pattern repeated during the region's turbulent history. And it was here that the French and Mi'kmaq learned to respect one another. "The alliance that was formed here would endure throughout the whole English-French rivalry for Acadia," Melanson points out. Without Membertou's friendship and support, he adds, the colony would not have survived as long as it did. "They were a few Frenchmen living in a Mi'kmaq world." Or, in the words of historian John Reid, a specialist in the colonial period, "Native people had the power in the decade of the 1600s to say 'yes' or 'no' to French colonization." Efforts to convert Native peoples to Catholicism, which began here, forged a further link between the peoples.

Despite the setbacks and the Habitation's fiery demise, the pioneering efforts of de Monts, Champlain, and Poutrincourt gave France a foothold on the East Coast of North America. And, as it turned out, a couple of the settlers Samuel Argall left homeless in 1613 would help Acadie rise from the ruins.

In his black suit and matching top hat, Alan Melanson looks like a villain drawn from the pages of a Charles Dickens novel. Long ribbons of black silk flow from his neck and hat, a Victorian-era accessory, called weepers, worn by men taking part in funeral processions. A candle inside the hurricane lantern he holds casts an eerie glow upward and frames his bearded face. As if to complete this sinister picture, it really is a dark and stormy night—the wind off the Annapolis Basin is spitting rain on a half-dozen people huddled under umbrellas. Only twice in a dozen summers has foul weather forced Melanson to cancel his summertime tours of the Garrison Graveyard adjacent to Fort Anne, and he's not about to let the dying gasps of a hurricane stop this one.

Melanson, president of the Historical Association of Annapolis Royal, has led thousands of tourists on candlelight walks through the moss-covered headstones of Canada's oldest English cemetery. He offers a thumbnail sketch of his town's turbulent history—peppered with a little black humor, in keeping with the setting—and introduces some of the soldiers, camp followers, and clergymen buried here. The older stones bear images of marching skeletons and winged skulls that would be a hit at any Halloween party. The 1830 marker for William Tomlinson is inscribed with a rather childish running rhyme: "Affliction sore I long time bore / Physicians were in vain / Till death did seize and God did please / To ease me of my pain." The oldest stone belongs to Bathiah Douglas, who died in 1720 at age thirty-seven, but it and the 233 others that survive only begin to tell the story of the people buried here. From 1636 until the English takeover in 1710, this was an Acadian cemetery. Hundreds of Acadians are buried here, but their wooden markers disappeared long ago. They lie among the trees in an area that stands out today because the English buried their dead in an L-shape to avoid it. "We have no stones," notes Melanson, who likely has ancestors buried there.

During the graveyard tour, and one he leads in the daytime along the town's waterfront, Melanson introduces visitors to more than four centuries of history, from the days when the Mi'kmaq camped here to the dawn of the twentieth century when a citizen's campaign saved Fort Anne from being razed to build a hotel. In between, he picks up the Acadian story where his brother leaves off. "This whole river basin is really the cradle of where the Acadians started," he explains. "Unfortunately, we got caught up in the middle of the whole struggle between France and England for control of the area. Although it's fairly tranquil—except for the rain here tonight—this is one of the most fought-over pieces of land in Canadian history. Thirteen battles were fought here; it [this land] changed hands seven times between the French and the English."

Melanson has time to offer only a condensed version of Acadian history on his tours, but a chat afterwards and a trip to the history books fill in the details. After the destruction of the Habitation two young French colonists, Jean Biencourt, Poutrincourt's son, and Charles de Saint-Étienne de La Tour, stayed on. Aided by the Mi'kmaq, they built posts in Maine and near the ruined Habitation and continued to send cargos of fish and furs back home.

After Biencourt died in 1623, La Tour took over the operation, married a Native woman, built a fort at Cape Sable—the southernmost point of the Nova Scotia peninsula—and settled in.

Back in Europe, people with powerful connections had designs on La Tour's little fiefdom. The Scots wanted a piece of the action. There was a New France, a New England, a New Spain, and even a New Netherland, so why not a New Scotland? The instigator was William Alexander, a highly regarded poet who had the good fortune of hitching his star to Scotland's King James, who ascended to the English throne in 1603. In 1621 Alexander wrangled a charter to colonize all of Acadie and the Gaspé Peninsula. But Alexander had trouble reconciling "the roles of a dreamer and a man of action," as one biographer put it. He was unable to scrape together money and colonists to settle what he christened Nova Scotia—New Scotland, in Latin—until he hit upon the idea of conferring the title of baronet on anyone willing to pay cash or support colonists. Enough noblemen and wannabes signed up to enable Alexander to dispatch his son and about seventy colonists to Port-Royal in 1629. About thirty settlers died during the first winter, but reinforcements enabled the outpost to muddle along for three years. A cairn and plaque honoring the "Scotch Fort" was erected in the 1950s on a hill overlooking the Habitation based on clues in old maps. A recent archeological dig, Melanson notes, confirmed that Alexander's post stood on the shoreline directly in front of Fort Anne.

By this time, the English and French were engaged in one of their favorite pastimes—war. When hostilities broke out in 1627, La Tour wrote to Louis XIII's chief minister, Cardinal Richelieu, pleading for help to keep Acadie from falling into English hands. As luck would have it, Richelieu had just organized a group of merchants to revive the fur trade and reinforce Quebec and other French posts with settlers and supplies. The Company of 100 Associates, as it was known, included the influential Richelieu, the trailblazing Champlain, and Isaac de Razilly, a naval captain who had won prominence, and lost an eye, in battle. The company bolstered La Tour's fort at Cape Sable and helped him build a new fur-trading post at the mouth of the Saint John River. Events took a bizarre turn after the Kirke brothers, English raiders who were harassing French settlements and convoys, captured a ship carrying La Tour's father, Claude. Shipped off to England, the elder La Tour threw in his lot with his captors. He had been at the old Habitation with Poutrincourt, and advised Alexander's 1629 expedition to head for the fertile lands at Port-Royal. Claude even accepted one of Alexander's baronetcies and, on the journey back to Acadie, stopped at Cape Sable and tried to convince his son to switch sides. Charles refused and declared, by Champlain's account, that he would rather die than "consent to such baseness as to betray his King." The English besieged his fort for a day or two before giving up and continuing to Port-Royal.

Charles de La Tour's choice proved to be astute. Under the Treaty of Saint-Germain-en-Laye that ended the war in 1632, the English ceded to the French all lands claimed under Alexander's charter. That year Razilly brought 300 settlers, mostly men, to La Hève—present-day LaHave, near Lunenburg—and took possession of Port-Royal. Alexander's little band of colonists handed over the keys to the Scotch Fort, and all but two families accepted a French offer of passage back to England. For years to come, map-makers designated the colony as "Acadia or Nova Scotia," making it clear that ownership remained in dispute.

With the English temporarily out of the picture, the French could afford to fight among themselves. In the fog of war, both La Tour and Razilly had been named governor of Acadie; in peacetime, they managed to keep out of each other's way. The fur trade expanded and Razilly is credited with establishing the first significant group of permanent settlers. The goodwill, however, died with Razilly in 1635. La Tour now faced an aggressive rival, Charles de Menou d'Aulnay, Razilly's cousin and lieutenant, who took command. D'Aulnay moved most of the La Hève settlers to Port-Royal, where the farmland was better, and refurbished the Scotch Fort as his headquarters. He brought in seventy new settlers in 1636, including families of Trahans and Martins from the Anjou region of France and men who knew how to build dikes to reclaim the Bay of Fundy's tidal marshes. D'Aulnay recruited more settlers from his family's estates near La Rochelle in western France—Belliveaus and Blanchards, Landrys and Bourgs, LeBlancs, Terriots, and Thibodeaus. Capuchin priests were imported to provide religious instruction, schools, and to convert the Native peoples. As Melanson points out to the tourists who have braved the rain for his graveyard tour, these settlers—and Port-Royal's revival—signaled the true beginning of Acadie. De Monts may have been "the pioneer of civilization in North America," but Razilly and d'Aulnay backed up France's claim to the region with people on the ground.

When it came to competing for territory and furs, d'Aulnay proved as ambitious and ruthless as La Tour. In 1638, some geographically challenged French officials complicated matters and granted control of the area south of the Bay of Fundy, including d'Aulnay's base at Port-Royal, to La Tour. The remainder of the region, and La Tour's main fort on the Saint John River, was given to d'Aulnay. D'Aulnay had powerful supporters in France, Richelieu among them, forcing La Tour to seek supplies and help from English merchants in Boston. The man who refused to betray his king in 1629 was now branded a traitor. The rivalry soon erupted into a civil war, with each side attacking the forts and ships of the other. La Tour's forces laid siege to the fort at Port-Royal in 1634 and destroyed an adjacent mill and killed several of d'Aulnay's men before withdrawing. The feud culminated in an attack on La Tour's stronghold at the mouth of the Saint John River in 1645. With La Tour away in Boston, his second wife, Françoise-Marie Jacquelin, took command, but the fort fell amid a barrage of cannon fire. D'Aulnay, in an act of surprising cruelty, is said to have forced Madame de La Tour to stand with a noose around her neck and watch as about two dozen of the surviving defenders were hanged. She died three weeks later, while still in his custody. D'Aulnay won the battle and was named governor of Acadie in 1647, but La Tour ultimately won the war. In 1650 d'Aulnay's canoe capsized in the Annapolis Basin and he died of exposure. La Tour returned to France, where he lobbied for an inquiry that condemned d'Aulnay's conduct. Reinstated as governor, La Tour returned to Port-Royal in 1653 and married d'Aulnay's widow.

The struggle was costly in terms of lives and money and lost opportunities. It sapped Acadie's strength, hindered settlement, and diverted attention from the real enemy, the growing English colonies to the south. New England boasted a population of some 13,000 by the 1650s compared to a few hundred Acadians, most of them in the Port-Royal area. "Had La Tour and d'Aulnay resolved their differences, poured wealth and energy into building a strong French presence on the Atlantic coast, the future might have been different," writer Marjorie MacDonald has noted in a compelling account of Acadie's civil war. "Then Acadia and Quebec together could have presented formidable opposition to the English in the close-run campaigns of the next century." The conflict certainly left Acadie vulnerable when the English, fresh from their own civil war, once again set their sights on the colony in 1654. Oliver Cromwell, Lord Protector of England's newly proclaimed Commonwealth, dispatched troops under the command of a Massachusetts merchant, Robert Sedgwick, to attack the Dutch colony at present-day New York. When a truce derailed the attack, Sedgwick decided to cruise north to raid the French. The undermanned fort at Port-Royal capitulated after a brief skirmish and Acadie was suddenly under English rule.

For the next three decades, as historian John Reid has observed, Acadie existed "essentially as a mercantile concept," more trading post than colony. The English were happy to claim new territory, but were too embroiled in domestic affairs to do much with it. The smooth-talking La Tour, who had been shipped off to England as a prisoner, put the Nova Scotia baronetcy he had spurned to good use. He convinced Cromwell that, as heir to the title William Alexander granted to his father back in 1629, he had the right to govern the colony. La Tour promptly sold his claim to two English merchants, Thomas Temple and William Crowne. Temple set up shop in Boston and ruled from afar, leaving the field open for Massachusetts merchants to develop trade ties with the Acadians that would endure for a century. War broke out again in 1666, and when the smoke cleared in 1667, England gladly swapped Acadie to regain its half of the Caribbean island of St. Christopher, which the French had seized. Temple, bankrupt and embittered, managed to delay the handover until 1670.

The return of French rule proved to be more of the same. A census in 1671 turned up only 389 people and little attempt was made to attract new settlers. Trade with New England continued despite halfhearted official attempts to stop it. Acadie was governed from a post in present-day Maine and for a time from Quebec, and was so weakly defended that in 1674 a band of Dutch raiders briefly took control and renamed the colony New Holland. Some stability was restored in the 1680s when Port-Royal was re-established as the capital. The population doubled to more than 600, thanks in part to the arrival of a garrison of French troops and an entourage of officials. Once again, French efforts came up short. When war resumed in 1689, Port-Royal's dilapidated fortress was still being rebuilt as a Massachusetts expedition of seven ships and more than 700 men sailed into the Annapolis Basin. It was under the command of Sir William Phips, a New England ship's carpenter who had earned a fortune and a knighthood by recovering Spanish gold from a Caribbean shipwreck. On paper, at least, Phips's attack was to retaliate against the French, who were providing guns and ammunition to Indian tribes responsible for ruthless raids that had killed scores of New England settlers. It was also infused with religious fervor, cast as a battle of Protestants—the true Christian faith—"against Popery and Paganism." In truth, it was just another treasure hunt. French governor Louis-Alexandre Des Friches de Meneval, his troops outnumbered ten to one, surrendered without a fight after negotiating a deal to protect the town and allow his troops to return to France. Phips reneged on his promises, imprisoned the troops, and set his men loose. Warehouses, homes, and the church were looted and gardens were dug up to recover stashes of valuables.

So began seven more years of absentee English rule. Before leaving, Phips rounded up as many residents as he could and forced them to take an oath of allegiance to the British Crown. He also appointed a French officer and six Acadians to act as the local government. Then the New Englanders demolished the fort and left the residents, as one French official put it, "between the hammer and the anvil." Their professed allegiance depended on whether the pirate ships or frigates sailing into Port-Royal were flying an English flag or a French one. What they really wanted was to be left alone. When an English force returned to Port-Royal in 1692 to demand that the Acadians agree to fight against the French and Indians if need be, they asked to be treated as neutrals. It was a plea that would be repeated many times in the decades ahead.

The war ended in 1697 and, with the stroke of a pen, treaty negotiators in Europe returned Acadie to France. The French rebuilt the fort at Port-Royal and organized Acadian men into a militia as tensions with New England continued at a fever pitch. The seizure of Massachusetts fishing boats in Acadian waters provided a direct affront, but the colony also bore the brunt of New

England's wrath after war, and Indian raids on their frontier towns, resumed in 1702. It mattered little that the French in Quebec were backing the raids—Frenchmen were Frenchmen, and it was easier to attack neighboring Acadie. After a bloody attack on Deerfield, Massachusetts, in early 1704—about fifty men, women, and children were massacred and more than 100 others were taken hostage—a force under the command of Major Benjamin Church was dispatched to exact revenge from the Acadians. Bypassing Port-Royal, Church attacked the outlying settlements of Minas and Chignecto, burning farms, slaughtering cattle, and seizing women and children to exchange for the Deerfield hostages. Two more New England expeditions laid siege to Port-Royal in 1707. Both were repulsed, but those victories would prove to be the last gasp of the French regime in Acadie.

Port-Royal remained the hub of Acadie at the dawn of the eighteenth century. Farms and villages dotted both sides of the winding Annapolis River for about 20 miles inland, from the town to Paradis Terrestre, a bucolic setting that immodest road signs still proclaim to be Paradise. More farms fanned out to the west of the town, along the north side of the Annapolis Basin. There, about a mile from where the Habitation stood, Alan and Wayne Melanson's ancestors settled on a stretch of rolling hills and farmed the marshland stretching down to the water's edge. The original Melansons, Pierre and Priscilla, arrived in Acadie with Thomas Temple's expedition in 1657. The best genealogical evidence unearthed to date suggests he was French, she was English, and both were Protestant. When the colony reverted to France in 1670, they fled to Boston. Their grown sons, Pierre and Charles, who had married local women and converted to Catholicism, remained on the farms they had established at what became known as Melanson Settlement.

Other families migrated to areas farther along the Fundy coast in search of new land or simply to escape the fighting. Jacques Bourgeois left Port-Royal with five other families in 1671 to found a village at Beaubassin, on the broad Chignecto marshes at the head of the bay. About 1680, Pierre Melanson said goodbye to his brother Charles and became one of the founders of the Minas-Grand-Pré region, which was destined to become the colony's largest and most prosperous settlement. The scattering of the Thibodeau clan was typical. Pierre Thibodeau was barely twenty when he arrived in Port-Royal from Poitou in 1654, under contract to work three years as a laborer. He stayed on, married Jeanne Theriot, and built a gristmill on his farm at Prée Ronde—now known as Round Hill—6 miles upriver from Port-Royal. The couple had sixteen children between 1661 and 1689. Pierre and four of his sons pulled up stakes in 1698 and moved to the mouth of the Petitcodiac River, on the New Brunswick side of the Bay of Fundy, no doubt to escape the turmoil. Another son settled in Grand-Pré, a sixth farther east in Piziquid. François Girouard, who arrived from the Loudun area of western France in 1642, was among the laborers d'Aulnay recruited to work at Port-Royal. Of Girouard's five children, two daughters and a son joined the migration to Beaubassin.

Founding new settlements meant diking and reclaiming new stretches of marshland. Sieur de Dièreville, a French doctor and writer who spent the winter of 1699–1700 in Acadie, was impressed with the skill and planning that went into making a dike. "An undertaking of this nature, which can only be carried on at certain Seasons when the Tides do not rise so high, costs a great deal, & takes many days." It was also a communal project, with the area's farmers pitching in to share the backbreaking work. The expertise came from France. In 1636 d'Aulnay imported five *sauniers*, or saltmakers, from the La Rochelle area, where marshes were drained to recover the salt used to preserve fish. Other Acadians traced their roots to the Poitou region, where freshwater marshes were drained and cultivated. Reclamation efforts usually started with the construction of small dikes alongside muddy rivers or streams. These "running dikes" were joined and extended over time, creating ever-larger fields. A typical dike was 5 feet high and 10 feet or more wide at its base, built using rectangular sods cut from the surrounding marsh. The matted roots of the marsh grass held the soil together in a solid, compact mass that one observer likened to a mortar. Fresh grass soon covered the surface of the dike, increasing its strength.

It was not enough to keep out the tide. Unless the land was properly drained, rainwater and backed-up streams would soon create freshwater lagoons on land that used to be awash in seawater twice a day. Drainage was an essential part of the reclamation process, as it took two or three years for rain and melting snow to flush brine from the soil and allow wheat to grow. This is where the Acadians displayed their ingenuity, inserting wooden sluices, called *aboiteaux*, at key points along a dike. Dièreville described the process: five or six rows of large logs were driven into the marsh mud, with a layer of logs stacked horizontally between each one to create a solid cribwork. Spaces between the logs were "carefully filled with well-pounded clay," he reported, to make them watertight. At the center of the structure was the *aboiteau* itself, and several well-preserved examples have been extracted from old Acadian dikes. Workers hollowed out a large log to create a U-shaped channel for freshwater to escape, covered the top side with boards, and installed a wooden door, suspended from a hinge, at the seaward end. The *aboiteau*'s operation was deceptively simple: When the door was exposed at low tide, it was forced open by the pressure of the fresh water backed up in the ditches and streams that cut through the marsh, draining the land. When the tide and the flow of water reversed, the valve snapped shut and the seawater was kept at bay. So it went, twice a day, as Fundy's mighty tides rose and fell like clockwork.

The effort was worth it. The rich soil of the marshes was up to 40 feet deep. "The abundant crop that is harvested in the second year, after the soil has been washed by Rain water compensates, for all the expense," Dièreville noted. In the meantime, as nature looked after desalination, the land produced marsh hay or was used as pasture for cattle. New England surveyor Charles Morris reported in 1748 that the reclaimed marshlands—which he coveted for his countrymen—were incredibly fertile and "so strong and Lasting" that the Acadians could plant grain season after season, for ten and in some cases twenty years, without depleting the soil or reducing the yield. There were also drawbacks. As dikes stretched farther out into bays and estuaries, higher and stronger barriers had to be built. More robust dikes were required as Acadians settled the upper reaches of the Bay of Fundy, where the tide reached its greatest height. There was always the threat that an exceptionally high tide or a storm would overflow or breach the dikes, flooding the hard-won fields. When Church's raiders looted and burned Acadian villages in 1704, they broke open the dikes at Minas as a coup de grâce. But floods, whether natural or human-made, were a temporary setback. Once the dikes were repaired, rainwater would once again wash out the salt and the land would be as good as new within a couple of years, if not better, since new layers of muddy silt and the break from cultivation sometimes made the land more fertile than before.

Besides wheat and hay, the marshes were used to grow oats, rye, barley, corn, flax, and hemp. Windmills and water-powered mills to grind grain were scattered among the villages. The ever-present risk of flooding prompted the Acadians to locate their farms and mills on higher ground at the edge of the adjacent uplands. Houses, barns, and garden plots were surrounded by fences to keep out the cattle, which roamed the fields and woods during the summer. Bread and milk were staples of the diet. Visitors remarked on the poor quality of the butter and likely were relieved to discover the Acadians did not try to make cheese. No Acadian garden was complete without peas, cabbages, and turnips. Acadians also hunted and fished, using canoes and small boats or erecting weirs along the tidal rivers, but preferred farm produce over wild game. Dièreville observed that they would rather drink milk than eat partridge or rabbit. Sheep were kept for wool rather than meat, and chickens and geese were prized for their feathers, which were used to stuff mattresses or sold to traders. Pigs feasted on table scraps and the discards from slaughtered livestock until their own day of reckoning. Dièreville found the Acadians to be "great lovers of fat bacon," and a popular wintertime dish was a soup made of cabbage, turnip, and slices of pork. Another visitor recorded the menu for one hearty meal—bonyclabber (a combination of buttermilk curds and oatmeal) with soup, salad, roast fish, and buttered bread.

Like their ancestors in France, the Acadians kept fine orchards. Homesteads were set among rows of apple, cherry, pear, and plum trees. By the closing years of the 1600s, census takers counted almost 1,800 fruit trees on about fifty farms. The Acadians planted well: when New Englanders began snapping up vacant land five years after the deportation, some orchards were still bearing fruit. Early names for some areas of the Minas region—Canning (Apple Tree Landing) and the marshland near Avonport (Pear Tree Dike)—

record what the new settlers found. One incredibly long-lived Acadian tree was reputed to be still producing apples when it was chopped down in the 1930s.

In *Evangeline*, Longfellow portrays Acadie as an arcadia, an idyllic place where men and boys toiled in the fields all day while their wives and sweethearts spun flax to make clothes, merrily singing as they worked. In the poet's imagination, frolicking children would stop in their tracks to kiss the hand of the parish priest as he made his rounds. The sun sank "serenely" each evening, a church bell tolled softly to enforce a nine o'clock curfew, and columns of pale blue smoke drifted from the chimneys of "homes of peace and contentment." No one locked their doors, of course, for the pious Acadians "dwelt together in love" and lived "at peace with God and the world," even tolerating the English heretics who passed through their villages from time to time. "Fear, that reigns with the tyrant, and envy, the vice of republics" were unknown on this fairytale landscape, where "the richest was poor, and the poorest lived in abundance."

Longfellow never visited Nova Scotia, and his lack of first-hand experience shows. First, a reality check on the climate. The Annapolis Valley is blessed with the warmest temperatures in Nova Scotia, enjoying a long growing season and plenty of days that are bathed in sunshine and finish with a serene sunset. But winters can be harsh along the Bay of Fundy, with deep snows and bitter winds howling across the exposed marshland. Summer can bring day after day of stifling heat and the scourge of black flies and mosquitoes. Robert Hale, a young Massachusetts doctor who hopped aboard the schooner *Cupid* for a cruise to Nova Scotia in the summer of 1731, was shocked at the onslaught of mosquitoes when he stepped ashore in the Chignecto area. On a calm, hot day, he claimed, "tis impossible to live, especially among the trees." He attributed the Acadians' dark complexions to "living in the smoke ... to defend themselves against the mosquitoes."

Most Acadian houses had French-style thatched roofs and may have been the "homes of peace and contentment" that Longfellow described, but they were far from comfortable. A house built near Rustico, Prince Edward Island, in 1770 by Acadians who escaped deportation, has been restored as a museum. Maison Doucet is primitive, its square timbers hewn by hand and held together with wooden pegs—not a single nail was used, no doubt because none were available. Gaps between the timbers were plugged with clay, seaweed, even animal dung—anything to keep out the winter wind. By modern standards, the house is barely the size of a one-car garage, but for years it doubled as the area's church and the Doucets somehow found room for a large brood of kids. There is a main kitchen and dining area facing the open stone hearth, two small bedrooms downstairs, and a loft that provided additional sleeping quarters. Most cooking and baking was done outside— and well away from the house to reduce the risk of fire—using a brick-lined oven or a large kettle suspended over an open fire.

Hale described the interior of an Acadian house he visited in 1731, and it sounds much like Maison Doucet—a single large room and a loft. The beds he saw resembled bunks on a ship, enclosed and accessed though a hole "just big enough to crawl into" and covered with a curtain. This appears to have been a common feature of Acadian homes, providing a measure of privacy as well as a cozy nighttime oasis in a drafty house. A thatched-roof Acadian house, circa 1670, reconstructed on the grounds of Annapolis Royal's Historic Gardens, features one of these chambers. Hale, a Harvard graduate who was later elected to the Massachusetts legislature, was obviously used to finer accommodations. He was taken aback by the lack of furnishing, which is a revelation as well for the modern visitor who steps inside the sparsely appointed Maison Doucet. The spartan decorating style can best be described as minimalist-meets-country primitive. Hale counted no more than two or three chairs to a house, all crudely built with uncomfortable plank seats. Utensils were just as sparse. In five days ashore at Chignecto, he saw a total of two drinking mugs in use, and one of those had a broken rim. When the locals broke out the "strong drinks"—the *Cupid* had brought 100 gallons of rum to trade for coal dug from Chignecto's seaside cliffs, so there was booze to be had—they served it in a large basin, handed Hale a dipping ladle, and invited him to help himself.

"The French entertained us with much civility and courtesy," Hale reported, as one would expect of such a contented people. He also confirmed

Longfellow's vision of a society in which "the richest was poor," at least in terms of cash. "Money is the worst commodity a man can have here and the people here don't care to take it," he groused. When he paid his room and board at the village tavern, he discovered the owner had five pennies to his name, "though he is one of the wealthiest in the place." Wealth accumulated, perhaps, by convincing gullible American tourists he could not make change.

Many Acadians were better off than the chair-deprived, mugless, basin-sharing crew that Hale encountered. Farms along the Annapolis River and Minas Basin were well established and prosperous, with good harvests of grain, large herds of livestock, and homes that were larger, yet equally rustic. Artifacts unearthed at Acadian sites over the years include shards of English and Chinese porcelain, French pottery and New England earthenware, evidence of prosperity and proof of the extent of trade between Acadie and the outside world. Archeologists have found English clay pipes, French wine bottles, and fancy buckles, along with oversized iron keys that show a few folks locked their doors. And Acadie's economy was not completely moneyless— eighteenth-century British, French, and even Spanish coins have been found. The basement of the harbormaster's house that stood at Port-La-Joye, near present-day Charlottetown, Prince Edward Island, until the 1740s yielded four weathered coins, including a gold piece the size of a quarter.

Acadians earned wages by building and supplying forts, and the troops stationed inside were let out now and then to spend their pay among the locals. But the true measure of wealth in Acadie was cattle, which could be sold for cash or swapped for imported goods. Acadian livestock and grain supplied the region's garrisons, both French and British, as well as the populous New England market. While much of this trade was illegal, officials on the ground lacked the manpower or will to enforce embargoes. Smuggling was so prevalent under French rule that, at one point, two French officials accused each other of profiting from illegal trade with New England. Each spring the merchants of Boston and other centers sent their vessels up the Bay of Fundy "as if it were an English gulf," one scholar has claimed. In addition to live cattle, the Yankees wanted salted beef, flour, and feathers to stuff bedding and pillows. In return, they peddled tools, other iron products, guns, cloth, sugar, and spices. Acadians developed a reputation as misers—as being "covetous of specie," as one American observer put it. Money was hoarded out of necessity, not greed, earmarked for the long list of items the Acadians could not grow or make themselves. "There is plenty of money in Acadia," Daniel d'Auger de Subercase, the last French governor, complained in 1710, "but that the inhabitants do not put it into circulation." Hale's tavernkeeper no doubt had only five pennies in his till because the rest of his cash was socked away for the arrival of the next Yankee trading ship.

Acadians tended to be do-it-yourselfers. Most farmers could turn their hands to carpentry and other tasks, and it was common for relatives and friends to join forces on major projects like building houses and dikes. French census records show that as early as the 1670s, there was an array of tradesmen within some villages, including blacksmiths, weavers, coopers, gunsmiths, masons, tailors, and—Longfellow would be surprised to discover—locksmiths. There was even a surgeon. Many of these specialists likely farmed as well, and it was common to trade labor for services, so a blacksmith might forge tools or nails for a farmer in exchange for produce or help in tending his own fields and herds. There were a few water-powered sawmills to cut boards for building houses, boats, and small ships, but such operations were modest. Many Acadians fished for a living and some, like Charles Belliveau, knew their way around a sailing vessel. Hale reports that a dozen Acadians manned two boats that ferried Chignecto coal to a central wharf for loading.

Much of their cloth and clothing was imported, but Acadian women made the rest from the flax and wool their farms produced, using homemade spinning wheels and looms. Linen shirts and dresses for women, woolen coats and pants for men, were standard issue. Visitors noted the Acadians had a penchant for wearing red and black, sometimes as a pants-leg stripe, while women adorned their skirts with ribbons. Hale appeared to have had an eye for the ladies because he made no mention of what Acadian men wore. The women's clothes looked as if "they were pitched on with pitchforks," he noted, "and very often their stockings are down about their heels." Dièreville was more charitable than his fellow traveler, noting simply that the Acadians did not "follow the fashion." To Hale's surprise, both men and women wore wooden shoes, which were unknown in New England. While leather shoes were common, these *sabots* were surprisingly comfortable for long days spent tending gardens and working the fields—"the original Birkenstocks," says an interpreter at the Port-Royal Habitation who swears by them.

The early Acadians, like their present-day Acadian and Cajun descendants, knew how to have a good time. Moses Delesdernier, a Swiss immigrant who lived among the farmers of Piziquid before the deportation, recalled them as "cheerful and light-hearted" and fond of "parties and merrymakings." Although Acadian women were "more assiduous workers," he recalled, they too took "a considerable part in the amusements." Given the unrelenting work of running a farm and raising a family, there's little wonder the Acadians welcomed a chance to blow off some steam and enjoy life. Delesdernier does not specify what these merrymakers were up to, but other accounts say Acadians often gathered to play cards, tell stories, sing songs, and dance to pass the long winter nights. Pipe-smoking was the Acadian vice of choice, confirmed by the numerous fragments of clay pipes found at Acadian sites. The diversions recorded in *Evangeline*—feasts, games, evening chats at the fireside, friends sharing a pouch of tobacco—appear to have a basis in fact. The ever-observant Robert Hale was surprised to see family members kneel to say their bedtime prayers as others in the room continued to talk and smoke without missing a beat.

And, as Hale noted, Acadians liked their "strong drinks." The impending marriage of Evangeline and Gabriel was toasted in verse with a tankard of ale, and real-life Acadians had plenty of imported rum, wine, and brandy to hoist. The Cajun party mantra—*"laissez les bons temps rouler"* (let the good times roll)—may have originated three centuries ago on the shores of the Bay of Fundy. Local priests complained, in a 1740s report to their superiors, of quarrels fueled by too much drinking. This may, in part, explain why the Acadians planted willows on their farms—the tree's bark has long been the basis for a folk-remedy for hangovers. The report implied that taverns remained open on Sundays and religious holidays, even during mass, and condemned the sinful practice of men and women singing lewd songs and dancing together after sunset.

This is not to imply the early Acadians were debauched party animals, or that Longfellow's frolicking children were more likely to thumb their noses at the parish priest than to kiss his hand. The clergy was an influential force in Acadian communities, as subsequent events would show. The parish registers of births, baptisms, marriages, and deaths were often the only written record of entire communities and families. Delesdernier claimed the Acadians were "the most innocent and virtuous people" he had ever encountered, and remarked on "the inviolable purity of their morals." While he could not recall hearing of a single illegitimate birth, it is clear that not all of those couples engaged in late-night dancing were married. Records of court proceedings in Annapolis Royal under British rule include cases dealing with illegitimate children. Priests were sometimes called on to grant permission for second cousins to marry, and a premarital pregnancy was the most common reason for couples to seek such dispensation. Acadians took their Catholic faith seriously, just not seriously enough for their priests. Communities relied on clergymen imported from Quebec or France, and there is no evidence of Acadians directing their children into the priesthood. "Religion among the Acadians seems to have been a matter of necessity but not a question of sainthood," Canada's pre-eminent Acadian scholar, Naomi Griffiths, has observed, "an important and vital ingredient in life, but not the sole shaping force of the social and cultural life of their communities."

Acadians certainly took to heart the Catholic belief that marriage was intended to produce children. Historians estimate that an average family consisted of between four and seven children, and larger families were common. A study of the Port-Royal area shows that women who married before the age of twenty, which was common, bore on average ten or eleven children. Alan and Wayne Melanson's ancestor who escaped the deportation, Ambroise, married twice and fathered twenty-one children, including triplets and two sets of twins. Dièreville remarked that "the swarming of Brats is a sight to behold." Griffiths cites one man, Claude Landry of Grand-Pré, who raised eight children and, when he died in 1747 at age eighty-six, was survived by at least forty-six grandchildren and eleven great-grandchildren. By the early 1700s the Acadian population was doubling every twenty years. Census records chart the Acadians' remarkable population growth. Between 1671 and 1701 their numbers tripled to 1,450. Port-Royal was still the largest community in 1701, with 450 people, but there were 300 in the Minas area, about 190 at Piziquid and the same number at Beaubassin. Another 115 people lived in the southern coastal settlements of La Hève, Cape Sable, and Pubnico. The population was nearing 10,000 when English Governor Richard Philipps noted in 1730, with some alarm, that the Acadians were spreading themselves "over the face of the province ... like Noah's progeny."

This population explosion was accomplished during a period when immigration to the colony was sparse. At a time when life expectancy in France was estimated to be as little as twenty-five years—and maybe half the population survived to celebrate a twenty-first birthday—two-thirds of the children born in Port-Royal reached adulthood. Acadians were blessed with good genes, and many men and women lived into their seventies and eighties. Households made up of three or four generations of one family were common. Acadian women had their hands full looking after large broods of children and elderly relatives as well as tending to their gardens and household chores. Longevity and low rates of childhood mortality are proof that life was good for most Acadians. Food was plentiful. Traders supplied necessities and luxuries that could not be grown on the farm or made at home. Acadie was not cut off from the rest of the world, but its remoteness and insular society shielded its settlers from the deadly plagues and epidemics that routinely swept through other populations of the time. Despite constant contact with itinerant merchants, soldiers, and priests, and a trickle of newcomers from France and neighboring French colonies, no major outbreaks of disease were recorded in Acadie prior to 1755.

A few Acadian families were related before they left France and lack of immigration meant the rest quickly became intertwined. After a few generations, it became increasingly difficult to find anyone who was not a second or third cousin to someone else. Pierre Melanson, who founded the Minas settlements, married into the d'Entremont family of Pubnico. One of Charles Melanson's daughters married the son of Charles de La Tour and Charles de Menou d'Aunlay's widow, Jeanne Motin, giving Alan and Wayne Melanson a distant family link to Acadie's bitter civil war. Other Melansons of that generation married into the Belliveau, Bourg, Robichaud, Landry, Comeau, and Babineau families. As his sixteen children married, Pierre Thibodeau became an in-law to the Landrys, Robichauds, Bourgs, and Comeaus, as well as the Boudrots, Heberts, Aucoins, and Lejeunes. François Girouard's oldest son,

Jacques, made him a grandfather fourteen times, and the third-generation marriages of this single branch of the family tree would link the Girouards to the Doucet, Labornge, Pettipas, Granger, Blanchard, Bernard, Bastarache, Comeau, Bourgois, and Richard families. A typical Acadian village was a small cluster of farms, like the Melanson Settlement, worked by members of extended families. These hamlets, in turn, were linked by ties of blood and marriage that crossed the generations and spanned the Fundy region.

While Acadians were overwhelmingly of French origin, there was diversity in their ranks. There was a smattering of Scottish, Irish, English, and Basque blood, thanks to the visiting fishermen who found Acadian wives and a few settlers and traders who were holdovers from the days of English rule. Acadians also intermarried with the Mi'kmaq, cementing the bonds of friendship and religion first forged at the Port-Royal Habitation. The harmony that prevailed between Acadians and Mi'kmaq stands in stark contrast to the clashes between Europeans and Aboriginal peoples in other parts of North America. This was not a matter of luck or getting off on the right foot—the two peoples were able to coexist because of their unique use of the land. The Mi'kmaq moved their villages with the seasons, using rivers and lakes as highways into the interior as they hunted and fished. The Acadians did not compete for the land the Mi'kmaq had been using for centuries—they were busily creating their own as they reclaimed Fundy's marshes.

Some historians and contemporary observers have looked down their noses at the Acadians, denigrating their work ethic and intellectual abilities. Even Delesdernier, a bit of a fan of all things Acadian, declared them "completely ignorant of the progress of arts and sciences." Apparently it took more than engineering an elaborate system of dikes to hold back the world's highest tides to impress him. A history of Canada, published for a general audience in the 1920s, offered a patronizing description of the Acadians as "simple-minded people ... a frugal, contented folk" who "knew or cared little" about the outside world. A decade later textbook writer James Bingay was telling impressionable Canadian high school students that the Acadians were "a humble, ignorant, fairly peaceable body of farmers." The victors write the history books, of course, and for a long time this was the popular image of the Acadians, at least in English Canada—simple French peasants who were so busy building dikes and having kids that they were oblivious to the imperial struggle engulfing their corner of the world.

Modern-day observers, however, have come to appreciate the Acadians as a complex people who were, in some respects, advanced in their thinking. American geographer Andrew Hill Clark, who in the 1960s published the definitive work on life in Acadie before the deportation, showed obvious affection when he described them as "dedicated, stubborn, resilient, pettifogging, inventive, exasperating, peace-loving, and, in many ways, altogether magnificent." Much of the earlier nonsense was based on the fact that most Acadians were illiterate. This was not by choice—there were no formal schools after the British takeover. The Acadians were a frontier people, among the first wave of European settlement in North America. Like other trailblazers of the colonial period, education was not always a priority. No books or hours spent in a school were going to put bread on the table. A system of public education was not instituted in Nova Scotia until a century after the deportation. Petitions and oaths of allegiance signed under English rule do show that a fair number of Acadian men could at least sign their names.

The idleness rap comes from the Acadians' approach to farming. They preferred to build dikes and drain marshes rather than clear the forests on the adjacent uplands. A French governor of the 1680s concluded that "fear of work" prevented the Acadians from expanding their farms inland. British observers reached similar conclusions. Major Paul Mascarene of the Annapolis Royal garrison, a French-speaking Huguenot who went on to become the colony's lieutenant-governor, described them in 1720 as:

> very little industrious, their land not improved as might be expected, they lieving in a manner from hand to mouth, and provided they have a good feild of Cabages and bread anough for their familyes, with what fodder is sufficient for their Cattle they seldome look for much further improvement.

Philipps, the English governor who fretted about the Acadian population explosion, wrote in 1734 that they were "a pest & Incumbrance" to the colony, "a proud, Lazy, obstinate and untractable people, unskillfull in the methods of Agriculture." In a century of settlement, Philipps claimed, they had cleared no more than a few hundred acres of woodland, and could not be bothered to spread cattle manure to fertilize their fields. Charles Morris, the surveyor, also considered them "indifferent" farmers who undertook "no more labour than what necessity urges them to."

What Mascarene, Philipps, and Morris considered laziness, though, was evidence of an intimate knowledge of the land and a shrewd assessment of how best to farm it. For starters, building, expanding, and maintaining the sprawling network of dikes was hard work in its own right, requiring careful planning and the joint effort of many families. "The ebb & flow of the Sea cannot easily be stopped," Dièreville declared after surveying the diked marshlands in 1699, "what labour is needed to make them fit for cultivation!" To stroll along the remnants of those dikes today, to witness Fundy's surging tide stopped in its tracks on one side, corn growing and cattle grazing many feet below sea level on the other, is to admire the Acadians for their foresight and achievement. They were already felling trees on the uplands to clear land for their homesteads and for timber and firewood; the famous opening line of *Evangeline*—"This is the forest primeval"—leaves an erroneous impression that the Acadians were tree-huggers who built their homes under towering pines and hemlocks. But making the uplands suitable for agriculture meant hauling away or burning the logs and brush, then uprooting the stumps or tilling the space between them. Since the land was not very fertile, manure would have to be spread to produce a worthwhile crop.

The Acadians saw the advantages of reclaiming the marshes—the land was flat, well drained, free of stones, and fertile enough to produce grain without fertilizer. Once the prep work of diking and draining was complete, the rain did the rest. Some forested land was cleared for cultivation over the years, but the results were disappointing. In the opinion of Andrew Hill Clark, the Acadians "simply observed the comparatively poor yields and short life of unfertilized upland soils and made, for their situation, a good judgment." The Acadians made a good living off their land by farming it their way—crop failures, Clark concluded, were rare. Could they have aspired to do more than live "hand to mouth," as Mascarene put it? They could and they did, producing enough food to sustain their families during the harsh winters as well as a surplus for export. Anyone who has ever dreamed of escaping the rat race can admire the Acadians for being content to live within their means, for finding the elusive balance between hard work and merrymaking.

Acadians were sophisticated—one might say ahead of their time—when it came to social and political structures. Visitors were struck by the egalitarian and communal nature of Acadian society. Longfellow described it as a land "where all men were equal, and all were brothers and sisters," and in this respect he seems to have hit the nail on the head. "They live in a state of perfect equality, without distinction of rank in society," Delesdernier observed, so laid-back and informal that men did not bother to address each other as *monsieur*. It was a world away—literally as well as figuratively—from the rigid class distinctions of Europe. Delesdernier detected little evidence of greed or lust for power during his sojourn among them. People "helped each other's wants with benevolent liberality; they required no interest for loans of money or other property." American historian Francis Parkman, writing a century ago, concluded that everyone was equal in Acadian society because everyone was equally poor. To him, they achieved nothing more than "the social equality which can only exist in the humblest conditions of society." But Parkman's rather smug view overlooks the fact that many Acadians were rich in terms of land and livestock, and wielded considerable power and influence within their tight-knit communities.

Acadians displayed an independent streak and a deep distrust of authority. Government, whether French or English, rarely touched their lives as they tended their farms, raised their families, and founded new communities along the Bay of Fundy. Governor François-Marie Perrot complained in 1686 that his unruly charges did as they pleased, with many young men living "an easy vagabondish and immoral life" among the Mi'kmaq. Count Louis de Baude Frontenac, the governor of New France, felt the Acadians displayed "parliamentary" leanings that he attributed to the influences of English rule and trade with Massachusetts. "They lived like true republicans," another official complained, "not acknowledging royal or judicial authority." Trying to collect taxes was often futile and surveyors dispatched to try to make sense of years of unregulated settlement faced resistence, if not outright hostility. When French officials conducted their first census in 1671, Pierre Melanson and another man flatly refused to supply any information about their families or farms. Melanson's wife, Marguerite, assured the census taker he was "crazy" to be walking around asking such questions. A succession of governors fired off letters griping about their tenuous grip on the population, but little was done to assert authority. Port-Royal's garrison was chronically understaffed, no matter which flag was flying over its modest fortifications. And although the town was the seat of power for most of Acadian history, it became increasingly isolated from the thriving settlements at Minas and Chignecto.

By the dawn of the eighteenth century, the Acadians were no longer French settlers in the New World. They were *acadiens* and *acadiennes*, a people that had called Acadie home for close to a century. They were North Americans who spoke French, not Frenchmen living in North America. Their families were large, close-knit, and interconnected in countless ways through marriage and friendship. The Acadians were fully adapted to their environment and deeply attached to the land. They had learned to reclaim its fertile marshes, tough out its winters, and get along with the Mi'kmaq. War and trade brought the outside world to Acadie, but the impact was minimal. The Acadians had evolved into a distinct people, an immense extended family that was hardworking, independent-minded, sometimes boisterous, and ever wary of authority. Griffiths put it best: "The Acadians considered themselves Acadian, the French considered them unreliable allies, and the English, unsatisfactory citizens." It was their misfortune, and their tragedy, to be on the front lines when these superpowers squared off, in the first half of the eighteenth century, in a final contest for control of North America.

3 "THE NEUTRAL FRENCH"

The french Inhabitants are certainly in a very perillous Situation, those who pretend to be their Friends and old Masters have let loose a parcell of Banditti to plunder them, whilst on the other hand they see themselves threatened with ruin & Destruction, if they fail in their allegiance to the British Government.

—Major Paul Mascarene to Governor William Shirley, July 28, 1744

"Saluting the Fort," Nicholson called it. The first two nights of the siege, his bomb ship—a rather grand name for a floating gun platform—maneuvered to the center of the river and lobbed mortar rounds over the walls of the fortress. Seven exploding shells rained down on the first night, another three dozen on the second, shaking Port-Royal like huge thunderclaps. All the while French gunners on the ramparts returned fire toward the British positions and camps, but scored few hits. On the third and fourth nights the wet and stormy fall weather kept the bomb ship at anchor and spared the defenders from further battering. The attackers used the interlude to continue to land their cannon and haul them within range of the fort. Those batteries would soon join the barrage.

This was the third British attempt to retake Port-Royal in as many years. After the colony's return in 1697, the French built what was, for the time, a state-of-the-art bastion on the site where the forts of Alexander, d'Aulnay, and Meneval had stood. Based on the designs of renowned military engineer Sébastien le Prestre de Vauban, its earthen walls and deep ditches formed a four-pointed star around the barracks and powder magazines inside.

Approaching soldiers literally faced an uphill battle, exposed to a deadly cross-fire from muskets and cannon stationed on the walls above. Twice during 1707, expeditions out of Boston laid siege to the fort, but both attacks foundered under the weight of inept leadership. Daniel d'Auger de Subercase, then barely eight months into his tenure as Acadie's governor, had his horse shot out from under him as he led one ambush. The New Englanders fled, reappeared with reinforcements two months later, and were sent packing a second time, but a lot had changed since those easy victories. France was faring badly in the latest war and there was no money to pay the troops. Subercase sold his silverware to finance repairs to the fort. The recruits sent to the garrison were mostly teenagers and, as for the officers, Subercase grumbled that he had "as much need of a madhouse as of barracks."

So when Subercase counted five warships and thirty troop transports at anchor in the Annapolis Basin on the afternoon of October 5, 1710, his alarm turned to dread. He was outnumbered, outgunned, and running out of miracles. There were about 150 soldiers in the garrison—many of them too sick or too jaded to put up much of a fight—plus about 100 Acadians and Native fighters. Morale was so low that he dared send no more than a handful of soldiers outside to harass the invaders as they dug in, for fear they would desert. At least ten men bolted for the British lines before the shooting even started. Subercase, though, was not the kind to cut and run. He was a veteran of backwoods campaigns against Native tribes, and the governorship of Acadie had been his reward for masterminding a series of raids on Newfoundland's British posts. But after two nights of bombardment and with enemy cannon encircling the fort, Subercase knew all he could do was buy a little time. A Vauban fort could keep soldiers at bay, but it would not last long in the face of bomb ships and siege batteries. Subercase had begged his superiors to send supplies and reinforcements, so there was a chance French warships would show up to save the day. On October 10, he dashed off a letter to the British commander Colonel Francis Nicholson. He had a small favor to ask, gentleman to gentleman. The wives of some of the French officers had fled to the woods, but others, along with their female servants, had chosen to remain in the fort as the siege began. "Sir," he wrote, "they did all along Flatter themselves that they could hear and bear the noise of your Bombs without fear, but they now find themselves a little mistaken." Would Nicholson be so kind to allow these fine ladies to leave the fort and ensure that "nothing that is uncivil or abusive" would befall them?

Nicholson had no feud with the ladies, but he smelled a rat. The French officer who delivered the letter walked into his camp without a drummer to announce his arrival, and had a good look around before he could be blindfolded. It was a serious breach of battlefield protocol and Nicholson arrested the officer as a spy. The attempt to parley may well have been a ploy to confirm the enemy's strength. Subercase was about to fold his cards and likely wanted to be sure he was not surrendering to some ragtag band of conscripts. He need not have worried. Nicholson, the former lieutenant governor of Virginia, was a seasoned campaigner who had seen action in Europe and North Africa. A physically imposing man in his mid-fifties, he evoked strong reactions from those around him—for every detractor who considered him quick-tempered, vain, and vindictive, there was an admirer in awe of his bravery and generosity. His second-in-command on this expedition, Samuel Vetch, later dismissed him as an illiterate madman. Mad or not, Nicholson had 400 redcoats and 1,500 colonial troops under his command. This time, the British meant business.

An extraordinary correspondence followed over the next three days as Subercase tried to delay the inevitable. Nicholson refused to hold back his bomb ship, but promised to protect the officers' wives if they took refuge at his camp. Fine, Subercase replied, but the detained officer must be released. Nicholson refused, insisting he was a spy. They engaged in a debate over the rules of war that applied to messengers entering an enemy camp under a flag of truce. Nicholson accused Subercase of being more interested in retrieving his officer than protecting the women inside the fort. Subercase suddenly complained he had no one to translate the incoming messages and asked Nicholson to write future letters in French. Nicholson found that hard to believe, since the officer in his custody spoke perfect English. "When you are pleased to write to me in English," he shot back, "I will answer you in French." The object of this petty squabbling, for Subercase at least, was to make sure Nicholson was a man of his word. He was well aware of the broken promises made to his predecessor, Meneval, to end the siege of 1690. "To prevent the spilling of both

English and French Blood," Subercase wrote at last, "I am ready to hold up both hands for a Capitulation that will be honourable to both of us."

Nicholson answered with a barrage from his shore-based guns to show he meant business, then issued a demand for Subercase to surrender the fort and the colony. A cease-fire was called while officers hammered out the terms. Subercase and his troops would be granted the honor of marching out of the fort, and the entire garrison, along with wives and children, would be given passage to France. Nicholson made good on his promise to look after the wives of the French officers, sending his men to retrieve those who were hiding in the woods and treated them to breakfast at his camp. The entire siege was a gentlemanly affair, with only a handful of casualties on each side despite the intense bombardment. More lives were likely lost before the attack began, when one of Nicholson's transports ran aground at the entrance to the Annapolis Basin and two dozen soldiers and sailors drowned.

On October 16, Subercase met Nicholson at the entrance to the fort. "I'm very sorry for the misfortune of the King my master in Losing such a Brave Fort, and the Territories adjoyning," he declared, "but count myself happy in falling into the hands of so noble and generous a General." He handed over the large iron key to the main gate and could not resist a last dig, telling Nicholson he hoped to pay him "a visit next Spring." Subercase then led his soldiers out of the fort with their muskets on their shoulders, "Drums beating, Colours flying," each man saluting Nicholson as he passed. The British marched inside, fired the cannon of the fort in celebration and drank a toast to Queen Anne. Nicholson immediately christened the fortress Fort Anne and renamed the town Annapolis Royal in her honor. Back in New England, a public holiday was declared to mark the long-sought conquest of Acadie.

Vetch was named governor and a small garrison was left behind to defend the British foothold in Acadie. Vetch was a shady figure, a soldier-turned-merchant from New England who was forever fending off allegations—most of them true—that he profited from illegal trade with the French. He had sold the queen's ministers on his vision of a "Glorious Enterprise" to conquer all of New France, giving new meaning to the term "hostile takeover." The conquest of Port-Royal, a pared-down version of the plan, almost unraveled during the winter of 1710–1711. The fort was still damaged from the siege and France and England remained at war. About seventy New England soldiers succumbed to disease over the winter and were buried at night, so the Acadians would not see that the garrison was becoming vulnerable. In the spring, making good on Subercase's threat to return, the French sent in a band of Native fighters to retake the fort. A June 1711 skirmish along the Annapolis River, at a site aptly named Bloody Creek, left at least eighteen British soldiers dead and incited some Acadians to take up arms. The British were pinned down in the fort for about a month, but reinforcements arrived from New England, the Natives withdrew, and the uprising withered.

Acadie had changed hands for the last time. In 1713, the Treaty of Utrecht formally ceded Port-Royal and Acadie, "with its ancient boundaries," to England. This inexact phrase clearly covered all of mainland Nova Scotia, but both sides continued to claim sovereignty over what is now New Brunswick. France retained the neighboring colonies of Île Saint-Jean (Prince Edward Island) and Île Royale (Cape Breton), making Nova Scotia a British enclave ringed by French territories. Under the treaty, the estimated 1,800 Acadians in the conquered territory could "remove themselves within a year to any other place, as they shall think fit, together with all their moveable effects." Those who chose to remain would be considered British subjects and would be free "to enjoy the free exercise of their religion, according to the usage of the Church of Rome, as far as the laws of Britain allow the same." This rather magnanimous gesture of religious tolerance came at a cost—the Acadians could keep their priests, but, like Catholics in Britain at the time, they were second-class citizens, barred from serving in the army and navy and ineligible to hold office in the new administration being formed to govern the colony. Queen Anne issued instructions to Nicholson, who had replaced Vetch as governor, that Acadians who chose to stay were to be treated as British subjects and were free to remain on their farms "without any Lett or Molestation as fully and freely as other our Subjects do." Those who chose to leave were free to sell their lands—a hollow concession, since there were no buyers waiting in the wings—and depart.

At first, it appeared the Acadians would pack up and leave. The French were establishing a fortress and town at Louisbourg and tried to lure the Acadians to their beachhead on Île Royale. French emissaries toured the colony in 1714 and convinced a few hundred families in the Annapolis Royal, Minas, and Cobequid areas to emigrate in exchange for land and free provisions. But the British were beginning to get cold feet—a mass exodus would deprive their garrisons of a source of food and supplies. The colonial authorities consulted Vetch, who was in England and believed the loss of the Acadians and their cattle would reduce Acadia "to its primitive state" and make Île Royale the most powerful French colony in America. The official in charge at Annapolis Royal, Thomas Caulfeild, added a warning that the friendship between the Acadians and the Mi'kmaq kept the latter in check, helping to protect the British from "ye insults of ye Indians, ye worst of enemies." Besides, Caulfeild predicted, the Acadians' children "in process of time will be brought to our Constitution."

The decision ultimately rested with the Acadians. If they chose to leave, the British did not have the manpower to stop them. For their part, the Acadians were having second thoughts. Agents sent ahead to Île Royale reported that the land was poor for farming, convincing many that it made no sense to leave their fertile marshlands. When the French failed to follow through on a promise to send ships to pick them up, most Acadians decided to stay put. The French saw advantages in this arrangement. When the time came to try to retake the mainland—as it most certainly would—they assumed the Acadians would join forces with them to drive out the British.

Meanwhile, it took Nova Scotia's new rulers several years to get their act together. Vetch managed to reclaim the governor's post from Nicholson, but never showed up to take charge. A new governor, Colonel Richard Philipps, was appointed in 1717. A Welsh-born career military officer, Philipps fought at the bloody Battle of the Boyne and, on another occasion, was captured during a clandestine mission and narrowly escaped being hanged. His appointment signaled a new resolve on the part of the British officials in charge of colonial affairs, the Lords of Trade and Plantations, to create a stable government in Nova Scotia. A system of military rule was established, with the governor and an appointed council, made up of garrison officers and local English merchants, calling the shots.

In 1721, in response to the "dayly cry ... for Justice" from the inhabitants, Philipps established the council as a court to hold criminal trials and to resolve civil disputes. Despite the Acadians' reputation, in some quarters, for living in peace and harmony, they were quick to take advantage of this crude legal system and instigated most of the civil actions tried at Annapolis Royal in the early 1730s. The council's detailed minutes reveal that two-thirds of these cases involved disputes over boundaries and ownership of land, which is to be expected in an agrarian society. While the Acadians preferred to deal with other disputes among themselves, they were pleased to turn to the British when it served their purposes. In a few instances, disgruntled Acadians appealed to the council to overturn a decision made by their local priest. In others, communities fed up with rabble-rousers or unable to restrain feuding families turned to the court to prosecute and punish those responsible for assaults or destroying property.

For the most part, though, the Acadians remained as wary of authority as they had been under French rule. They resisted British demands for surveys and formal grants of land. The Acadians tended to settle where they liked, diking new marshland in remote areas "contrary to the orders often repeated to restrain them," groused one exasperated official. The garrison's authority was so weak that the eminent American historian John Bartlet Brebner dismissed it as "phantom rule." A few hundred soldiers camped at Annapolis Royal could do little to impose their will on the scattered and growing population. One report to London complained that the inhabitants of Minas "scoffed and laughed" when served with orders and "put themselves upon the footing of obeying no government." Philipps was only facing facts in 1720 when he noted that his authority extended no further than the range of the cannon mounted on the ramparts of Fort Anne. To prove the British meant business, he pleaded with the Lords of Trade to post another 600 soldiers to the colony "to curb the insolent temper of the present Inhabitants." The show of force never materialized.

In an effort to impose some order on this chaos, the British relied on elders within the Acadian communities to act as go-betweens. Even during the tense winter of 1710–1711, Vetch summoned Acadian representatives to the fort to help settle disputes between residents and to record land transactions. The idea of a crude form of representative government may have originated with the Acadians themselves—the residents of Minas sought permission to choose deputies "to represent the whole" as early as 1713. Philipps formalized the system, dealing with the Acadians through a group of deputies chosen to represent their communities. He selected a half-dozen representatives from the Annapolis Royal area in 1720 and more deputies were summoned from Minas and Cobequid the following year. They were appointed at first, but by the 1740s Acadians along the Annapolis River and residents of Minas, Piziquid, Cobequid, and Chignecto were holding annual elections to choose a body of twenty-four deputies to represent their interests. For the independent-minded Acadians, this experiment in democracy reinforced a sense that they were able to govern their own affairs. Deputies assumed a host of official duties over time, even though their Catholic faith barred them from formal appointment to public office. They acted as a justice of the peace and a con-stable rolled into one, adjudicating minor disputes and enforcing the orders and judgments of the council. They also oversaw repairs to roads and bridges, verified land surveys, and at times were called on to make arrests or to keep an eye on suspects.

The main role of the deputies, though, was to stickhandle the govern-ment's incessant demands for their people to take an oath of allegiance to the British Crown, a political quagmire that culminated in the events of 1755. In the eighteenth century an oath of fidelity to the monarch was a prerequisite for owning land and claiming the rights of a citizen. In a conquered territory like Acadie, it was considered vital to ensuring the inhabitants would not rebel or side with their former rulers in a future war. The matter first arose in 1714 when George I assumed the throne upon the death of Queen Anne. Since most Acadians had chosen to stay put and become British subjects, the authorities at Annapolis Royal demanded that the head of each family sign an oath of allegiance to the new sovereign. Much to their surprise, the Acadians considered the matter to be negotiable. The residents of Beaubassin refused to sign, pointing out that "while our ancestors were under English rule such an oath was never required of them." The blunt reply from Minas was that the people there would promise to remain neutral as long as the British were in power. Acadians along the Annapolis River proposed that they take an oath vowing not to take up arms against England or France.

The Mi'kmaq were a major stumbling block. The Natives were the most powerful military force in the colony and completely loyal to the French; the Acadians were convinced their old friends and allies would turn on them in a heartbeat if they aligned themselves with the British. Most of all, the Acadians were hedging their bets. The mighty citadel the French were building at Louisbourg was casting a long shadow over the puny British presence at Annapolis Royal. Acadie had changed hands on several occasions within the lifetimes of the older residents and it looked as if the French would be back, and soon. Caught in the middle, the Acadians and their deputies understood that their best hope lay in striving to remain neutral until one side prevailed. "From the Acadian viewpoint," Naomi Griffiths has observed, "it would have been folly indeed to engage in any action which would bind them irrevocably to one Great Power when the other was still not only obviously in the neighbourhood, but even more obviously still interested in the future status of the colony and its inhabitants."

Philipps returned to England in 1722—indeed, he spent most of his tenure there—but in his absence the lieutenant governor, Major Lawrence Armstrong, made a breakthrough. Armstrong was a hothead whose Irish temper once compelled him to smash a wine decanter over the head of a fellow officer to settle an argument. He summoned Acadians in the Annapolis area to the fort in 1726 and convinced them to take an oath that exempted them from bearing arms against the king's enemies. Armstrong, who reasoned that Catholics could not serve in the army anyway, agreed to scribble the proviso in the margin of the French translation of the oath, "in order to gett them over by Degrees." It does not appear that the Lords of Trade were apprised of this strategy. After George I died in 1727, Armstrong demanded that the Acadians take a new, unqualified oath of allegiance to the new monarch, George II. When they again demanded an exemption from fighting for the British, Armstrong and the council briefly imprisoned three of their deputies to show they meant business. So much for winning hearts and minds by degrees.

Armstrong tried another tack, dispatching an officer of his regiment and a detachment of soldiers to administer the oath in the outlying communities. When Ensign Robert Wroth's boat landed at Chignecto in October, a large crowd turned out, "every one shewing their Loyalty & Affection." A new king was as good an excuse as any for a party. The Acadians loudly cheered George II, drank "frequently" to his royal health, and fired their muskets into the air as a salute, Wroth recalled. They were less enthusiastic about swearing the oath and Wroth agreed to a modified one that exempted them from bearing arms. A couple of weeks later the residents of Minas extracted a similar concession, as well as a caveat that they were free to leave the colony whenever they wanted. At their insistence, a reference to "obeying" the king was dropped from the translated version of the oath. The Piziquid Acadians swore the same watered-down oath as their neighbors in Minas. When Wroth reported the results to the council upon his return, he was raked over the coals. In light of Armstrong's new get-tough policy, the concessions were "unwarrantable & dishonourable" and, as a result, the oaths were declared "Null & Void." Armstrong forwarded a copy of Wroth's report to the Lords of Trade, so "His Majesty may see the presumption and unparalleled imprudence of those people." The Acadians, for their part, thought the matter was settled.

Philipps returned to Nova Scotia in 1729, determined to extract an unconditional oath from every Acadian over the age of sixteen without resorting to "threats or compulsion" or "making a scandalous capitulation"—an obvious swipe at the efforts of Armstrong and Wroth. A couple of hundred residents of the Annapolis area signed the following unconditional oath:

> I sincerely promise and swear on my faith as a Christian that I will be utterly loyal, and will truly obey His Majesty King George the second, whom I recognize as the sovereign lord of Acadia or Nova Scotia. May God so help me.

Philipps traveled to Minas, Chignecto, and other communities along the Bay of Fundy and administered the same oath. By September 1730 he was able to send the Lords of Trade oaths signed by about 800 heads of families, which he estimated accounted for some 4,000 people, the majority of the population. How had he succeeded where others had failed? By using "plain reasoning and presents" to placate the Mi'kmaq, Philipps claimed, he was able to reassure the Acadians that they would not face reprisals if they signed. Philipps took another swipe at Armstrong, whom he detested, telling the Lords of Trade with little modesty that the Acadians preferred his style of governing to what they had experienced in his absence.

The truth was that Philipps was lying and had made a "scandalous capitulation" of his own. The Annapolis oath appears to have been unconditional, but there was no sudden change of heart in the outlying areas. There is convincing evidence that Philipps gave Acadians in those settlements a verbal assurance that they would not have to take up arms against the French or the Mi'kmaq. According to two French priests, who were present when the Minas residents signed, Philipps exempted them from fighting for the British. The Lords of Trade quibbled about the wording of the French translation of the oath, but Philipps's reports and letters contain no mention of a side deal about not bearing arms. It was "a spectacular and portentous lie," in the words of a biographer, that would "haunt the masters of Nova Scotia for 25 years and contribute significantly to the tragic elements of the expulsion of 1755." Later governors acknowledged that Philipps, to their chagrin, had saddled them with the concession. After 1730, British officials often referred to the Acadians as "the Neutral French" or as simply "the Neutrals," but there was no official record or recognition that they enjoyed this special status. In his zeal to succeed where his rival Armstrong had failed, Philipps misled his superiors and sowed the seeds of disaster. The Acadians and their deputies were convinced they had won their long-sought neutrality.

Philipps did not stick around to face the consequences of his ruse. He was recalled to England in 1731 amid allegations of mismanaging the garrison's finances and never returned. He remained the absentee governor until 1749, leaving Armstrong in charge once again. Even though Armstrong considered the Acadians "a very ungovernable people" and distrusted their French priests, he was responsible for giving the deputies a greater role in the day-to-day administration of the colony. He was also prone to bouts of depression that culminated just before Christmas 1739 when he grasped his sword and stabbed himself five times in the chest. His fellow officers held an inquest and attributed his suicide to "lunacy."

The exact terms of the oaths sworn before Philipps made little difference as long as peace prevailed, and it did for a generation after the conquest, a period of growth and prosperity, and would be remembered as the Acadians' "golden age." The population explosion continued and new settlements sprang up after 1730 in the Petitcodiac and Memramcook valleys of southern New Brunswick. Geographer Andrew Hill Clark sifted through conflicting population estimates and concluded there were 10,000 Acadians in what is now the Nova Scotia mainland and southern New Brunswick by the 1750s. Grand-Pré and the surrounding area formed the largest community, with 2,500 people. Another 2,500 Acadians lived in the neighboring French territories of Île Saint-Jean and Île Royale. Trade with New England brought in the tools, cloth, and other manufactured goods that made frontier life easier. There was also a lucrative but illegal market for Acadian produce at Louisbourg. As early as the 1720s herds of cattle were driven overland to the north shore of Nova Scotia and taken by ship to the fortress. The Acadians developed a three-way trade—cattle and produce were forwarded to Louisbourg in exchange for sugar, cotton, and molasses, as well as rum, brandy, and wine. If the French paid cash, the money was used to buy goods from New England. With British officials powerless to stem the trade, enterprising New Englanders joined the rush to supply the fortress. In 1740 alone, New England's shipments of bricks, furniture, and other goods to Louisbourg were worth twice as much as the livestock, flour, fish, and other products the Acadians managed to smuggle to Île Royale. The peace, prosperity, and good times, though, soon came to an end.

"My Lord," the letter began, "I beg to represent the difficulties we shall labour under in case of a rupture with France." It was the first day of December 1743 and Paul Mascarene knew it was just a matter of time until France was drawn into the war being waged between Britain and Spain. Seated at his desk in the governor's quarters at Fort Anne, the stone walls offering little comfort from the cold weather, Mascarene also knew he was composing one of the most important letters of his long career as a soldier and colonial administrator. It was imperative that the secretary of state, the duke of Newcastle, and his government appreciate Britain's tenuous position when war once again came to Nova Scotia. "The Inhabitants of this province ... are all French Roman Catholics who were allowed on their taking the Oaths of Allegiance to keep their possession and enjoy their religion," he wrote. "These Inhabitants cannot be depended on for assistance in case of a Rupture with France, it is as much as we can expect if we can keep them from joining with the enemy or being stirred up by them to rebell." His fort was in rough shape, its earthen walls requiring "continual patching" as sections collapsed during heavy rains or spring thaws. It had long been recognized that hundreds more soldiers were needed to keep the Acadians in line, yet he had a garrison of no more than 110 officers and men, "much short of what is necessary for the defence of the Works in time of War." Mascarene had made no secret of his appeals to Massachusetts governor William Shirley to send troops and supplies. The prospect of reinforcements from New England, he reported, was having a sobering effect on the Acadians and keeping them "in some awe." It was anybody's guess whether they would remain in awe when an attack came.

The story of the deportation of the Acadians has been told and retold over the past 250 years, and each time Paul Mascarene emerges as a hero. Of all the British officials who dealt with the Acadians, he alone was sympathetic to their plight as a people trapped between rival empires. Mascarene was a Huguenot born in France in 1685, the year the Edict of Nantes was revoked and his fellow Protestants were banished from the country. Relatives smuggled the young Mascarene to Geneva, where he was schooled in the classics before moving to England. He joined the army in 1706 and first saw action in 1710 at the siege of Port-Royal, where he commanded the artillery units that hammered Subercase into submission. Mascarene posted the first guard after the British took possession of the fort and was a key figure in the garrison for the next forty years, even though he spent long sojourns in Boston. He was fine-featured and oval-faced and, while his official portrait depicts him in a suit of black armor, he was more diplomat than warrior. Fluent in

French, he was the go-to guy when Vetch and other governors needed documents and orders translated or advice on how to deal with the Acadians. Philipps, who was the first to recognize Mascarene's talents, named him to the council in 1720.

After Armstrong's suicide in 1739, Mascarene was named president of the council and lieutenant governor. With Philipps governor in name only—he was nearing eighty and ensconced in a fashionable London neighborhood— Mascarene was the right man for the job as war loomed. Brebner has been lavish in his praise, describing him as "a gentleman officer ... competent, modest, and tactful," the perfect choice for tasks that demanded "industry and judgment." What's more, "he showed unusual ability and sympathy in direct dealing with the Acadians." Shirley, for one, feared that Mascarene could be too accommodating—in "danger of too much tenderness" toward the Acadians, as he put it. Mascarene, though, was no pushover. He had mulled over the idea of expelling them as early as 1720 and had tried, without success, to recruit Protestant New Englanders to settle among them. He distrusted the French priests and missionaries operating in Nova Scotia as much as anyone, and often took a hard line when their words or actions seemed to undermine British authority. In refusing to take a harder line, he was merely being pragmatic: his position was precarious and, until Britain committed settlers and more soldiers to the colony, the wisest course was to win over the Acadians by degrees, as Armstrong had put it. "My study has been to make these French Inhabitants sensible of the difference there is between the British and French Government," Mascarene explained to Newcastle in 1740, "by administering impartial justice to them and in all other respects treating them with lenity and humanity, without yielding anything wherein His Majesty's honor or interest were concerned."

War broke out between Britain and France in May 1744. The news reached Louisbourg first and the French promptly seized the key fishing center of Canso, near Île Royale. Annapolis Royal would be next, and there seemed to be little hope of repelling the attack. A third of his soldiers were "utter Invalides," Mascarene reported, and only a few of his dozen officers "had ever seen a gunn fir'd in anger." On July 1 Mi'kmaq fighters, led by a French officer and a renegade priest, Abbé Jean-Louis Le Loutre, surrounded the fort. Acadian men hired to rebuild the crumbling walls fled at the first sign of trouble, staying true to their promise of neutrality. Mascarene rallied his troops to drive the Mi'kmaq from the town, but the Natives regrouped and demanded a surrender. Mascarene rejected the demand just as a British warship sailed into the basin behind him, along with seventy New England militiamen. Shirley had heeded Mascarene's plea for help—if Fort Anne fell, he feared, New England would be exposed to renewed Indian attacks and more seizures of its merchant ships and fishing boats. The timing was perfect and the attackers withdrew.

More reinforcements arrived just ahead of a second attack. This time Captain François Du Pont Duvivier, fresh from the capture of Canso, spearheaded the attack with fifty French soldiers from Louisbourg. Duvivier, the son of a French officer and an Acadian woman, had been born at Port-Royal and had hoped to recruit Acadian men as his forces trekked overland through Minas. No more than a handful of Acadians had heeded the call by the time Duvivier reached the outskirts of Annapolis Royal. He was a wily adversary, slipping into town in disguise one night to spy on British soldiers as they worked by lamplight to shore up their defenses. The next morning he surrounded the fort, having spread the word that his force was double its actual strength of less than 300 men. He stretched his men into longer rows and lit extra campfires each night to create the illusion of growing strength. Mascarene was fooled, later claiming he had faced an enemy force of more than 650.

There was a long standoff. Duvivier's snipers picked off redcoats manning the ramparts and made nightly forays to test defenses and rattle nerves. Mascarene spent most of each night patrolling the walls to boost morale. Duvivier thought that time was on his side because at any moment French warships were expected to appear in the basin to tip the balance in his favor. Mascarene rejected a demand to surrender, but if the French ships arrived, it was game over—as one of the architects of the victory of 1710, he knew as well as anyone that the fort could not withstand a heavy naval bombardment. "I must say they are already masters of the whole province, except this Fort, which I am determin'd to defend to the utmost of my power," he declared in a letter smuggled out to London at the height of the siege. Mascarene, Duvivier, and their men eagerly scanned the horizon on September 15 when three ships were spotted in the basin. To Duvivier's disappointment, they carried more soldiers from New England. Shirley, again showing impeccable timing, saved the day. The demoralized attackers could only look in disgust as the British celebrated their good fortune. "The British yelled out many hurrahs," a disappointed Duvivier noted in his journal. "They were singing and enjoying themselves thoroughly; they probably spent the whole night drinking." This time Mascarene was the sly one—the party atmosphere masked the fact that the reinforcements had shown up "almost naked, & most without arms." Duvivier learned the following week that the French warships were not coming, and the attackers retreated. The ladders they left behind, built to scale Fort Anne's walls, became fuel for bonfires as Mascarene's men celebrated their unexpected victory.

The reprieve was short-lived. In May 1745 a large force of soldiers and Natives from Quebec mounted a new siege. A mild winter had enabled Mascarene to whip the fort into shape, and the attackers did not have the cannon needed to wear down the defenses. Again, the Acadians withdrew to the sidelines, withholding support to the garrison, but also resisting French demands for horses, food, and other supplies. For a third time, Massachusetts came to Mascarene's rescue, this time indirectly. The attackers were ordered to rush to Louisbourg, which was surrounded by New England troops and British warships that Shirley cobbled together in a bold offensive against the French. Louisbourg and its formidable bastions, the seemingly impenetrable "Gibraltar of North America," capitulated at the end of June after being peppered with shells and cannon balls for more than a month. Île Saint-Jean also fell, dealing a body-blow to French power in the region.

The battle for Louisbourg was won, but not the war. The French mounted a massive counterattack in 1746, assembling half of France's navy and 7,000 soldiers and sailors under the command of Duc d'Anville, the head of naval forces. His mission was to capture Annapolis Royal, retake Louisbourg, and attack Boston, if possible. More than 700 troops and Natives, under the command of Lieutenant Jean-Baptiste-Nicolas-Roch de Ramezay, left Quebec to provide ground support. Ramezay surrounded Fort Anne, the first target, but the French fleet was battered by severe storms during the Atlantic crossing. Damaged ships were forced to turn back and the rest limped into Chebucto harbor—the future site of Halifax—in mid-September. D'Anville collapsed and died soon after his arrival, and within a month scurvy and a smallpox epidemic killed hundreds of men and put another 2,000 out of commission. As the disaster unfolded, the admiral who replaced d'Anville tried to commit suicide. The fleet dispersed to Quebec and France, and Ramezay lifted his seige and withdrew his troops to Minas for the winter.

Mascarene, his unlikely winning streak intact, was content to let them go. But Shirley, rattled by this brush with a powerful French armada, demanded action. In mid-December, 500 men, most of them from Massachusetts, set out to drive Ramezay from Minas and spend the winter there, giving Fort Anne some breathing room. Their commander was Lieutenant-Colonel Arthur Noble, a tannery owner and trader who had been a minor player in the capture of Louisbourg. Upon learning that Ramezay had retreated to Beaubassin, Noble settled in for the winter, billeting his officers and men in about two dozen houses strung along the road through Grand-Pré. Assuming weather and distance insulated his camp from attack, he did not bother to erect a palisade or blockhouse.

Those decisions proved fatal. Ramezay received word of Noble's arrival and launched a daring attack. Captain Nicolas-Antoine Coulon de Villiers led 300 soldiers and Natives on a grueling march from Beaubassin on snowshoes, over mountains and ice-clogged rivers in bitter cold. On the eve of the attack they sought shelter in Acadian homes in the Gaspereau Valley, a few miles from Grand-Pré, interrupting a wedding feast and apparently learning from the guests precisely where Noble's men were quartered. Villiers attacked at three in the morning on January 31, 1747, in a blinding snowstorm. A sentry managed to sound the alarm, but otherwise the surprise was complete. Some of the New Englanders died in their beds. Noble was wounded twice, but brandished his pistols, refused a demand to surrender, and was shot through the forehead. His brother Francis also died, vainly defending the same house. Villiers was relieved of command after a musket ball shattered his left arm.

The battle raged until noon, with most of the remaining defenders holed up in a stone building next to Noble's quarters. With few rations and little ammunition, they surrendered and were allowed to march back to Annapolis Royal. The "Massacre at Grand-Pré," as it came to be called, left seventy

New Englanders and forty-four Frenchmen dead, according to Mascarene; the French claimed to have killed 130 and lost only 7. It was a stunning defeat for the British and "one of the most gallant exploits in French-Canadian annals," according to Francis Parkman. The lives lost on both sides were in vain. The French promptly withdrew to Beaubassin and the British reoccupied Grand-Pré in the spring.

The war ended in October 1748 with the signing of the Treaty of Aix-la-Chapelle. The British returned Louisbourg to the French in exchange for the port of Madras in India. Shirley and the rest of New England were outraged—100 colonial troops died storming the fortress and another 1,000 succumbed to disease while stationed there during the winter of 1745–1746. The war in North America had been a "side-show" to the main event in Europe, historian George Stanley has noted, and four years of death and sacrifice "changed nothing." Louisbourg was once more a menace to New England, Annapolis Royal was an isolated British island in an Acadian sea, and Nova Scotia was as vulnerable as ever to attack.

Mascarene, meanwhile, had launched a crackdown on traitors and collaborators. The Acadians had been under tremendous pressure to take up arms and to supply the armies that besieged Fort Anne. Duvivier posted an order to the residents of the Minas area when he passed through in August 1744, demanding gunpowder as well as teams of horses and men to drive them. He threatened that those who refused to help would be turned over to the Natives to "be punished as rebellious subjects" and "enemies of the state." When the French retreated to the area after lifting the siege of Fort Anne, ten representatives of the area's Acadians signed a letter refusing to supply meat and grain. "We live under a mild and tranquil government, and we have all good reason to be faithful to it," they pleaded. "We hope therefore, that you will have the goodness not to separate us from it; and that you will grant us the favour not to plunge us into utter misery."

Mascarene had warned the deputies of Minas and Piziquid that anyone who took up arms was "guilty of rebellion." Those who traded with Louisbourg or supplied the invaders would be punished unless they could show they were the victims of "pure violence" at the hands of the French and Natives. It was clear a few Acadians sheltered or passed information to

Villiers's forces before the battle of Grand-Pré; the attackers knew which houses were being used to billet soldiers and, by some accounts, Acadian guides led them to the door. But it was also known that residents had warned Noble about the impending attack. The French strategy of threats and intimidation attracted a few Acadian converts, but alienated the rest. No one under the age of forty could remember life under French rule; those who could were hard-pressed to explain what difference it made whether the flag flying at Annapolis Royal was French or British. And after the fall of Louisbourg and the disastrous demise of the d'Anville offensive, it made little sense to back the losing side.

Mascarene recognized that the vast majority of Acadians had lived up to their promise to remain neutral. "We owe our preservation," he assured the Lords of Trade, not only to Shirley's timely interventions but "our French Inhabitants refusing to take up arms against us." If the Acadians had chosen to fight, he reckoned they could have added 3,000 to 4,000 men to the attack, creating an overwhelming force. The ever-conciliatory Mascarene was determined the many innocents should not be punished for the acts of the guilty few. He even risked Shirley's wrath when the Massachusetts governor launched a retaliatory raid, in the fall of 1744, against Minas and other settlements along the Bay of Fundy. Three ships were dispatched from Boston to burn homes and seize hostages, who would be used to ensure the rest of the population was kept in line. Mascarene was convinced such brutal tactics would drive the Acadians into the hands of the French. When the ships reached Annapolis Royal, he persuaded the commander it was too late in the season to risk a journey deeper into the bay and the mission was scrubbed.

Yet Mascarene knew there were Acadians who had aided the French. The most notorious was Joseph-Nicolas Gautier, a wealthy shipowner who traded with Louisbourg and put his ships and pilots at the disposal of the French. Since his daughter was married to Duvivier's brother, another French officer, he kindly invited Duvivier's troops to camp on his large estate overlooking Annapolis Royal during the siege of 1744. Gautier evaded capture, but his wife, Marie Allain, and son Pierre were arrested in 1745 on suspicion of "holding Correspondence with the enemy." They were imprisoned at the fort, their feet clamped in irons, for almost a year before they staged a breakout. Two men from Minas, Armand Bigeau and Joseph Le Blanc, had furnished supplies and boats to the invaders and acted as scouts and couriers. A few others had taken up arms, the most prominent a forty-five-year-old firebrand from the Chignecto region, Joseph "Beausoleil" Broussard, who took part in the raid on Noble's forces at Grand-Pré. In all a dozen men—including Gautier and two of his sons, Bigeau, Le Blanc, Broussard, and Pierre Guidry, who helped to pilot French ships—were declared outlaws in 1747, with £50 reward offered for their capture. The Gautiers fled to Île Saint-Jean, but Mascarene confiscated their vessels, land, and cattle. The homes of Bigeau and Le Blanc were burned. Le Blanc spent six months in custody at Annapolis Royal—"in a frightful dungeon, laden with chains," he later claimed—but also escaped. Broussard retreated to French-occupied southern New Brunswick to fight another day.

In four years of war, and in the face of four enemy incursions into the heart of Nova Scotia, only a handful of Acadians—out of a population of more than 10,000—violated their promise of neutrality. They had, in the words of historian George Rawlyk, a specialist in North America's colonial past, "carefully walked the knife-edge of neutrality." Mascarene concluded that, despite concerted "cajoling & threatning," the French "could not prevail above twenty to joyn with them." He emerged from the war with a renewed faith in the Acadians, satisfied they "possess still the same fidelity they have done before, in which I endeavour to encourage them." He had always thought of the Acadians as "an unsound limb ... grafted in the Body of the British Nation," to be nurtured over time, "first to become Subjects and after that good Subjects." But Mascarene would not be around to nurture and encourage those who had remained neutral, and all Acadians were about to pay a terrible price for the acts of a few renegades.

The *Beaufort* rocked gently at anchor, one of more than a dozen ships that created a thicket of masts and spars to defy the dense forests on the surrounding shoreline. The month was July, the year was 1749, and, given the vagaries of the summer weather along Nova Scotia's southern coast, the ships were either bathed in sunshine or shrouded in fog. The Mi'kmaq called this place Chebucto, "the great harbor," and the reason was obvious. The globe-trotting British officers in charge of the flotilla agreed it was the finest harbor they had ever seen, extending miles inland to become a wide, sheltered basin. They were here to establish, at long last, British settlers and a strong military presence on Nova Scotia soil. The return of Louisbourg had been a wake-up call for officials in London, who earmarked a small fortune to build a fortified city to keep the French in check and protect New England and its fishermen. It would be named Halifax, in honor of Lord Halifax, the president of the Lords of Trade and a promoter of an aggressive policy to keep Nova Scotia in British hands. Advertisements in London newspapers recruited settlers with generous offers of free land, free tools, food for a year, and freedom from taxes for a decade. Some 2,500 answered the call, many of them discharged soldiers and sailors and their families.

The ambitious enterprise was placed in the hands of Edward Cornwallis, a colonel with the influential connections needed to snag such a plum assignment. His father was a baron, his mother the daughter of an earl, his twin brother a future archbishop of Canterbury, and he was careful to marry the daughter of a viscount. Cornwallis became a royal page at twelve, then joined the army and rose through the ranks during campaigns against the French and Scots. In 1747 he was tapped for the ultimate insider's job—a groom of the royal bedchamber. Cornwallis was in his late thirties when he was appointed governor of Nova Scotia, replacing Philipps and superseding Mascarene. Outspoken and impatient, he was a good leader but a poor follower; in the months ahead, when London questioned the growing expense of building and fortifying Halifax, he fired off responses that were condescending and blunt. His connections would insulate him from criticism or recall, and he knew it.

For now, though, he had more important things to do than bicker with his bosses. The land was "one continual wood," he noted upon his arrival in June 1749, but was soon alive with the clatter of axes as settlers cleared a town site (and, tradition has it, made the grisly discovery of the remains of some of Duc d'Anville's unfortunate men). There was also the pressing business of forming a government. Cornwallis was empowered to form a new council, establish courts, and create the bureaucracy needed to run the settlement and maintain law and order. Mascarene and five of his councillors sailed down from Annapolis Royal for the formal changing of the guard. The handover took place on the deck of the *Beaufort*, not at the old capital, and the symbolism of the locale was unmistakable. Cornwallis and his entourage were the new broom that would sweep away the neglect and inaction that had been the hallmarks of British rule since 1710. On June 25 a new council was sworn in, with Mascarene and one holdover from the old regime joining Cornwallis and four other newcomers. The announcement of the new government's formation, according to one account, "was received by a salute from all the ships in the harbor, and the remainder of the day was devoted by the settlers to festivity and rejoicing."

On board the *Beaufort*, however, the remainder of the day was devoted to business and the Acadians were the first item on the agenda. Mascarene's conciliatory policy toward them was also a thing of the past. Cornwallis believed Mascarene had "sold out, and is worn out." He was definitely worse for wear at age sixty-five, but the charge of selling out was a low blow to the man whose courage and diplomacy had preserved Nova Scotia for the British. None of that mattered. Mascarene was yesterday's man and the new crew from Britain had their own ideas about how to handle the bothersome Acadians. Mascarene attended two council meetings, then retreated to Annapolis Royal. He retired in 1751 to his brick mansion in Boston, where he read, played chess, and doted on his grandchildren until his death in 1760. "No man in British America ever served his country better," claimed an early Nova Scotia historian, Thomas Beamish Akins, "and no man ever received less support in his necessities or less remuneration for his services." And so little credit from his successors.

Cornwallis opened the first council meeting by reading a declaration denouncing the Acadians who had "openly abetted or privately assisted" the French during the war "by furnishing them with quarters, Provisions and Intelligence and concealing their designs." These acts were a slap in the face to the "many indulgences" the king had shown in allowing them to keep their religion and their lands. Those privileges would continue, Cornwallis added ominously, only if they took a new oath of allegiance to George II. Mascarene, in one of his last official acts, took the floor and read the oath Philipps had administered two decades earlier. While it made no mention of conditions, Mascarene revealed that the Acadians had understood when they took the oath that they would be exempted from bearing arms. Cornwallis was taken aback, noting bitterly that Philipps "did not do his duty." The council decided to make it clear that this oath would be sworn "without any Conditional Clauses ... or any reservation whatsoever." With that, three Acadian deputies—two from Minas, one from Piziquid—were called in and the declaration and oath were reread. Asked for a response, the trio sputtered that they had come to make a courtesy call on the new governor and to ensure their religious freedoms would continue. Cornwallis handed over copies of the declaration and oath, ordered the deputies to spread the word to other communities, and to return within two weeks with an answer.

Ten deputies from a half-dozen settlements returned to the *Beaufort* in mid-August, bearing a letter asking the council to amend the oath to exempt them from bearing arms, as Philipps had done. The council rejected the request, insisting the Acadians would not be freed from "the natural obligation to defend themselves, their habitations, their lands and the government under which they enjoy so many advantages." The deputies asked whether those who opted to leave the colony could sell their land and possessions. No, Cornwallis warned, anyone who left or failed to swear the oath by the end of October would forfeit his lands and possessions. The deputies requested, and were granted, time to consult with their communities. They were back within five weeks with a letter bearing 1,000 signatures—most of the names marked with an X—refusing to take an unconditional oath. The reason was the same as in the 1720s—the Mi'kmaq already viewed them with suspicion, and a stricter oath was certain to make them "victims of their barbarous cruelty." They would swear a conditional oath, the deputies replied; otherwise "we are resolved, every one of us, to leave the country."

This was brinkmanship of the highest order. A small delegation of Acadians, trapped on a ship and surrounded by British soldiers and sailors, was playing hardball with His Majesty's representative. A succession of historians have viewed this response as evidence of Acadian insolence, the naivete of simple peasants, or proof of the influence of their pro-French priests.

Cornwallis and his council considered it a combination of all three. "Gentlemen," the governor replied, "it appears to me that you think yourselves independent of any government; and you wish to treat with the King as if you were so ... you deceive yourselves if you think that you are at liberty to choose whether you will be subject to the King or no." By choosing to remain in the colony after the Treaty of Utrecht, he continued, they had become British subjects and the time for swearing allegiance to their monarch was long overdue. "It is only out of pity to your situation, and to your inexperience in the affairs of government, that we condescend to reason with you," he added haughtily, "otherwise, Gentlemen, the question would not be reasoning, but commanding and being obeyed."

It was a great speech, but Cornwallis's tough talk was just that—talk. His bargaining position was extremely weak. The Mi'kmaq, alarmed at the sudden buildup of British strength and egged on by the French, had launched raids that would keep Cornwallis and his troops busy for the foreseeable future. In the meantime, the Acadians remained trapped between the British hammer and the French anvil. French troops occupied the northern side of the disputed Chignecto Isthmus, and Le Loutre, the renegade priest who attacked Fort Anne in 1744, was pressuring Acadian families to move north to French territory. Cornwallis was spot-on when he told the duke of Bedford, the British secretary of state, that "'tis necessary to show them that 'tis in our power to master them or to protect them." He could do neither.

The main problem, as Cornwallis saw it, was Le Loutre, whom he considered "a good for nothing Scoundrel as ever lived." Many English-language accounts of the Acadian tragedy cast Le Loutre as the villain, a rabble-rouser who would stop at nothing to prevent the Catholic Acadians from submitting to the Protestant heretics. An early writer dubbed him "the black priest." Francis Parkman said Le Loutre "more than any other man was answerable for the miseries that overwhelmed" the Acadians. He was, Parkman wrote, "a man of boundless egoism, a violent spirit of domination, an intense hatred of the English, and a fanaticism that stopped at nothing." Le Loutre was all that, a zealot capable of ruthlessness that left some French officers who knew him shaking their heads in disgust. Sent to Nova Scotia in 1738 to run a Mi'kmaq mission, he became fluent in the language and the unofficial general of a

Native army that fought alongside the French. He was twice captured by the British while traveling under assumed names, and released both times before his identity was discovered. After the founding of Halifax, Le Loutre unleashed his followers on the British and offered bounties for British scalps.

But insecurity and even Le Loutre's threats do not fully explain why most Acadians—those who refused to flee their homeland—balked at Cornwallis's demand to take an unqualified oath. Their intransigence sprang from a deep, collective sense of independence. The Acadians had considered the terms of their governance to be negotiable long before the British takeover. Independence and resisting authority were Acadian traditions, a reflection of their long history of isolation from government control. Neutrality had served them well in the past, and there was no reason to think it would not continue to serve them well in the future. As the perceptive Naomi Griffiths has stressed, the Acadians were a border people and reacted with the survival instincts of a border people—they wanted to remain above the fray. Those who fled to French territory, by choice or coercion, faced harsher treatment than those who remained behind. The governor of Quebec issued an order in April 1751 demanding that refugees swear an oath of allegiance to France and sign up for militia duty; those who refused would be "declared rebels ... and as such expelled from the lands which they hold." The Acadians were still caught in the middle and, as they had for more than a century, did their best to remain on the sidelines as the outsiders squabbled for control. What they failed to appreciate, though, was that this time the British meant business. Within a few years Halifax would eclipse Louisbourg as the regional powerhouse and the British would have the troops and settlers needed to impose their will. Until then, though, the old rules still applied. The Acadians considered the latest demand for an oath to be open to negotiation and, if the past was a guide, the British could be expected to give in or drop the matter.

Cornwallis, following the familiar script, blinked. After showing his fist at the August council meeting, he met privately with the deputies and they left for home "in good spirits promising great things." The October deadline passed with no oath taken or demanded. The Acadians elected a new slate of deputies in the fall, as they had for almost thirty years. Cornwallis forwarded a copy of the Acadians' letter to London, and said he would seek further instructions from the Lords of Trade if they were "still obstinate" in the spring. By March, he had changed his tactics, telling Bedford that he would defer the oath until the colony could be made secure. When the Acadians' deputies from Minas, Piziquid, and Annapolis brought forward a request in April to leave the province, Cornwallis denounced them for being "seduced" by French agents and priests who would "lead you to your ruin." Cornwallis faced the same dilemma as Philipps before him—allowing the Acadians to leave would strengthen the French territories at Nova Scotia's expense. Permission to leave was denied, on the pretext he could not throw open his borders in the face of the French menace on his doorstep. Cornwallis dispatched one of his officers, Major Charles Lawrence, to Chignecto in 1750 to build a fort near the village of Beaubassin, on the British side of the isthmus, to stare down the French. In response, Le Loutre sent his Natives to burn the village and force its inhabitants to seek refuge on the French side, flouting Cornwallis's ban on emigration. The French built their own fort, Beauséjour, and Chignecto's marshes became no-man's land where a winding river marked the unofficial boundary between empires.

The stalemate over territory and the oath continued for the remainder of Cornwallis's tenure. In late 1752, after butting heads with the Lords of Trade over the mounting costs of defending Nova Scotia, he resigned and returned to England, where he served in Parliament before ending his days as governor of Gibraltar. His replacement, Peregrine Hopson, was a career military officer who was as measured and cautious with the Acadians as Cornwallis had been impatient and blunt. Hopson asked the Lords of Trade to shelve a fresh demand for an oath until "a more convenient opportunity." Cornwallis, he said, could attest to "how useful and necessary these people are to us, how impossible it is to do without them," and "how difficult, if not impossible, it may be to force such a thing upon them." One of Hopson's first acts was to direct his officers to treat the Acadians like any other British subject and to pay them a fair price for supplies. Hopson was no fan of the Acadians—he considered them as an "ignorant" and "bigotted" people—but he understood the intense pressure they faced from the French and Natives. And, like every governor since Vetch's time, Hopson did not have enough soldiers to keep his enemies in check. If he could secure the colony and stamp out "all hopes of any change," he told the Lords of Trade in July 1753, he was confident the Acadians would make "proper submission to His Majesty's Government."

Hopson's go-slow approach echoed Armstrong's 1720s strategy of winning the Acadians over by degrees. Given time and a little luck, it might have worked. Le Loutre was in France drumming up support for his guerrilla campaign, creating a lull in hostilities with the Natives, and easing the pressure on both the British and the Acadians. But a new war was on the horizon and it was clear that Nova Scotia, the meeting point of the tectonic plates of empire, would be on the front lines. Hopson, who suspected the French were regrouping for a new offensive, would not be around when the shooting started. Severe eye problems forced him to return to England in November 1753. In his absence, the governor's powers passed to the president of the council. For the third time in four years, a new military officer with new ideas would be responsible for defending the colony and dealing with the Acadians. And he would prove far worse a rogue, and far more of a villain, than the black priest Le Loutre. That man was Charles Lawrence.

4 BETWEEN THE HAMMER AND THE ANVIL

> As they possess the best and largest Tracts of Land in this
> Province, it cannot be settled with any effect while they remain
> in this situation, and tho' I would be very far from attempting
> such a step without your Lordships approbation, yet I cannot
> help being of opinion that it would be much better, if they
> refuse the Oaths, that they were away.
>
> —Lieutenant Governor Charles Lawrence to Lords of Trade,
>   August 1, 1754

It was a public spectacle designed to dazzle and impress the citizens of Halifax, the rowdy and the genteel alike. The procession that set out from the governor's house on the morning of October 22, 1754 was as finely scripted as any theatrical performance even if, to modern eyes, it would look more like a theater of the absurd. The man of the hour was Jonathan Belcher, a forty-four-year-old lawyer newly arrived from England and about to be installed as Nova Scotia's first chief justice and the head of the first superior court within the boundaries of the British colonies that would become Canada. Portly and double-chinned, Belcher was decked out in the scarlet, fur-trimmed robes of an English High Court judge, his bald head hidden under an enormous white horsehair wig that dangled to his chest. Ahead of him marched Halifax's sheriff and constables and a man carrying a ceremonial staff. Alongside Belcher strode Lieutenant Governor Charles Lawrence—wearing the red dress uniform of a British officer and a fashionable wig of his own—and members of his council. Bringing up the rear were other town notables and a half-dozen "gentlemen of the Bar attending in their gowns."

Lawyers were in short supply, and so were citizens to be awed. Halifax's population had ebbed and flowed in the five years since its founding—many settlers had fled to less rustic New England, and tales of scalpings and the constant threat of war made it tough to attract replacements. Halifax in 1754 was home to a couple of thousand people, not quite the number who had accompanied Cornwallis in 1749. A patchwork of shops, houses, and warehouses huddled between the harbor and the hilltop fortress that guarded this British foray into the land of the Acadians and the Mi'kmaq. In the middle of town the spire of St. Paul's Anglican Church, built in 1750 of timbers imported from New England, poked above the surrounding roofs and chimneys. St. Paul's and a few other public buildings were stately jewels of Georgian symmetry, but the town still had a wild frontier feel. Belcher was disappointed to discover the streets, while "of a very convenient Breadth," were "not yet levell'd or paved." Halifax was a military town, its fortunes rising and falling in proportion to the presence of soldiers and sailors to spend their pay on food and drink. A wry observer of the time was not far off the mark in suggesting that the occupation of half the population was selling rum to the other half.

Belcher's job was to bring stability and the rule of law to an outpost with aspirations of becoming a stately and well-mannered colonial capital. Nova Scotia already had a rudimentary court system, with magistrates to deal with disputes over property and unpaid bills. As under the Annapolis Royal regime, the governor and his council dealt with crimes. In fact, within weeks of arriving in 1749, Cornwallis and his colleagues were called on to try, convict, and hang a sailor for murder. The whole process took about a week, and Cornwallis was confident that meting out swift justice would "convince the settlers of the intention of conforming to the Laws and Constitution of the Mother Country in every point." But none of the councillors and magistrates sitting in judgment had legal training. Concerns about the legitimacy of laymen's rulings, coupled with complaints of bias and a troubling reliance on New England legal precedents, prompted British authorities to create a common law court. Belcher, a Harvard graduate who had practised law in England and Ireland for two decades, was tapped to be the court's first judge and chief justice.

The procession of scarlet uniforms and black gowns filed through the dirt streets along the waterfront to the Great Pontac tavern. Named after a London club, the Pontac was the town's fanciest watering hole and the venue of choice for important meetings and gala balls. The dignitaries sat down to "an elegant breakfast" and, after "a gathering of ladies, army officers and merchants tendered congratulations" and fawned over Belcher, the procession regrouped outside. Falling in behind a man bearing a copy of Belcher's commission as chief justice for all to see, they marched up the hill for a service of thanksgiving at St. Paul's, at the southern end of a public square known as the Grand Parade. The next stop was the courthouse, an unimposing building with a steeple-like cupola over the entrance, just off the Grand Parade and "very handsomely fitted up" for the occasion. Belcher, seated under a canopy with Lawrence at his right side, listened as his commission was read aloud. When it was his turn to speak, he offered "a few directions for the guidance of [law] practitioners." Twenty-three merchants and officials—citizens of the better sort—were sworn in as grand jurors for the inaugural session of the court. Belcher lectured them on the need to respect the law and the government. The court's establishment showed the king's "Concern for the Rights and Liberties of his Loyal Subjects," he declared, exhorting the jurors to wield the "Sword of Justice" for the "protection of the innocent, and to the terror of the noxious and guilty."

What must have most pleased Lawrence, as he watched his new colleague in action, was Belcher's tirade against dissent and its potential "to sap the very foundations of Government." The chief justice drove home the link between loyalty to the Crown and political stability:

> No considerate Person will suffer himself to conceive, that any loyal Subject of His Majesty residing in this Province ... can be so weak and infatuated, as to disturb and interrupt our Peace and happiness, by introducing distinction and Parties against the Government of this Province .... If this spirit should ever arise in this Province ... we may boldly conclude that as such persons are not with us they are against us, and enemies to our Peace and Order.

Court was adjourned for the day and, as a finale, Belcher and his entourage paraded back to Lawrence's residence. As he walked, Lawrence may have replayed Belcher's words in his head, the stuff about us and them, about loyal subjects not rocking the boat, about dissenters and troublemakers being "enemies to our Peace and Order." Yes, he must have thought, under that long white wig is the mind of a kindred spirit.

Lawrence had been named lieutenant governor in April 1754 once it became clear that illness made it impossible for Peregrine Hopson to return to Nova Scotia. While not commissioned as a full governor, Lawrence wielded the power of the colony's top civic official and the military's commander-in-chief. Early on he lobbied London to appoint a judge who could give him legal advice and lend credibility to the justice system—someone who, as he put it, could "lay a solid foundation for that concord and tranquillity that is so necessary to the well-being of this infant settlement." The answer came in the form of Belcher, the well-educated and somewhat pompous son of the governor of New Jersey. Belcher earned a couple of master's degrees before he headed to England in 1730 to study law. A small colonial fish in London's tight-knit legal pond, he headed to Dublin and made a name for himself as a compiler of Irish statutes. He eventually caught the eye of Lord Hardwicke, Britain's chief justice, who lined him up with the Nova Scotia post. Belcher's commission made him a one-man court with the power to preside over all major lawsuits and serious criminal cases. His real ambition, though, was to secure an appointment as a governor, preferably as his father's successor, and Nova Scotia was a convenient place to hang his hat for the time being. The judgeship also offered an introduction to colonial governance—Belcher was sworn in as a member of Lawrence's council shortly after his arrival in early October.

A week after his elaborate welcome, Belcher presided over the court's inaugural session. There was the usual array of petty thieves and highway robbers, but one case stood out. Three crewmen from the New England sloop *Nancy and Sally* were charged with murdering two sailors from HMS *Vulture*. The British warship intercepted the vessel in the Bay of Fundy the previous summer, suspecting it was trading illegally with the French at Beauséjour. After exchanging warning shots in the course of a day-long chase, the sloop was cornered in a shallow cove and the *Vulture's* captain sent over a boarding party. As the *Vulture's* longboat drew near, it was raked with small-arms fire from the sloop, killing one sailor and fatally wounding another. The *Nancy and Sally's* captain, John Hovey, and three crewmen were charged with murder, but Hovey broke out of the Halifax jail before he could be prosecuted. The November trial of the crewmen, described as "a politically-charged affair," convened just as Lawrence's government imposed new regulations to stamp out trade with Beauséjour. Witnesses disagreed about who fired first and there were suggestions the crew of the *Nancy and Sally* acted in self-defense, fearing the boarding party was a press gang. Belcher was having none of this, and told the jury the evidence "appeared plain and sufficient to support the indictment for murder."

The jury retired, conferred briefly, acquitted all three of murder, but found them guilty of the lesser offense of manslaughter. They may have viewed the navy's actions as high-handed or, like many jurors of the time, they may have balked at the notion of sending someone to the gallows. Whatever their reasons, Belcher was outraged. He launched into a tirade, telling the sailors they had killed in cold blood "in the cause of treachery to your sovereign." They were guilty not only of murder, but of supporting enemies of the king who were bent on "the destruction of the province"—in other words, high treason. "Your Crimes," he fumed, "are attended with such circumstance of indignity to the Crown, of treachery and ruin to His Majesty's faithful subjects of this province." The verdict meant the trio could claim the benefit of clergy and escape "the just sentence of death," as Belcher put it, but they would have the letter "M" branded on a thumb so, in future, they would be "publicly marked out as offenders and criminals in blood." Belcher also imposed the maximum prison term provided under the law, nine months behind bars, and upon release ordered them impressed into service on a British man o' war—the irony of the latter punishment apparently lost in his outrage.

The courtroom meltdown cemented Lawrence's belief that he had found a staunch ally in his quest to root out and destroy the king's enemies. The men were very much alike. Almost the same age, they were obsessed with maintaining law and order. They shared a black-and-white view of the world that equated political dissent with treason. Their career paths differed—Belcher chose books and the law as his route to the top, Lawrence opted for guns and swords—but each man coveted a governorship as his reward for faithful service to His Majesty.

Little is known, however, about Lawrence's background. A lifelong bachelor, he was in the army by age eighteen, served in the West Indies during the 1730s, and received back-to-back promotions to lieutenant and captain in the early 1740s. One biographer says he was popular with his comrades and "strong, energetic, and direct in his methods," an apt description of his future actions as a colonial administrator. In May 1745, during the War of the Austrian Succession, Lawrence fought the French at the battle of Fontenoy in Belgium. British troops under the command of George II's son, the twenty-four-year-old Duke of Cumberland, and their Austrian allies—50,000 strong—faced a French army of about 56,000. The French, dug in on a well-defended plateau, mauled the advancing cavalry and foot soldiers with cannon fire as the young duke became increasingly impatient with the sluggish advance. It was only when the British fought their way to the crest of the hill that they discovered they were facing a superior force. The British withstood wave after wave of horsemen and soldiers, but the battle quickly turned into a rout. The British withdrew, leaving more than 1,200 dead and 2,400 wounded, among them the thirty-six-year-old Lawrence. The severity of his injuries is unknown, but one suspects the deep suspicion and hatred he would display toward the French population of Nova Scotia was born in the blood and mud of Fontenoy.

Lawrence's family was related to the Montagus, and his rise through the ranks of the military was aided by the patronage of George Montagu Dunk, the president of the Board of Trade, the second Earl of Halifax, and namesake of the Nova Scotia capital. That may have been his ticket to Nova Scotia. His regiment occupied Louisbourg in 1747 and moved on to Halifax when the fortress was handed back to the French two years later. Lawrence was immediately named to the council and Cornwallis sent him to Chignecto with 400 soldiers in April 1750 on a sensitive mission to stop French encroachments into British territory. With French troops occupying the north side of the isthmus and no orders to dislodge them, Lawrence withdrew. He was back in the fall with a larger force and, after a skirmish with some of Abbé Le Loutre's Mi'kmaq followers, built a palisaded fort on a ridge beside the burned village of Beaubassin. He christened it, rather immodestly, Fort Lawrence. The French responded by building Fort Beauséjour on the opposite ridge as the battle lines were drawn for a war both sides considered inevitable.

A crude and rather unflattering portrait dating to Lawrence's time in Nova Scotia depicts a stern figure with a pronounced nose, baggy eyes, and a broad, jowly face. Lawrence by now held the rank of lieutenant colonel and his next mission was to establish a new settlement for German-speaking Protestants who had assembled in Halifax. The idea had been to grant them land among the Acadians, in hopes of hastening the assimilation of that fractious lot into loyal British subjects. But Acadian resistance to having the newcomers as neighbors and the continuing threat of Mi'kmaq raids scuttled the plan. In 1753 the so-called Foreign Protestants were shipped farther along the province's South Shore to found the town of Lunenburg. Lawrence oversaw the operation and, by one account, relied on "a mixture of bribery, bullying and verbal persuasion" to convince the settlers that they needed to build defenses first and homes later. After more than a year spent staring down the French and Mi'kmaq on the Chignecto frontier, Lawrence had good reason to be obsessed with security.

He returned to Halifax in August 1753 to take over from the ailing Hopson. Lawrence had been present for the early council meetings with the Acadian deputies—including the August 1749 session when they stood firm against Cornwallis's demand for an unconditional oath of allegiance—so he knew something of their stubbornness and resolve. He clearly disliked and distrusted the Acadians, and some Acadians clearly felt the same way about him. Lawrence had spent the summer of 1750 in Piziquid, where he oversaw the construction of a modest square-timbered blockhouse that, remarkably, is still standing more than 250 years later. A local priest would later claim that Piziquid's Acadians "personally hated" Lawrence, and would never be at ease under his government because he had "treated them so harshly when amongst them." It is easy to imagine the forceful, blunt, and bullying Lawrence ruffling feathers among people accustomed to dealing with British overseers who were all talk and no action.

In December 1753, after Hopson's departure, Lawrence wrote to the Lords of Trade with an update on the colony's affairs. He also made it clear that, unlike Hopson, he was not prepared to treat the Acadians with kid gloves. While the Acadians were "tolerably quiet ... they seem to think we only wait a convenient opportunity to force (an oath) upon them," an apprehension that would prove well founded. Lawrence believed the Acadians were exaggerating the threat of a Native backlash if they took the oath, no doubt because he was convinced the Acadians and Natives were in cahoots. As for the requirement to bear arms, he had no intention of putting guns into the hands of the untrustworthy Acadians, oath or no oath. He felt it was time to force the issue, as "it would be of great advantage, both to them and us, that this matter was one way or another, cleared up to them as soon as possible."

In a reply written the following March, the Lords of Trade were unequivocal: If an oath were sworn, it should be "absolute and unqualified with any reservation whatever." The Lords advised Lawrence to proceed with "great Caution," for fear of sparking a mass exodus to French territory. But he should also avoid instilling "an improper and false confidence in them, that by a Perseverence in refusing to take the Oath of Allegiance, they may gradually work out in their own way a Right to their Lands, and to the Benefit & Protection of the Law, which they are not entitled to but on that condition." For the Acadians, the "false confidence" was already there, instilled by more than four decades of weak and inept British rule.

This was exactly what Lawrence wanted to hear. Emboldened, he issued a proclamation forbidding Acadians from crossing the border to work on a massive dike that Le Loutre was building near Fort Beauséjour, then outlawed the export of grain to the French territories. The Lords of Trade later endorsed both initiatives. In an August 1754 letter to London, Lawrence poured out his frustration with the "obstinacy" and "treachery" of the Acadians, their "affected" neutrality, and their "ingratitude" for their lenient treatment at the hands of the British. They would never take an oath "till they are forced." They were funneling their livestock and produce away from Halifax to feed the French and Natives, "whom they have always assisted with provisions, quarters, & intelligence." Perhaps, he suggested, it was time to renew the demand for their allegiance. "As they possess the best and largest

Tracts of Land in this Province, it cannot be settled with any effect while they remain in this situation," he noted, "and tho' I would be very far from attempting such a step without your Lordships approbation, yet I cannot help being of opinion that it would be much better, if they refuse the Oaths, that they were away."

While a succession of writers have tendered this comment as proof of Lawrence's dark designs, it seems clear he was alluding to the likelihood the Acadians would rather leave than take an oath. Note his wording, "that they were away," not "that they be taken away" in a wholesale deportation. Like the Lords of Trade, he was concerned that a fresh demand for an oath would force the Acadians into the French camp. In fact, the only "ill consequence" was that the Acadians might be goaded into taking up arms against the British, which he considered unlikely. "I believe," he wrote, "that a very large part of the inhabitants would submit to any terms rather than take up arms on either side." Scoff as he might at the Acadians' "affected neutrality," he was willing to bet on it. There remained one barrier—his superiors might feel "that we are not sufficiently established to take so important a step."

It was late October 1754 before the Lords of Trade replied to Lawrence's August musings about how much better life would be if the Acadians "were away." It's doubtful the letter crossed his desk much before Christmas. The Lords expressed disappointment that the "Lenity which had been shewn to those People ... has had so little Effect." The fact that virtually all Acadians had remained neutral during the last war counted for nothing; London had swallowed Lawrence's all-or-nothing approach to loyalty. The Lords offered some musings of their own, noting they were not yet ready to make a recommendation to the king on how to deal with the Acadians. In the meantime, "Provisional Measures" were in order. Lawrence should consult his new chief justice for a legal opinion on whether Acadians who refused to take the oath of allegiance lost their rights as British subjects and title to their lands. Belcher's opinion "could serve as a foundation for any future measure it may be thought advisable to pursue with regard to the Inhabitants in general." While he was at it, Lawrence should ask Belcher whether residents of Chignecto who defected to the French had forfeited their lands. If so, those farms should be granted to New Englanders or "any persons desirous of settling there."

The idea, they realized, was "absurd" until Beauséjour was destroyed, the Natives subdued, and "the French driven to seek such an Asylum as they can find in the barren Island of Cape Breton and St. Johns and in Canada." The frustrated tone and uncharacteristically tough talk emanating from Whitehall may have steeled Lawrence's resolve to deal decisively with the Acadians. Like his predecessors, Lawrence lacked the troops needed to secure the colony and force the Acadians into submission. That, however, was about to change.

The notion of solving the Acadian "problem" once and for all, through a full-scale deportation, was not new. John Bartlet Brebner, after an extensive review of colonial-era archives on two continents, concluded that "the idea of the total expulsion had existed, expressed or latent, by the English in Nova Scotia since 1658." After 1713 the Treaty of Utrecht, with its promises of religious tolerance and civil rights, obliged the British to try to turn the Acadians into British subjects and led to the prolonged haggling over the terms of an oath of allegiance. As the Acadians balked at an unconditional oath and their numbers passed the 2,000 mark, even the soft-hearted Paul Mascarene took the view they should either shape up or ship out. In 1720, at Governor Philipps's request, he drafted a long report for the Lords of Trade on the state of their new colony. He was pessimistic about the prospects of winning over the Acadians, describing them as heavily influenced by their priests and "entirely wedded" to the French, "tho' they find a great deal more sweetness under the English Government." Mascarene weighed the pros and cons of forcing them to leave, noting that land and cattle confiscated from Acadians who refused to swear allegiance could be used to entice British colonists to take their place. The British had been threatening to bar Acadians from trading and fishing if they did not swear the oath, but lacked the ability to impose such sanctions. Give us 600 more soldiers, Mascarene said, and the Acadians could be forced into submission.

In a terse response dated December 1720, the Lords of Trade expressed disappointment, noting that since the Acadians were "so wavering in their inclinations we are apprehensive they will never become good subjects to His

Majesty." As a result, "we are of opinion they ought to be removed as soon as the Forces which we have proposed to be sent to you shall arrive." It was a green light to deport, but the Lords warned Philipps "not to attempt their removal without His Majesty's positive order, for that purpose." The order and the troops never materialized, thoughts of deportation were shelved, and Armstrong and Phillips renewed their efforts to extract an oath.

The outbreak of war in the 1740s and fears of an Acadian rebellion revived the idea in London and Boston. The Lords of Trade dipped into their files and produced a report for George II in 1743 that declared it "absolutely necessary ... That these French Inhabitants should be removed." They were convinced the Acadians would never become loyal subjects and warned "there is all the Reason in the World to apprehend, that upon any Rupture between the two Crowns, They may openly declare in favour of France." While that did not happen—only a handful of Acadians defected to the French side once war erupted in 1744— Governor William Shirley of Massachusetts was convinced he could never secure the New England coast without ridding Nova Scotia of its French-speaking inhabitants. He found an ally in Peter Warren, commodore of the British fleet that supported the capture of Louisbourg. Warren, who was overseeing the removal of captured French officials and some Louisbourg-area Acadians to France, offered the unsolicited opinion that the Acadians "will ever be a thorn in our side" until removed to the "remotest of our colonies from the French."

Mascarene, who was now acting governor, was pushed to the sidelines as Shirley, Warren, and officials in London debated the future of his colony. The low point came in late 1745 when Mascarene's own council sided with Shirley and endorsed a report asking London to consider whether the Acadians should be "transported out of the Province of Nova Scotia and be replac'd by good Protestant Subjects." Mascarene had said the same thing in 1720, but after dealing with the Acadians for more than two decades, he was convinced that, with time, they could become loyal subjects. Their neutrality in wartime, in the face of intense pressure from the French, confirmed his faith in them. Mascarene cautioned London that replacing the Acadians with British settlers would be costly, difficult, and a possible violation of the Treaty of Utrecht. He also estimated there were 20,000 Acadians to be removed, an inflated figure no doubt calculated to make his superiors think twice.

It did. The Duke of Newcastle and his successor as secretary of state, the Duke of Bedford, balked at the expense. Shirley backed off for the time being. Deportation, he conceded in late 1746, "may be deem'd too rigorous a Punishmt" as it would "involve the innocent with the Guilty in the Loss of their Estates, and the Expulsion of their Families out of the Country." Shirley's new plan was to secure Nova Scotia with new forts and to disperse "the most obnoxious" Acadians—namely, the implacable residents of Chignecto—to neighboring British colonies. The rest could be assimilated through an influx of New Englanders and other Protestant settlers. To that end, Shirley dispatched a surveyor, Captain Charles Morris, to choose the most promising sites for new settlements. Morris, a survivor of the massacre at Grand-Pré with no love of the Acadians, filed a report advocating the utter destruction of the French presence in the Chignecto region. The Acadians should be "rooted out ... by some stratagem" and the settlements destroyed "by burning down all the houses, cutting the dykes and destroyg all the Grain now growing." His vision of an Acadian apocalypse would prove to be chillingly accurate.

Mascarene and Shirley had more immediate concerns. The colony was rife with rumors of a possible deportation, which threatened to undo all of Mascarene's diplomacy and push the Acadians into the enemy camp. Shirley, at Newcastle's behest, issued a proclamation in October 1747 assuring Acadians "there was not the least foundation for any Apprehensions of His Majesty's intending ... to remove them from their Settlements"—an outright lie, given the debate raging behind closed doors. Furthermore, Shirley insisted, the king was determined "to protect and maintain all such of 'em as have adher'd to, and shall continue in their Duty and Allegiance to him, in the quiet and peaceable Possession of their respective Habitations and Settlements, and in the Enjoyment of all their Rights and Privileges as his Subjects." This, too, was far from the truth. Newcastle was still pondering the idea of at least deporting the troublesome residents of Chignecto. "His Majesty ... thinks it right to postpone any Thing of this kind, for the present," he informed Shirley the very month the proclamation was issued, "tho' His Majesty would have you consider, in what manner such a Scheme may be executed, at a proper Time, and What Precautions may be necessary to be taken, to obviate the Inconveniences that are apprehended from it." The reassuring words of Shirley's proclamation were hollow indeed.

Events of the next half-dozen years—the uneasy peace, the struggle to establish and secure Halifax, Cornwallis's attempts to bully and then befriend the Acadians—temporarily suspended thoughts of deportation. But by 1754, in Lawrence's mind at least, the day of reckoning was approaching. Shirley was as adamant as ever that securing Nova Scotia was vital to protecting Massachusetts, and proposed a preemptive strike to capture Beauséjour, "wounding the Serpent in the head," as he phrased it. Under his latest plan, Chignecto's Acadians would be removed to the Annapolis River area and the border secured with settlers from New England or Northern Ireland. He was not advocating a general expulsion—the uprooted Acadians would remain within the colony and be introduced to "English manners, customs, and language." The British secretary of state, Sir Thomas Robinson, endorsed the scheme and advised Shirley to work in concert with Lawrence, who also was pressing for an expedition against Beauséjour. Lawrence had his own plans for settling accounts with the Acadians—once the fort capitulated, those in the immediate area would be repatriated to Nova Scotia or, he added with startling vindictiveness, "driven totally away by Fire and Sword." A deal was done. Lawrence would supply the cash and a force of British regulars, and Shirley would convince the Massachusetts assembly to raise a force of 2,000 volunteers to provide the backbone for the campaign.

Major-General Edward Braddock set out from Britain in early 1755 with money, guns, and 1,500 redcoats to quarterback a series of campaigns against the French in America. The French, meanwhile, were reinforcing garrisons and arming their Native allies in the river valleys to the west of the American colonies. This was war, even if monarchs and politicians had yet to go through the formalities of declaring one. In mid-April, Braddock met with Shirley and other colonial governors at Alexandria, Virginia, to finalize the plan of attack. Braddock and an up-and-coming Virginia officer, George Washington, would lead the main attack on Fort Duquesne, deep in the wilderness of the Ohio River Valley. Shirley, who had no experience as a field commander, nevertheless would direct one of two thrusts against French posts in what is now upstate New York. The fourth prong—and, as it turned out, the only successful one—was a joint New England–Nova Scotia attack against Beauséjour.

All the signs were there, and yet the threat of war seemed remote to Jacau de Fiedmont. The snippets of news reaching Fort Beauséjour were ominous, but, at the same time, reassuring. The British were shoring up their defenses at Halifax, but what else was new? As for the arrival of Braddock's regiments in Virginia, it was obvious they were headed inland to claim the Ohio Valley. With France and Britain at peace, at least on paper, Fiedmont was confident "all these warlike preparations would be nullified" by negotiations underway in Europe. Not even the irritating presence of Fort Lawrence, barely a mile and a half across the marshes, could shake his belief that if fighting broke out, it would not begin in this backwater. "The confidence that peace would continue was so deeply impressed on the minds of those who lived in the district," Fiedmont confided to his diary in April 1755, that the signs of trouble failed "to awaken the slightest alarm, and we continued to enjoy a sense of security as perfect as though we were residing in the centre of Paris."

Fiedmont had been stationed at Chignecto for three years. He held the rank of lieutenant in the French army and, like his father, Thomas, before him, was a gunner. With no engineer in the small garrison, he was pressed into service to oversee the construction and maintenance of Beauséjour's defenses. It was a thankless task, hindered by superiors more interested in lining their pockets than in spending Louis XV's gold on earthworks. Even when they coughed up the money, laborers were hard to find—Le Loutre had almost every able-bodied Acadian in the area working feverishly to complete a dike on the marshes behind the fort. Fiedmont was half Acadian himself, the grandson of the Pierre Melanson who founded Minas. His father had married Anne Melanson at Port-Royal in 1705, and was on hand for the fireworks when Nicholson's forces captured Acadie.

Now, forty-five years after the fall of Port-Royal, Fiedmont was about to witness the beginning of the end of French power in North America. Beauséjour's slumber was shattered on June 2 when a settler rushed into the fort with word that about forty British ships were anchored in a nearby cove. Louis Du Pont Duchambon de Vergor, the commander, sent messengers to Louisbourg and Quebec to plead for reinforcements, then summoned Acadian men in the area to gather at the fort. The fleet pulled into view late in the afternoon and Lieutenant-Colonel Robert Monckton landed his troops at Fort Lawrence the next day. They quickly captured the ridge behind the French fort—its vulnerable flank—and turned to the unglamorous work of digging trenches and getting cannons and mortars in place. Fiedmont led a frantic effort to repair neglected walls and cut trenches to slow the British advance. "It is not the ramparts however, which, as a rule, defend a fort, but men," Fiedmont later noted. If defenders "show good will and courage," he believed, they could throw an attacker's plans into disarray and win the battle.

But there was little courage within Beauséjour's walls. Vergor, corrupt and barely literate, was unfit for command; it was said the commandant's post was his reward for keeping a superior supplied with women. He was so indecisive that his own officers dismissed him as a coward. He was also outnumbered. Vergor had just 150 soldiers and 21 cannon inside his pentagon-shaped fort. The call to arms evoked little enthusiasm in the surrounding villages. About 300 Acadians turned up—less than half the number living in the area—after hiding their wives and children in the woods. Most were reluctant to do battle, fearing if they were captured or the fort fell, the British would hang them as traitors.

Vergor lured them inside with assurances he could hold the fort until help arrived, and issued an order compelling them to defend the fort "under pain of dire punishment if they disobeyed," an insurance policy of sorts against British reprisals. "As soldiers," historian George Stanley concluded in a painstaking account of the fall of New France, the Acadians "were of small value to the garrison. At the best they carried out their duties sullenly and without heart; at the worst they deserted and returned to their homes." Fiedmont complained that soldiers and Acadians alike had to be forced to build earthworks, and "vanished like smoke" when the officers were not looking. While Acadians volunteered for patrols and scouting parties, Fiedmont considered this a ploy to avoid the heavy work of building defenses. He dismissed them as "a people who are little adapted to warfare and who were already intimidated by the mere sight of the enemy's fleet."

There were exceptions, Fiedmont conceded, "honest folk who did their duty with much zeal." He singled out Joseph Broussard, "reputed to be one of the bravest and most enterprising of the Acadians." Known to everyone as Beausoleil—the literal translation is "beautiful sun"—Broussard had always been a rebel in search of a cause. Born in Port-Royal, he likely witnessed Nicholson's siege as a boy of eight. He was an avowed enemy of the British all his life, his hatred and sense of injustice fueled, perhaps, by his father's brief imprisonment in 1713 in retaliation for the kidnapping of a British soldier.

In his twenties, Broussard was twice hauled before the council at Annapolis Royal to answer for his actions. The first time, in 1724, he was accused of threatening another settler and aiding a Mi'kmaq raid on Fort Anne. He was arrested and imprisoned, but not before he assaulted the official who served him with the summons. Broussard was released after local Acadian deputies agreed to keep him in line. Two years later, soon after his marriage, he was arrested for failing to support an illegitimate child; despite his contention he was "very innocent and not the father," he was ordered to pay maintenance. His reputation shot in Port-Royal, Broussard and his older brother, Alexandre, moved their families—their wives, Agnès and Marguerite Thibodeau, were sisters—to the remote Petitcodiac River Valley. The site of present-day Moncton, New Brunswick, and deep within the area claimed by France, the marsh-lined river was about as far from British rule as an Acadian could get.

The Broussard brothers spoke the Mi'kmaq language, were said to live like the Natives, and were skilled at wilderness warfare, making them natural leaders of the local militia. Beausoleil Broussard, who still had a price on his head for his support of the French during the 1740s, was likely among the first to answer Vergor's call to defend Beauséjour. Three days into Monckton's attack, when Le Loutre called for volunteers to harass the advancing British and to take hostages as bargaining chips, Broussard "promised to do everything he could to capture a few prisoners." True to his word, Broussard and a band of Acadians and Natives turned up on June 8 with a captured British officer.

Vergor did not mount a serious counterattack until June 12, when he mustered about 200 soldiers, Acadians, and Natives for a raid on the British positions. They were easily repulsed, but sporadic fire from the fort's cannons kept the British pinned down and slowed the advance. Monckton unleashed his heavy artillery on June 13. "We threw Bumb^s all Day," John Thomas, a surgeon's assistant with one of the New England regiments, noted in his journal. The batteries "Kept up a warm fire (and) Got our Large Mortar to Bair on ye Enemys Foart." The defenders sought cover in underground casements to escape the shelling as the French returned heavy cannon fire—more than 150 volleys in a single day. The gun battle raged for three days, creating more din than damage. There were few casualties on either side and the British scored few direct hits on the fort. In the midst of the shelling, a courier arrived with a message that no help would be coming from Louisbourg. The devastating news soon leaked out—a servant, who was in the room when Vergor broke the news to his officers, told his wife and soon the whole fort knew. By Fiedmont's count, about eighty Acadians deserted that night. Vergor averted a further exodus by ordering his troops to shoot anyone who fled. If his initial order compelling the Acadians to fight was just for show, the threat was now real.

The end came about nine in the morning on June 16 when a shell pierced the roof of a supposedly bombproof casement, killing two French officers, two Acadians, and the unlucky British officer that Broussard had taken prisoner. The explosion blasted a gaping hole in the ramparts and shattered what little resolve the defenders had left—if another shell penetrated the powder magazine, the entire fort might be leveled. Water was running low, half-buried corpses littered the grounds, and the Acadians had no place to take cover from the incoming rounds. Fiedmont, who was urging his gunners to keep firing, recorded the dramatic final showdown: the panicked Acadians confronted Vergor and demanded that he surrender. It was not a request; it was mutiny. If he refused, they threatened to turn their guns on the French soldiers and hand over the fort themselves. The ever-zealous Le Loutre urged them to continue the fight, proclaiming "it was far better to be buried in the Fort than to surrender it." There were no takers. The fort's supply clerk, Thomas Pinchon, had been sowing doubt among the Acadians for days and took credit for inciting the uprising. The French later discovered, to their chagrin, that Pinchon was a spy who had funneled information, including the plans to the fort, to the British.

Vergor conferred with his officers, then sent a message to Monckton asking for a cease-fire to discuss terms. The capitulation came as a surprise to Monckton, who had no inkling of the havoc one of his shells had unleashed. Realizing he had the upper hand, he gave the French two hours to surrender. Monckton took control of the fort on June 17 and renamed it Fort Cumberland, after the royal duke who had been sent packing at Fontenoy. Fort Gaspereau, a palisade with only twenty defenders on the Île Saint-Jean side of the isthmus, surrendered without a fight. The defeat shattered the balance of power in the region. The overland communication and supply route between Quebec and Île Saint-Jean and Île Royale was disrupted, and Louisbourg was likely the next British target. Acadians who had fled to Chignecto to escape British rule were again at the mercy of the British.

The hasty surrender sickened one French officer, who was convinced the fort, "bad as it was, could have held out a little while." Louis de Courville, a French official stationed at the fort, agreed, contending that Vergor should have taken the offensive and mounted more attacks to disrupt the British offensive. If Vergor "really meant to engage in warfare," he contended, "he could have held his ground for a considerable period of time." Fiedmont, too, felt more resistance could have been offered, but he conceded that Vergor's hand was forced once the Acadians revolted. The French military, stung by the defeat, convened a court martial to try Vergor and his officers on charges of failing to mount an adequate defense. The charges were dismissed in 1758 after the court concluded that the "faulty construction" of both forts had rendered it impossible "to make a more active or a longer resistance." The testimony of several officers accused the Acadians of avoiding service or ignoring orders. A Lieutenant Faber, who led a detachment of about 100 Acadians out of the fort on a sortie, described himself as "the most astonished man in the world" when only two turned up at the staging area, "all the others having taken to flight."

Few Acadians wished to die for the king of France or be hanged as a traitor to the king of Britain. Beausoleil Broussard and his followers were an exception, and even launched a daring but futile raid on the main British camp on the day the fort fell. The terms of surrender called for the French troops to be transported to Louisbourg. Monckton agreed that the Acadians, "inasmuch as they were forced to take up arms under pain of death, shall be pardoned for the part they have taken." Broussard, bold as brass, showed up at the fort two days after the surrender and offered to help barter a deal with the Native fighters in exchange for amnesty. Monckton agreed, subject to Lawrence's approval. The fate of the Acadians, in Chignecto and throughout Nova Scotia, was in the hands of the lieutenant governor.

Lawrence was elated to learn of the swift victory, but outraged at the number of Britain's "inveterate Enemies," as he called them, who had rallied to Beauséjour's defense. He praised Monckton for making no promises to the Acadians, other than to spare their lives. "Their pretending to have been forced to take up Arms is an insult upon Common Sense," he scoffed, and deserved "the severest treatment." He was determined to drive them out, declaring himself satisfied that if "suffered to remain," the Acadians "will prove for ever a sore Thorn in our Side." He reported the surrender to the Lords of Trade at the end of June, noting that British and New England losses had been "very inconsiderable"—no more than twenty soldiers killed and roughly the same number wounded. He wanted London to know that some 300 Acadians had been among the defenders. These and other "deserted French inhabitants" were handing over their weapons and had been conscripted to rebuild the captured fort and its barracks. Once this work was done, and in keeping with the pre-attack plan to clear out Chignecto, he had ordered Monckton "to drive them out of the country."

It was an ominous phrase, and it caught the eye of the secretary of state, Robinson, when a ship bearing the letter arrived in London more than a month later. In his reply, written on August 13, Robinson asked whether Lawrence meant "to drive away all the French inhabitants of the Peninsula, which amounts to many Thousands." He assumed Lawrence intended to expel only those who had taken up arms at Chignecto. Administering far-flung colonies in the Age of Sail was a slow and frustrating process, giving officials on the ground considerable latitude to act first and seek instructions or approval later. No matter what Lawrence had meant, Robinson acknowledged that action would be taken long before his query reached Halifax in the fall. "It is not doubted, but you will have acted upon a Strict Principle of immediate and indespensible Security to your government," he wrote. He hoped Lawrence had carefully considered the alarm an expulsion from Chignecto would cause within "the whole Body of French Neutrals, and how suddenly an Insurrection may follow from Despair." He also assumed Lawrence had taken into account the possibility that "useful Subjects" would be driven into the hands of the French. His belated advice was to proceed with care:

> It cannot, therefore, be too much recommended to you, to use the greatest Caution and Prudence in your Conduct, towards these neutrals, and to assure such of Them, as may be trusted, especially upon their taking the Oaths to His Majesty, and His Government, That They may remain in the quiet Possession of their Settlements, under proper Regulations.

It was the king's desire, Robinson added, to retain as many Acadians as possible. In May 1755 the French ambassador to Britain had proposed that the Acadians be given three years to leave Nova Scotia with their possessions. George II had instructed his ministers to reject the offer, Robinson noted, telling the French that allowing such a migration would deprive Britain "of a very considerable Number of useful Subjects."

By the time Lawrence read these words, it was too late for caution and prudence. A showdown between the British and the Acadians was already in the works. Lawrence had ordered a colony-wide clampdown in advance of the assault on Beauséjour, impounding canoes and boats that could be used to carry supplies to the fort and ordering all Acadians to surrender their guns.

The heavy-handed measures provoked a backlash, perhaps the backlash Lawrence was seeking. On June 10, twenty-five deputies from Minas and Piziquid signed a petition asking Lawrence to return their boats and guns. They needed boats to fish and guns to protect their livestock from wild animals. They denied providing supplies to Beauséjour and complained of being lumped in with those who had. "We are grieved, Sir, at seeing ourselves declared guilty without being aware of having disobeyed." Seizing firearms was "but a feeble guarantee of our fidelity," the petitioners contended. "It is not the gun which an inhabitant possesses, that will induce him to revolt, nor the privation of the same gun that will make him more faithful; but his conscience alone must induce him to maintain his oath."

Lawrence's order, they were suggesting rather bluntly, was wrongheaded and unnecessary to maintain order. Their sincerity and loyalty was in question, despite their neutrality and "unshaken fidelity" to the British monarch. They begged Lawrence to review their past conduct, believing it proved that "far from violating that oath we have taken, we have maintained it in its entirety, in spite of the solicitations and the dreadful threats of another power." Lawrence immediately summoned the signatories to come to Halifax and appear before the council. Sensing the petition had been worded too strongly—and aware that the fall of Beauséjour would embolden the British—forty-five residents of the same areas signed a second petition on June 24, apologizing in advance for any errors or "want of respect" in their initial missive.

Lawrence and the council convened in Halifax on July 3 to discuss the petitions. They gathered as usual at the governor's house, near the waterfront. This rather modest structure—"small and low, being but one story high" by one description—was a mini-fortress, its august occupant defended by small cannon mounted on a perimeter of sand-filled barrels.

Nova Scotia was three years away from having an elected assembly; in the meantime the administration of colonial affairs rested with the governor and his handpicked council, who were answerable only to London. Lawrence's council was a motley crew, dominated by soldiers and ex-soldiers. Belcher, who was eight months into his job as chief justice, had no military background, but shared Lawrence's alarm about the French menace. John Collier, a member since Cornwallis's time, was a retired army officer who also held the posts of militia captain, justice of the peace, and admiralty judge. Collier often clashed with the boss—he would later complain to London about Lawrence's dictatorial behavior—but he was onside on this issue, and wound up with large tracts of vacated Acadian land in the Piziquid area for his trouble. Benjamin Green was a Harvard dropout and former Boston merchant who was now a Halifax port official. He later faced censure in London for awarding contracts to a business partner, and a posthumous audit determined he had helped himself to a small fortune in public money. William Cotterell, another former captain, had been in charge of the colony's military police and served as the council's secretary. These four—Belcher, Collier, Green, and Cotterell—were present for the July meetings with the Acadian deputies.

John Rous returned to Halifax in time for the final meetings that sealed the Acadians' fate, and brought yet another military viewpoint to the table. His exploits as a New England privateer landed him commands in the Royal Navy. Lawrence knew him well—Rous provided naval support to Lawrence's missions to Chignecto in 1750—and appointed him to the council in 1754. Rous showed up on July 25 fresh from the front, after taking part in the siege of Beauséjour and a subsequent raid to drive the French from the Saint John River.

The councillors reviewed both petitions and unanimously agreed that the first one was "highly arrogant and insidious," an "Insult" to the king's authority and deserving of "the highest Resentment." Were it not for the protestations of innocence and apologies in the second petition, its authors would have been "severely punished for their Presumption." The deputies, who had been waiting outside, were called into the room. Fifteen had answered the summons and the council was told the other ten were too sick to attend. The offending petition was read aloud and, according to the minutes of the meeting, the deputies "were severely reprimanded for their Audacity in Subscribing and Presenting so impertinent a Paper." In light of the groveling follow-up petition and their "Weakness and Ignorance" in matters of government, they were told, the council would let their impertinence pass. Then the petition was reread, paragraph by paragraph, and Lawrence refuted each point. The Acadians had been treated with "the greatest Lenity and Tenderness," allowed free exercise of their religion and possession of "the best Soil of the Province," despite failing to swear allegiance to the British. As for their past conduct, Lawrence dismissed it as "undutifull" and "ungratefull." He accused the Acadians of providing food and ammunition to Britain's enemies, overcharging the British for supplies, and neglecting their farms. They were "of no use to the Province" and "an Obstruction to the King's Intentions" to promote settlement. The deputies were asked to point to a single instance of service to the government. "To which," the council's minutes record, "they were incapable of making a reply." The browbeating continued. Lawrence lectured them like schoolboys for having the audacity to debate matters of loyalty and fidelity with the king of Britain. He accused them of joining with "another Power" in the past, and claimed they would do so again as soon as the opportunity presented itself. The attack was relentless and humiliating; not even the matter-of-fact tone of the minutes and the passage of two and a half centuries can mask Lawrence's venom.

The deputies were offered a chance to redeem themselves. They could prove their loyalty by swearing the oath of allegiance on the spot. Still reeling from Lawrence's tongue-lashing, they protested that they had not come to Halifax prepared to deal with that issue. The council was unmoved, pointing out that the demand for a new oath had been hanging over their heads for six years, giving them plenty of time to make up their minds. The deputies asked to be allowed to return home to consult with the other members of their communities. The request was denied and the council persisted. No matter what their constituents might say, the deputies could decide for themselves whether to submit to the oath. Would they take it or not? The atmosphere in the room was electric as the irresistible force of the council collided with the immovable resistance of the Acadians. The deputies asked for time to consider their answer. They were excused and huddled outside for an hour. Upon their return, they said they could not take an unqualified oath without consulting their communities. But they were prepared to swear an oath "as they had done before," on condition that they were not required to fight. The council demanded that they take the same oath as any other British subject. When the deputies still refused, the councillors gave them until the following morning to think it over.

When the council reconvened on July 4, the answer was the same. The deputies insisted they could not swear an unqualified oath without consulting their constituents. They were ushered outside while the councillors plotted their next move. The Acadian communities would be ordered to send new slates of deputies to Halifax to respond to the demand for the oath. This would be their last chance—anyone who refused would be removed from the colony, but the Acadians would not be told this in advance. The deputies were recalled and, when told they would be expelled for refusing the oath, there was an immediate change of heart. They offered to take the oath, only to be told the council could have no faith in the sincerity of an oath extracted under duress. The deputies had lost their rights as British citizens and would be dealt with as subjects of the king of France. The group was seized and imprisoned on Georges Island, a heavily fortified speck of land in Halifax harbor normally reserved for thieves, pirates, murderers, and the other dregs of society.

The standoff in the council room sealed the fate of thousands of Acadians. An issue that had festered for forty-five years culminated in decisive action. The demand for the oath had been debated and then dropped, only to be resurrected and then ignored. Why now? What had changed?

For the Acadians, nothing had changed—they remained caught in the middle. Nova Scotia could face a French counterattack and Acadians who swore the oath would be branded as traitors to the king of France or, worse, forced to fight for the British. But what was really at stake was the Acadians' hard-won neutrality and their loyalty to themselves. They had sworn a conditional oath to Governor Philipps fifteen years earlier and, with very few exceptions, they had honored that pledge. In their minds there was no need for the British to seek further assurances of their neutrality.

The accommodation of Philipps, the patience of Mascarene, the hollow threats of Cornwallis, the mildness of Hopson—nothing in the past prepared the Acadians and their deputies for Lawrence's inflexibility and imperious demands for deference and obedience. "The Acadians," Naomi Griffiths has observed, "seem to have been unable to comprehend what government by Colonel Lawrence, who was experienced only as a soldier in the field, would demand in terms of diplomacy." Arthur Doughty, a Canadian historian and archivist writing in the 1920s, sized up Lawrence as a man "unaccustomed to compromise .... To him, the Acadians were as an enemy in the camp, and as such they were to be treated."

To the American historian Francis Parkman, a true Anglophile, Lawrence was an impatient man and the stubborn Acadians taxed what little patience he had. The closest Parkman came to criticism was noting that Lawrence's "energetic will was not apt to relent under the softer sentiments." His fellow American, Brebner, concluded that Lawrence was neither evil nor cruel, but motivated by personal ambition and by what he saw as his duty to his country. "The times were warlike," Brebner wrote, and Lawrence "resolved the situation with a soldier's cold and arbitrary logic into the mathematics of military terms. He knew allies and enemies, not 'neutrals'."

Lawrence's decision to settle the oath business, once and for all, rested on a consideration that had never before factored into the Acadian equation. He could settle it. For the first time since 1710, Nova Scotia's chief administrator had the means at his disposal to force the Acadians into submission or, if they refused, to take punitive action. The swift victory at Beauséjour left close to 2,000 New England troops at Lawrence's disposal. In mid-July, Admiral Edward Boscawen and his second-in-command, Rear-Admiral Savage Mostyn, sailed into Halifax with a fleet of Royal Navy warships. They bolstered the military might at Lawrence's disposal and the opinions of such high-ranking officers, newly arrived from Britain, carried considerable weight. Lawrence, who was operating well beyond his instructions to proceed with caution in his dealings with the Acadians, asked Boscawen and Mostyn to meet with the council to discuss measures to secure the colony. On July 15, the admirals appeared as requested and Lawrence briefed them on the impasse over the oath. Boscawen and Mostyn approved of the steps the council had taken and, according to the minutes, agreed that "it was now the properest Time" to oblige the Acadians to take the oath "or to quit the Country."

With the admirals onside, Lawrence decided it was time to break the news to the Lords of Trade. His July 18 letter to London reported that, as the Acadians had never taken the oath, "I thought it my duty to avail myself of the present occasion"—his position of military superiority—"to propose it to them." He described the meetings with the deputies, their insistence on an exemption from bearing arms, and the demand for new deputies to provide an answer from the wider population. A copy of the minutes would be sent as soon as one was available, he noted, but in the meantime he withheld a crucial fact—the deputies now in prison were not told the consequences of refusing the oath until it was too late. Lawrence concluded with a chilling promise: "I have ordered new Deputies to be elected ... and am determined to bring the Inhabitants to a compliance, or rid the province of such perfidious subjects." The letter was a courtesy, not a request for advice or approval.

As Lawrence signed his name at the bottom, he was well aware that, by the time his words were read in London sometime in September, he would have the Acadians' answer.

The council, with Boscawen and Mostyn in attendance, reconvened a week later to meet with deputies from the Annapolis River. They bore a letter signed by more than 200 residents who refused to swear a new oath, but assured the council they had adhered to their past oath and would do so in future. The delegation was brought into the room and confirmed the community's refusal to take an oath. If the government intended to force them to leave their lands, the deputies asked that their people be given time to arrange an orderly departure. The council dredged up the well-worn accusations of rebellion and collusion with the king's enemies and repeated its demand: "[T]hey must now resolve either to Take the Oath without any Reserve or else to quit their Lands." There would be no more delays, they were told—America had been plunged into crisis and no one knew where or when the French might attack. The deputies remained adamant. "They were determined One and All, rather to quit their Lands than to Take any other Oath than what they had done before." The refusal of the Acadians to compromise at such a late date, with more than a dozen of their deputies languishing in prison, defies an easy explanation. Was it obstinance? Naivety? Defiance? All of the above would account for their rigid position, but so would political maturity, national pride, and a strong collective identity, a sense that they were dealing with their rulers as equals, Acadian to Briton. We will stay, they were saying in a united voice, but on our terms; if that is unacceptable to the government, allow us to gather our possessions and leave. The minutes suggest this group, unlike the first slate of deputies, was warned in advance that if they persisted in refusing the oath, they would not get a second chance. It was a Friday. The council gave them the weekend to consider what their final answer would be.

The final act in this battle of wills was played out the following Monday, July 28, at Lawrence's residence. Outside, the weather was sunny and hot; inside, Nova Scotia's only judge was turning up the heat on the deputies. Belcher tendered a lengthy report on the legality of deporting the Acadians, an astonishing document that was replete with hearsay, conjecture, and distorted facts. Describing it as a legal opinion is a stretch—Belcher failed to cite a single statute or precedent in his headlong rush to condemn the Acadians and condone their removal. It was little more than a work of political propaganda, tailored to justify Lawrence's decision to conduct a wholesale deportation. The report was dated July 28, 1755 and read to the council that day, but its real purpose was to tie up a loose end. The Lords of Trade had directed Lawrence, many months before, to seek Belcher's advice on the legal status of Acadians who refused to take the oath. Lawrence saw no need to bother until the eve of the council meeting to rubber-stamp his decision to deport. He was making a monumental decision affecting the lives of thousands of people, and the future of the colony, without authorization. He could at least show London that he had obeyed their instructions to consult his chief justice.

Belcher's report built on the us-against-them theme of his speech at the opening of the Supreme Court in the fall of 1754, and resurrected his courtroom rant about stamping out traitors and dissidents. The conduct of the Acadians under more than forty years of British rule, he asserted, cast them as "Rebels to His Majesty" who had lost the right to take an oath of allegiance. He convicted the Acadians—without trial, and with little or no evidence—of duplicity in every act of aggression committed by French soldiers and Native warriors since 1710. They had committed "acts of Hostility," instigated others, failed to warn the British of impending attacks, and provided provisions to French forces during the 1740s invasions. Through their support of the Natives, they forced British settlers to live in fear, huddled in garrison towns, and prompted many newcomers to move on to safer colonies. He believed they were "more and more discovering their inveterate enmity to the English and their affection for the French."

His most damning allegation appears to be pure fantasy—that two-thirds of the New England soldiers who died with Noble at Grand-Pré were "sick Persons ... murdered by the French Inhabitants." That some Acadians had aided the French and Mi'kmaq was a fact, and a handful had been declared outlaws as a result; that an entire community should be punished for their misdeeds—real or imagined—was a grave injustice. Belcher claimed his information about events at Grand-Pré came from soldiers who escaped the bloodshed, but surviving accounts of the battle make no mention of Acadian fighters, let alone Acadians slaughtering soldiers. Belcher was practising law on the other side of the Atlantic at the time, so he could only repeat what he was told. The source of the damning allegation may well have been Lawrence.

There was more. Belcher advanced the specious argument that to administer the oath at such a late date would violate "the spirit and letter" of the governor's royal instructions of 1749. Cornwallis had demanded an oath, the Acadians had refused and, in doing so, had breached the Treaty of Utrecht and forfeited their lands and possessions. Once a demand to take an oath was refused, he argued, the person should not get a second chance—there could be no assurance the change of heart was genuine. Belcher proceeded to put words in the Acadians' mouths. The oath had been tendered, and their reply was to this effect: "That they would not take the Oath unless they were permitted not to bear arms against the King of France, and that otherwise they desired Six Months to remove themselves and their effects to Canada, and that they openly desired to serve the French King that they might have priests." Then he put words in the mouths of the Lords of Trade, speculating that in response to the Acadians' position, as he articulated it, "orders and possibly a Force would be immediately sent for banishing such Insolent and dangerous Inhabitants from the Province."

Finally, Belcher warned, allowing the Acadians to remain would squander the victory at Beauséjour and jeopardize the colony's safety and prosperity. Their presence offered a temptation to the French to attack and their questionable loyalty was a barrier to immigration. They persisted in refusing the oath, he pointed out, even in the face of the large force of New England troops at Chignecto and Boscawen's fleet at anchor in Halifax harbor. Once this show of force was gone, he predicted, "they will, unquestionably resume their Perfidy and Treacheries and with more arts and rancour than before."

The report was read to the council, adding a veneer of legality to the proceedings. Deputies from Piziquid, Minas, and River Canard had arrived in Halifax over the weekend with responses from those communities, which were read into the record. One hundred and three residents of Piziquid signed a letter stating they were resolved, "with one consent and voice, to take no other oath." The Minas deputies carried a letter from 203 residents declaring they would "never prove so fickle" as to swear an oath that altered the privileges "obtained for us by our sovereigns and our fathers in the past." Both groups begged Lawrence to release the jailed deputies. The letters said the Acadians considered the oath sworn under Governor Philipps to remain in force and promised they would honor its terms—in other words, they would remain neutral. The residents of Minas even resurrected Shirley's 1747 proclamation assuring them the right to remain on their lands. Neither letter indicated the Acadians in these communities had adopted the hard-line approach of the Annapolis deputies, who would rather leave the colony than submit to an unconditional oath. It is also unclear whether these deputies were aware they would be forced to leave the colony if they refused the oath. The delegations were summoned into the meeting separately, and may not have had a chance to confer before facing the council. Tragically, the Minas and Piziquid deputies may not have realized that the oath was no longer negotiable. Even more tragically, hundreds of signatories who had rejected the oath, men who were still on their farms awaiting word from Halifax, had no inkling what was at stake.

The stage was set for the final confrontation. Years later, the rabidly anti-British Le Loutre would describe a dramatic scene in which the deputies dropped to their knees in prayer before one of the older men rose and declared they would never take an oath against France:

> The Admiral Boscawen, astonished by such a reply, wished to intimidate them, drew his Sword and said to them: 'It is thus that you reply to a general? I know of nothing which should prevent me from plunging my Sword into your bodies.' One of the elders bared his breast and said to him: 'Strike, my general, strike if you dare! You can kill my body but you have no power over my soul, and you will never rip from my Heart my Allegeiance to my religion, nor my loyalty to my first and legitimate Sovereign Louis.'

Le Loutre met Acadian exiles in France in the 1760s, so it is possible he heard an eyewitness account of the meeting. But the story appears embellished and smacks of wishful thinking on the part of a man who had tried and failed to sway the Acadians by force. The Acadians were trying to preserve the terms of their existing oath of loyalty to Britain, not cling to loyalty to a French regime that had caused them nothing but grief. The minutes of the meeting—the most credible record that survives—are succinct: The deputies from Minas and Piziquid were brought before the council and refused to take the oath. The Annapolis deputies were then called in and also refused. "Whereupon," the minutes relate, "they were all ordered into Confinement." Lawrence, his council, and the admirals then debated how to proceed. Sending them to the neighboring French colonies would strengthen the enemy on the eve of war. Finally, the minute-taker, Jonathan Duport, was directed to record the following resolution:

> After mature Consideration, it was unanimously Agreed That, to prevent as much as possible their Attempting to return and molest the Settlers that may be set down on their Lands, it would be most proper to send them to be distributed amongst the several Colonies on the Continent, and that a sufficient Number of Vessels should be hired with all possible Expedition for that purpose.

With those words, the Acadian nightmare began.

5 "A Sceen of Woe & Distres"

Began to Embarke the Inhabitants who went of Very Solentarily and unwillingly, the women in Great Distress Carrying off Their Children In their arms. Others Carrying their Decript Parents in their Carts and all their Goods Moving in Great Confussion & appeard a Sceen of woe & Distres.

—Lieutenant-Colonel John Winslow, *Journal*, October 8, 1755

The church of Saint-Charles-des-Mines was jammed with men and boys. There were 400, maybe more. What news could possibly be so important to cause the English soldiers to summon the head of every family, and every boy over the age of ten, to be here? A proclamation had been read out in Grand-Pré and the surrounding villages a day earlier, but it revealed little. "His Excellency the Governor has Instructed us of his Last resolution respecting the maters Proposed Lately to the Inhabitants," it read, "and has ordered us to Communicate the same to the Inhabitants in General in Person." At the appointed time—three o'clock in the afternoon of September 5, 1755—those who heeded the command would learn "his Majesty's Intentions." Almost all of the men of Grand-Pré, Minas, and the other villages turned out as ordered, even though the weather was perfect and there was grain to be harvested. Those who refused, the proclamation warned, risked being stripped of their possessions.

Rumors had been rife for two weeks, ever since about 300 soldiers marched into Grand-Pré without warning. They commandeered the church as their headquarters, but at least had the decency to allow the priest to remove the sacred trappings before moving in with their muskets and supplies. The commander, Lieutenant-Colonel John Winslow, a plump man with a wry smirk, moved into the priest's house next door while his men pitched their tents on top of the cemetery. Within days the soldiers erected a log palisade that enclosed the church, the priest's house, and their tents. Grand-Pré had not played host to so many soldiers since Colonel Noble and his men arrived for their ill-fated occupation. Some said they planned to stay for the winter, and their fort was insurance against another surprise attack. Others were convinced the meeting at the church had something to do with the governor's latest demand to take a new oath of allegiance. The arrival of three ships in the basin at the end of August set off more rumors and prompted a few Acadians to row out to greet the visitors. The crewmen would say only that they were here to transport the troops. It was a strange response because these troops did not seem to be in a hurry to go anywhere.

The men and boys of Grand-Pré were startled to see their familiar churchyard transformed into an armed camp. They filed through the main gate of the palisade and were confronted with long lines of soldiers, armed with muskets. More soldiers stood guard inside the church. Once everyone had assembled—418 answered the summons—a table was placed in the center of the room. Winslow, in his best brass-buttoned uniform, entered with a bevy of officers. The church fell silent. Winslow appreciated the gravity of what he was about to say and preserved his exact words in his diary. "Gentlemen," he began:

> I have Received from His Excellency Governor Lawrence. The Kings Commission which I have in my hand and by whose orders you are Convened togather to Manifest to you his Majesty's Final resolution to the French Inhabitants of this his Province of Nova Scotia. who for almost half a Centry have had more Indulgence Granted them, then any of his Subjects in any part of his Dominions. what use you have made of them. you your Self Best Know.

The Part of Duty I am now upon, is what thoh Necessary is Very Disagreable to my natural make & Temper as I Know it Must be Grevious to you who are of the Same Specia.

But it is not my Buisness to annimedvert, but to obey Such orders as I receive and therefore without Hessitation Shall Deliver you his Majesty's orders and Instructions.

Winslow paused several times as he spoke, giving an interpreter a chance to repeat his words in French. His roundabout delivery and the delay in translation put everyone on edge. The wait was excruciating. What plans did King George have for them? Winslow finally got to the point:

your Lands & Tennements, Cattle of all Kinds and Live Stock of all Sortes are Forfitted to the Crown with all other your Effects Saving your money and Household Goods and you your Selves to be removed from this his Province.

The church erupted in shouts and cries. Every well-tanned face was frozen in shock or twisted in rage. What had they done to deserve such punishment? Where were they being sent? What would become of their wives and children? At first, few could grasp the enormity of what was happening. Weeks later, Winslow would note, many still found it hard to believe they were being stripped of their property and banished from their homeland. As the din subsided, he forged ahead:

I Shall do Every thing in my Power that all Those Goods be Secured to you and that you are Not Molested in Carrying of them of and also that whole Familys Shall go in the Same Vessel. and make this remove which I am Sensable must give you a great Deal of Trouble as Easey as his Majesty's Service will admit and hope that in what Ever part of the world you may Fall you may be Faithfull Subjects, a Peasable & happy People.

I Must also Inform you That it is his Majesty's Pleasure that you remain in Security under the Inspection & Direction of the Troops that I have the Honr. to Command.

Winslow marched out, leaving the frightened and outraged Acadians huddled in a church that was now a prison. A dozen soldiers circled the building to prevent escapes. Not long after Winslow returned to his quarters, he received a message from the elders locked up in the church. They expressed "Great Greif ... that they had Incurd his Majty's Displeasure," and asked that most of the men and boys be allowed to return home to tell their families what was happening. A few would remain as hostages to ensure they returned. Winslow conferred with his officers and agreed to release only twenty prisoners, who had until the following morning to spread the news and assure the women and children they would not be harmed. By now night had fallen. Winslow began drafting a list of his prisoners, but was too tired to finish. "Thus Ended the Memerable fifth of September," he scribbled in his journal, "a Day of Great Fatigue & Troble."

Lawrence had set the wheels in motion on July 31, three days after the council's decision to deport. Since the Chignecto Acadians had been found under arms, he noted in a letter to Lieutenant-Colonel Robert Monckton, they were "entitled to no favour from the government" and would be deported first. Ships would be sent to the Bay of Fundy as soon as possible with more detailed orders and the destination of each vessel and its deportees. It was imperative, Lawrence cautioned, that the plan be kept secret to ensure that no one escaped or made off with their cattle. Monckton should "endeavour to fall upon some stratagem to get the men both young and old (especially the heads of families) into your power and detain them till the transports shall arrive." Monckton was also directed to confiscate every boat and canoe and to patrol the roads to prevent escapes. Lawrence had thought through the mechanics of the deportation in considerable detail—evidence, perhaps, that he had resolved to rid himself of the Acadians long before the order was issued on July 28. The Acadians would be allowed to take only their "ready money and household furniture" into exile. His instructions for the provisioning of the transports were explicit: each deportee would be entitled to 1 pound of flour and a half-pound of bread each day, plus a weekly allotment of 1 pound of beef per person.

Monckton might have raised an eyebrow at the scale of the deportation, but his personal role had not changed—the local Acadians had been marked for exile all along as punishment for siding with the French. He forged ahead "with characteristic efficiency but no apparent enthusiasm," according to a biographer. As he pondered the best way to lure the Acadians into custody, it may have dawned on Monckton that this was a win-win situation. A wider deportation meant he could shake off the Acadians as well as most of the rag-tag colonial troops squatting in a tent city alongside Fort Cumberland. Winslow and his New Englanders would be needed to round up Acadians at Minas and Piziquid. Monckton was taking all the credit for the capture of Beauséjour and had not spoken a single word to Winslow since the shooting stopped in mid-June. Relations hit rock-bottom when Monckton cut off the supply of rum to Winslow's troops, creating an uproar in the camp and almost sparking a mutiny. "A very haughty man," in the estimation of one writer, Monckton "held no sympathy for the Acadians and very little respect for Winslow and his volunteers." Historian George Rawlyk was more blunt, describing Monckton as "an arrogant and basically stupid man." Rawlyk may have mistaken inexperience for aloofness. Monckton marked his twenty-ninth birthday barely a week after capturing Beauséjour. He was posted to Nova Scotia in 1752, but may have met Lawrence much earlier—both had fought at Fontenoy, where Lawrence was wounded. Monckton was named to the council in 1753 and later that year helped Lawrence quell riots among the German settlers at Lunenburg. After earning Lawrence's gratitude for his "moderate and most judicious" handling of that delicate mission, he was chosen to command the assault on Beauséjour.

August 1755 opened with a spell of hot, dry weather. Monckton chose August 10 as the day of reckoning, and summoned all men and boys older than sixteen to the very fort many of them had reluctantly defended weeks earlier. The turnout was poor and Monckton elected not to tip his hand just yet. Those who answered the call "were ordered to Tarry all Night under the Guns of the Garrison" while soldiers swept the nearby villages for stragglers. By the following morning some 400 men and boys had been assembled. For Winslow, this was a dry run for the speech he would make a few weeks later in the church at Grand-Pré, and he carefully recorded the scene in his journal:

the Male Inhabitants or the Principal of them being Colected togather In Forte Cumberland To hear the Sentence which Determind their Property from The Govr & Council of Hallifax, which was that they were Declared rebels. There Lands Goods & Chattels Forfitt to the Crown and thir Bodys to be Imprisoned. Upon which the Gates of the Forte was Shut & they all Confined ...

About half of the prisoners were transferred to Fort Lawrence. Winslow does not record the Acadians' reaction to being stripped of their property, or whether they were told they were about to be deported. Many had no intention of going quietly into exile.

Unaware that the trap had been sprung, Lawrence wrote again on August 11, urging Monckton to use force if necessary to round up the Acadians. Word had just reached Halifax of General Braddock's stunning defeat in the Ohio Valley. Braddock's troops, overconfident and unaccustomed to wilderness warfare, had been surrounded and attacked just outside Fort Duquesne in July. Hemmed in on a narrow trail and encumbered by their wagons and artillery, the British had been ambushed by a smaller force of French soldiers and Natives. Braddock and almost 500 British and American soldiers died and the survivors had scurried back to Virginia. The news sent shock waves through the Nova Scotia garrisons and, for Lawrence at least, proved the wisdom of clearing out the Acadians. He directed Monckton to "embark every person if possible" and to disregard the pleas of anyone seeking to remain. He clarified his earlier directive by noting that the deportees could take their furniture with them, but "they must not put on board quantities of useless Rubbish to encumber the vessels."

In the weeks that followed, patrols scoured the countryside in search of more prisoners and to round up livestock. Families still at large took to the woods as the soldiers approached, as did the wives and children of men locked up in the fort. The soldiers were under orders from Lawrence to burn every house and barn in a campaign to deprive the holdouts of shelter and to force them to surrender. "Destroy all the villages ... and use every other method of distress" to flush out anyone hiding in the woods, he instructed Monckton. Day after day columns of smoke rose over the ridges and marshes, charting the soldiers' path of destruction. John Thomas, the surgeon's mate with the

New England troops, recorded in his diary that one patrol returned to camp with several prisoners after having "Burnt Several Fine Viliges." Another detachment bragged of torching 200 buildings in just three days. The search-and-destroy missions continued well into the fall. Thomas accompanied a large force deep into the river valleys of southern New Brunswick in mid-November. His diary entries are sparse on detail, but still evoke stark images of a war-ravaged countryside dotted with empty, desolate villages and blackened ruins. In the Memramcook area, the troops surrounded a group of houses at daybreak, muskets at the ready. All were vacant except one, where nine women and children were found cowering in the cold, most of them sick. The soldiers set fire to about thirty houses, rounded up as many cattle and horses as they could, "Brought away one woman," and apparently left the rest of the miserable Acadians to fend for themselves.

More soldiers were sent to clear out villages along the shoreline of Northumberland Strait, an area within sight of French-held Île Saint-Jean. After a long journey by canoe and portage—with unsuspecting Acadian settlers welcoming and feeding them along the way—they arrived in mid-August at a pair of remote villages, now known as the communities of Tatamagouche and Wallace. After soldiers went house to house to seize firearms, the Acadian men were told the grim news: they were to be taken to Fort Cumberland and their houses would be burned. The men protested, demanding to know why. "One of the french Askt me for what Reason for he said he never had Taken up arms against the English," recalled Abijah Willard, a young captain from Lancaster, Massachusetts. The men offered to take an oath of allegiance on the spot, but Willard, echoing Lawrence, said they were rebels who had aided Native raiding parties. He rejected their pleas to be allowed to move to Île Saint-Jean and gave them two hours to decide whether they would take their families to the fort. The men, unaware they were never to return, made the heart-wrenching decision to leave their wives and children behind. Willard's men filled their canteens with rum found in a storehouse, then burned it and every other building in the area. They marched away with about 100 prisoners, unmoved by the thought of leaving women and children to fend for themselves without shelter. The wails and cries that filled the air unnerved even the cold-hearted Willard, who confessed he was shocked at the outpouring of grief and sorrow.

The transports were slow to arrive at Chignecto and, when they did, two were earmarked to ferry Winslow and his men to Piziquid. As a final slap in the face, Monckton withheld extra pay promised to some of the New Englanders and refused to allow them to march off with their regimental colors—an honor, Winslow complained bitterly, granted to the defeated Beauséjour garrison. Monckton did not begin boarding his prisoners until September 10, when about fifty were transferred to ships anchored in the basin. The weather turned cold and rainy and, a week later, a gale ripped across the isthmus, bringing rain and an unwelcome lashing of wet snow. It was an ominous warning that time was running out. Lawrence, frustrated at the slow work of chartering ships, advised Monckton in mid-September to send away as many people as he could as soon as he could, even if it meant separating the men in custody from family members still in hiding. "I would have you not wait for the Wives & Children coming in but ship off the men without them." In almost the same breath—and in a telling insight into his priorities—Lawrence asked Monckton to make every effort to salvage the cattle and grain that had been seized "for the public benefit."

By the end of the month, Lawrence had lost what little patience he had left. On September 27 he scolded Monckton like a schoolboy, allowing he was "much surprised as well as extremely sorry and uneasy" to discover that the transports had yet to sail. Enough was enough. "You will immediately order all the people on Board which you have," he commanded, "whether all the Women be come in or not so as they may be in readiness for sailing." Lawrence was determined to set the deportation in motion: if the Chignecto rebels were separated from their wives and children, so be it. The delay in embarking, he complained, had used up so many provisions that he was obliged to ship more food from Halifax for Monckton's troops "at this dangerous season" and at great expense. The risk of cramming thousands of people into the holds of ships and sending them to sea at such a "dangerous season" appear never to have crossed his mind.

Monckton's troops faced perils of their own. A number of Acadian escapees, Native fighters, and French troops under the command of Lieutenant Charles Deschamps de Boishébert lurked in the woods. Boishébert, a veteran of French incursions into Nova Scotia during the

1740s, was under orders from the governor of New France to rally the Natives and Acadian refugees to ensure that neither group "might think themselves abandoned and might yield to the English." Boishébert was waiting for a chance to strike. At the end of August, about 200 New Englanders under the command of Major Joseph Frye boarded ships and set out to destroy villages along the Petitcodiac and Memramcook Rivers. On September 2, after a profitable morning of burning buildings on either side of the river, a detachment landed at a village nestled below a newly built church. As the soldiers went about their work, a smaller group headed uphill to set fire to the church. At that moment, as many as 300 of Boishébert's fighters charged out of the woods, firing as they ran. A battle raged for three hours, leaving more than twenty New England soldiers dead and several more badly wounded. Boishébert lost only one man. The British casualties—eclipsing those of the entire siege of Beauséjour—put the entire camp on edge. In the words of Captain Thomas Speakman, one of the survivors, they were "in the Heart of a Numerous Devilish Crew." A second disaster was narrowly averted in late October. A patrol herding sheep and cattle toward the Chignecto forts came under fire. Troops set out in pursuit of the snipers, only to discover 100 more fighters lying in ambush. A brisk firefight erupted, but the attackers were driven off with no serious casualties on either side.

Back at Fort Lawrence, prisoners still in the fort were taking advantage of the delay in loading the ships. Day after day they burrowed beneath their barracks and under the wall of the fort, reputedly using spoons and tools smuggled in by wives and mothers. On October 1, under the cover of what Thomas termed a "Stormy Dark Night" long before the phrase became a cliché, eighty-six prisoners disappeared into the 30-foot tunnel. Emerging outside the wall, they bolted into the rain and darkness "& Got Clear undiscovered by ye Centery," as Thomas put it.

By the time the breakout was discovered the following morning, they were long gone. The escapees were mostly from Petitcodiac and Memramcook, the area where Frye's patrol was ambushed. Their wives and children remained at large and Monckton realized a ready-made resistence force had been unleashed. Among the intrepid escapees were Beausoleil Broussard and several of his grown sons. Alexandre Broussard, his brother and comrade-in-arms, remained locked up in Fort Cumberland. He was deported, but escaped from custody in South Carolina and returned to the Petitcodiac area on foot. The Broussards rallied other Acadians to join forces with Boishébert to harass the British in a campaign that lasted four years. Beausoleil, commissioned as a privateer by the governor of Quebec, fitted out a small schooner and prowled the coasts in search of cargoes to plunder.

The deportation continued despite the setback. During the first week of October a violent storm lashed the fleet and its human cargo, with gusts and waves powerful enough to toss the ships like corks and drag several from their anchorage. Captain John Rous showed up two days later, Thomas reported, "In order to Hurrey ye Fleet with ye Prisoners from this Place." Another storm blew through on October 11 as the last of the prisoners were put on board. After riding out another cold and stormy day at anchor, the fleet finally sailed on October 13. Most of the women and children had been captured or surrendered—left behind without food or shelter for the winter, they would have faced almost certain death—bringing the number of deportees shipped out that day to just shy of 1,000. Lawrence had decreed that the Chignecto Acadians, "who have always been the most Rebellious, shall be removed to the greatest distance." They were bound for ports in South Carolina and Georgia.

John Winslow's volunteer army had been sent to Nova Scotia to fight the French. The farm boys, carpenters, blacksmiths, and laborers of Massachusetts were making a habit of saving the colony. Winslow, who resented the way Monckton and other arrogant British officers treated his men like second-rate soldiers, believed that Nova Scotia would have reverted to French rule long ago without their timely aid. He was right. But the French were defeated and Winslow's men had been ordered to stop fighting soldiers and start waging war on civilians. A Frenchman was a Frenchman, and the New Englanders had no love of these Acadian peasants, who were papists to boot. "You Know our Soldiers Hate them and if they Can Find a Pretence to Kill them, they will," an officer warned Winslow at the height of the deportation. But most of the men standing guard outside the church at Grand-Pré were farmers or farmhands, just like the shell-shocked Acadians cooped up inside. These sons of Massachusetts had signed up to protect their families and farms back home. Now they were under orders to remove the Acadians from *their* lands and ship the whole lot into exile. It was a "Disagreable Business," Winslow noted, "to remove People from their Antient Habitations."

While Winslow did not relish the work ahead, he also understood that it was not his place to second-guess Lawrence and the Nova Scotia council. A biographer would later write that Winslow carried out his orders "with care, military precision, and as much compassion as circumstances allowed." Winslow was fifty-two, the blue-blood descendant of two governors of the Plymouth Bay colony. He became a soldier in his late twenties and spent several years in the British army as a member of the Annapolis Royal garrison. He was a favorite of Shirley and the Massachusetts governor's first choice to command the New England forces sent to capture Beauséjour. "He hath the best reputation as a military man of any officer in this province," Shirley gushed, "and his character in every respect stands high with the Government and people and he is particularly well esteem'd and belov'd by the Soldiery."

Francis Parkman has left a less-than-flattering description of Winslow: "double chin, smooth forehead, arched eyebrows, close powdered wig, and round rubicund face, from which the weight of an odious duty had probably banished the smirk of self-satisfaction that dwelt there at other times." Winslow may have appeared self-satisfied, but the journal he kept while serving in Nova Scotia reveals a sensitive soul who was deeply troubled by the "odious duty" he was forced to perform. The journal also records, in vivid detail, the deportation of the Acadians from Grand-Pré.

The timing of Winslow's September 5 announcement inside the church was worked out in advance with the commander at Fort Edward. Captain Alexander Murray, perched in a blockhouse overlooking the farms of Piziquid, had his own Acadians to round up. In the days before the traps were sprung, Winslow and Murray spent hours planning how best to take the men and youths into custody. Murray was Scottish-born and one of those redcoats that Winslow distrusted, but the two men clicked as they mapped out a strategy. Winslow was desperate for inside information about the Acadians and Murray was the man to provide it. He had been showing the British flag at

Piziquid for four years and knew as much about the Acadians as anyone. Murray, who prided himself on being a good soldier who did as he was told, had been the front man in Lawrence's battles with the Acadians. When Lawrence ordered guns and boats confiscated in the spring of 1755, Murray and his garrison did the dirty work of seizing and impounding. Murray and Winslow plotted in secrecy, even keeping their officers in the dark for several days for fear of being compromised. Together they could muster only a few hundred soldiers to gather up and deport some 3,000 Acadians. Surprise was essential to avoid an uprising. As he read out his order and surveyed the stunned faces in the church, Winslow knew he had succeeded. At that very moment, Murray was reading a similar declaration to 183 men trapped in Fort Edward.

Lawrence's orders to Winslow and Murray were lengthy, detailed, and nearly identical. They were to gather up as many Acadians as possible, secure the livestock and grain, and burn every building to the ground to deny shelter to stragglers and escapees. Once Monckton was satisfied he had enough ships to accommodate his deportees, the extra transports and provisions were to be sent to Minas and Piziquid. Winslow was told the Acadians could pack up their household furniture, but, like Monckton, he must ensure the ships were not encumbered with "useless Rubbish." People could take their bedding aboard, Lawrence said, "and if afterwards there is room for other articles Suffer them to Carry what they Conveniently Can." Even with the Acadians stripped of their firearms, Lawrence realized the soldiers sent to Minas and Piziquid were outnumbered and vulnerable. He gave Winslow and Murray a free hand to respond with lethal force and to show no mercy if the Acadians resisted or incited the Natives to attack. "You have my orders," he assured them, "to take an Eye for an Eye, a Tooth for a Tooth and in Shorte Life for Life from the nearest Nighbours where Such Mischiefe is Performed."

Organizing the expulsion of so many people in such a short time was a logistical nightmare. Ships were delayed and supplies failed to show up on time. Lawrence coordinated the entire operation from his desk in Halifax. He appointed a commissary to oversee the distribution of food and water to the transports, but personally handled almost all other arrangements. He chartered ships from Boston merchants and decided, to the pound, how much food would be doled out to each deportee. He decided how many people would be sent to each colony. Messengers arrived from Halifax with copies of orders, paperwork, and forms to be passed along to the captain of each transport. Lawrence was the executive director of Nova Scotia's Department of Deportation, an agency responsible for destroying the Acadians and their way of life, with branch offices in Chignecto, Grand-Pré, Piziquid, and Annapolis Royal. Winslow and Murray were required to send reports to head office twice a week. And like any bureaucrat, Lawrence was obsessed with cost cutting. He knew he would have to account for every penny of His Majesty's money being spent without authorization. One way to save money was to slash the food allotment to the deportees. The Acadians would be entitled to 5 pounds of flour a week, not the 7 pounds set out in his initial letters to Monckton, and 2 pounds of bread each week instead of a half-pound per day. These arbitrary amounts were "Equally Sufficient," he reasoned, "and Less Exspence to the Government." Busy as he was, Lawrence found time to send an emissary to Grand-Pré to round up six of the Acadians' finest horses, specifying a black one for himself and a gray one for his secretary.

Lawrence also decided how many Acadians would be allotted to each vessel, based on the ships' cargo capacity. To Lawrence's defenders, this was evidence of careful and meticulous planning; to his detractors, it afforded proof of a criminal mind working overtime to maximize the Acadians' suffering. Lawrence settled on two people per ton, "Or as Near it as Possible," as he instructed Winslow. If there were too many people and not enough ships to stay within that limit, Winslow was to inform Lawrence immediately, "but Make No Delay in the Embarkation upon that account."

Lawrence's letters and orders offer no hint of how he arrived at this ratio. It was likely based on a rough calculation of the estimated number of deportees—somewhere between 6,000 and 7,000—and the tonnage of all the ships he could scare up on short notice. One group of refugees later complained there had not been enough room for everyone to lie down at the same time. Immigrant ships of the era usually carried no more than one person per ton of cargo capacity. But unlike settlers headed across the Atlantic, the Acadians were not paying passengers—or willing ones, for that matter. The fear of mutiny prompted Lawrence to instruct the captain of each transport to keep their prisoners locked up in the hold. Only small numbers were to be permitted to come on deck for air at any given time "to Prevent the Passengers from Making any Attempt to Seize Upon the Vessells." British commanders were well aware that soldiers shipped from England or between colonies suffered the ill effects of being tossed around at sea; overcrowding vastly increased the likelihood of sickness, disease, and death. Lawrence knew he was putting lives at risk or, as a court would put it, he was reckless or willfully blind to the harm he was inflicting.

There was no time to consult officials in the colonies that were about to receive shiploads of unwelcome guests, and no plans to feed or house the Acadians once they arrived in the American seaports. Since the ships were hired by the month, Lawrence ordered the master of each transport to land his passengers as soon as possible to save money. Each ship carried a form letter from Lawrence, addressed to the governor, providing a blow-by-blow description of his efforts to bring the Acadians "to a Proper Obedience to His Majesty's Government." He smeared the entire population as rebels and traitors, accusing them of "Pretending" to be neutral while either assisting the enemy or engaging in "Open Rebellion." He stressed that hundreds had taken up arms to defend Beauséjour. They had "Audaciously as Well as Unanimously Refused" to take an unqualified oath, he claimed, leaving his council no option but banishment. To add a veneer of imperial approval, he told his fellow governors that Admirals Boscawen and Mostyn had backed the decision as "Indispensibly Necessary To the Security of this Colony." As for their destinations, the Nova Scotia authorities had decided:

> to Divide them among the Colonies, where they May be of Some Use as Most of them Are Healthy Strong People, And as they Cannot easily collecte themselves together Again it will Be out of their Power to Do any Mischief, And they May Become Proffitable and it is Possible in time Faithful Subjects .... I have not the Least Reason to Doubt of your Excellency's Concurrence And that [you] will Receive the Inhabitants I now Send and Dispose of them in Such Manner as May Best Answer Our Designs in Preventing their Reunion.

In short, Lawrence was washing his hands of the Acadians. In future they would be someone else's problem.

For the time being, though, most of them were still John Winslow's problem. On September 9, four days after detaining the men in the church, he detected some "Uncommon Motions" among his prisoners. Fearing that an uprising was in the works, he decided to move a couple of hundred of the most able-bodied men to ships anchored in the Minas Basin.

The transfer had to be made in haste in order to catch the high tide. The Acadians filed out of the church and were arranged into rows, with 140 young, unmarried men—the ones most likely to cause trouble—assembled to one side. The entire garrison stood at attention in a show of force. Winslow ordered the young men to march toward the gate. No, they said, they would not go without their fathers. "I Told them that was a word I did not understand for that the Kings Command was to me absolute & Should be absolutely obeyed & That I Did not Love to use Harsh Means." There was no time, he said, for parleys or delay. He ordered his troops to fix bayonets and advance. Metal clinked and scraped as the soldiers drew and attached their bayonets. As they leveled their muskets and stepped forward, Winslow shoved the young man who appeared to be the ringleader and ordered him to march. "He obeyed & the rest followed," Winslow was relieved to report, "althoh Slowly." Soldiers escorted the prisoners on the mile-and-a-half walk to the seashore, where boats waited to ferry them to the ships. A tableau of heartache and anguish unfolded as mothers, brothers, and sisters lined the route, fearing they would never see their loved ones again. The men went off "Praying, Singing & Crying being Met by the women & Children all the way ... with Great Lamentations upon their Knees praying &c." With "the Ice being Broke," as Winslow put it, ninety of the married men assembled without incident and were escorted to the boats.

Even with half of the men under guard on the ships, Winslow was obsessed with the vulnerability of his makeshift garrison. In his letters and journal, he fretted about not having enough soldiers to pull off the deportation. The Acadian men outnumbered his soldiers two to one, he reminded Lawrence and anyone else who would listen. "Things are Now Very heavy on my harte and hands," he noted in one letter to Murray, "wish we had more men." He spent his days dealing with problems "from Every Quarter," from complaints about soldiers playing cards to the protests of Acadian women who claimed their children were going hungry without fathers to provide for them.

The constant stress made for a few sleepless nights. His troops were low on gunpowder and the ever-difficult Monckton ignored pleas to send him more. Even the elements seemed to be conspiring against him—flour was in short supply because there was not enough water in the creeks to run the gristmills. Then there were the troops to keep in line. Two soldiers were whipped for stealing chickens. An order issued on September 13 hinted that the Acadians were being looted, harassed, and possibly molested. Winslow decreed that no officer or soldier was permitted to leave the camp after sunset because "bad" things done at night were "Distressing the Distressed French Inhabitants." Soldiers who ventured out for water during the day were to be accompanied by an officer to make sure the men did not "Intermeddle with the French or their Effects." The order was later extended to crewmen on the transports, but Winslow still struggled to maintain order. In mid-October he posted a reminder of the nighttime curfew because it had "Lately been violated and the French Inhabitants thereby Injured."

The scale of the operation meant the element of surprise was soon lost. Winslow's orders included rounding up about 300 Acadians living along the Cobequid Bay to the east to Grand-Pré, now the Truro area, but then an isolated bay. Abijah Willard's soldiers passed through the community in August on their way to wreak havoc along the Northumberland Strait, and that seems to have been all the warning the residents needed. They fled with whatever they could carry. When Willard returned a couple of weeks later on his way to Fort Cumberland with his prisoners, he found the villages deserted. Winslow's soldiers showed up a month later and, with the Acadians still in hiding, forged ahead with their orders to burn the houses and barns. Most of the escapees apparently retraced Willard's route to the opposite shore and made their way to Île Saint-Jean.

With loading at a standstill and additional transports nowhere in sight, a mood of complacency seemed to settle over the "Poor Devils," as Murray called them. The Acadians "are more Patient then I Could have Expected for People in their Circumstances," he told Winslow. He was even more surprised at the indifference of the women, "who really are or Seem Quite unconcerned." Winslow suspected the delays were creating doubts that the British could pull off a deportation before winter set in. The prisoners, he told

Lawrence in mid-September, seemed to have fully recovered from the initial shock of his announcement in the church. "I believe they did not then Nor to this Day do Imagine that they are Actually to be removed." They felt confident enough to appeal to Winslow's sense of fair play. "The French are Constantly plying me with Petitions & remonstrances," Winslow complained. They produced a copy of the oath of allegiance signed in 1730, when Philipps was governor, with a certificate attached from two priests who confirmed the exemption from bearing arms. A petition followed, begging Winslow to intervene to protect those who had been faithful to that oath. If the king wanted them gone, they offered to leave at their own expense so they could resettle among "their Kindred" and "Preserve their Religion, which they have Verry much at Harte." Winslow, under orders from Lawrence to ignore such pleas, refused to forward the petitions to Halifax.

He did, however, have a few complaints of his own about the delays in securing transports. "The Season Growing Every Day worse," he warned Lawrence at the end of September, "and we Gaine Nothing Forward for want of Vessels am Greatly Mortifyed that we Loose Time." In early October, with 330 Acadian men on board the ships in the basin, Winslow decided he could wait no longer. He conferred with the captains of the transports he had on hand and directed that, where possible, families should be kept intact and villagers should be put aboard the same vessel as their neighbors. This appears to have been Winslow's idea. Lawrence's elaborate instructions make no mention of keeping families together and he issued a direct order to Monckton to send off his transports even if wives and children were still at large. Other officers on the ground did not have the time or the inclination to take similar precautions—Abijah Willard, for one, thought nothing of separating the men of Tatamagouche and Wallace from their wives and children. Brook Watson, a merchant who assisted in deporting the residents of the Chignecto area, later acknowledged that the operation was rushed and "some families were divided and sent to different parts of the globe, notwithstanding all possible care was taken to prevent it." Winslow, who seems to have taken the most care to keep families together, spread the word around Grand-Pré on October 6 that it was time to prepare to embark. Even on the eve of the deportation, he "Could not Perswade the People I was in Earnest." Heavy rain scrubbed plans to begin boarding the following day. The weather cleared and, on October 8, Winslow's men herded women, children, and the elderly to the ships. Winslow compressed a day of confusion and sorrow into a single, graphic sentence: "Began to Embarke the Inhabitants who went of Very Solentarily and unwillingly," he wrote, "the women in Great Distress Carrying off Their Children In their arms. Others Carrying their Decript Parents in their Carts and all their Goods Moving in Great Confussion & appeard a Sceen of woe & Distres."

The night before, two dozen men on the transports escaped under the noses of their guards. The men's families were allowed on board for visits and to deliver food, leading Winslow to suspect women's clothes had been smuggled aboard and the group had escaped dressed as women. His retaliation was swift and brutal. After questioning the remaining prisoners, Winslow was satisfied that one of those left behind, Francis Hebert, was "Either the Contriver or abettor." Hebert was taken ashore and forced to watch as soldiers burned his house, barn, and all his belongings. Winslow threatened to mete out the same punishment to the friends of the escapees unless they surrendered. The local priest, Father Landry, offered to plead with the men to return in exchange for Winslow's promise to impose no further punishment. In the meantime, a search party stumbled upon one of the escapees, who tried to flee on horseback. The soldiers ordered him to stop and fired warning shots over his head; when he continued to ride away, a soldier took aim and shot him dead. Another man apparently was killed when searchers fired on a group of escapees as they ran into the woods. After six days on the run, the remaining twenty-two turned themselves in and were put aboard the ships.

With time running out, the two-people-per-ton rule fell by the wayside. Murray, fed up with waiting for more ships, finally packed about 1,100 people from the Piziquid area onto his five ships in mid-October. He was desperate to be rid of his "Rascals" and "affraid the Govr. will think us Dilertory" if he did not forge ahead. "They will be Stowed in Bulk but if I have no more Vessels I will put them aboard let the Consequence be what it may." The consequence, for the Acadians, was descending into overcrowded holds for long journeys to Boston, Philadelphia, Maryland, and Virginia. Winslow, too, was forced to cram as many people as he could into the ships he had on hand. "I put in more then Two to a Tun & the People Greatly Crowded," he told Lawrence. Despite the promise that the Acadians could take their possessions with them, there simply was not enough room. When New England farmers arrived to resettle the Acadians' lands five years after the deportation, beaches in the Minas area were strewn with the remains of carts, furniture, and household goods discarded in the rush to load the ships. By the third week of October, Winslow's troops had cleared out Grand-Pré and the Gaspereau River Valley and were loading residents brought over from the Canard and Habitant Rivers. Nine ships bearing 1,500 people sailed for ports in Pennsylvania, Maryland, and Virginia. Hundreds more collected from the outlying villages were billeted in the empty houses of Grand-Pré to await more ships.

With fewer people to guard, Winslow's men were free to roam the countryside, burning everything in their path. By the end of November, the tally was 255 houses destroyed, along with 276 barns, 155 outbuildings, and 11 mills. The Acadians stoically awaiting deportation in Grand-Pré gazed across the marshes and, like the unfortunate Hebert, stood in stunned silence as smoke and flames rose from their own homes. The heartland of Acadie was reduced to a wasteland, a vista of yellowed fields and bare trees pockmarked with countless blackened cellars. The remaining 732 deportees were dispatched to Boston, Connecticut, and Virginia in mid-December. As operations wound down, Winslow retreated to the comforts of Halifax, leaving Captain Phineas Osgood to send off the last of the deportees. They assembled as ordered and "without great difficulty," Osgood assured Winslow, "and we Embarked them with as much of their Effects as I Could." The final ships passed beneath the cliffs of Blomidon just five days before Christmas, as Osgood's men put Grand-Pré to the torch. Saint-Charles-des-Mines, the church that became a prison, was likely the last building set on fire as the soldiers marched away.

Major John Handfield read the handwritten orders from Lawrence, and likely had to read them a second time. It was not the wording that gave him pause.

There was no mistaking what he was being commanded to do, and that was why the words left him cold inside. The instructions to the commander of His Majesty's garrison at Fort Anne, dated August 11, were almost identical to those issued to Winslow and Murray. Handfield was to oversee the expulsion of the Annapolis area Acadians, who were to be dispersed to New York, Philadelphia, Connecticut, and Boston. As soon as the transports arrived, he was to "use all the means proper and necessary" to collect and embark the inhabitants. If there was resistance, Handfield was authorized to resort to "the most vigorous means possible" to force them onto the ships. Escapees were to be deprived of shelter and support "by burning their houses and destroying every thing that may afford them the means of subsistence in the Country." As Handfield pored over Lawrence's detailed blueprint for the deportation, he thought of only one thing: What about his wife and her family?

An accident of geography and a rebel streak drew the Chignecto Acadians into the orbit of the French. In Minas and Piziquid, their cousins had grown accustomed to being left alone by both sides. But the Annapolis Acadians had lived beside the British garrison at Fort Anne for almost half a century. Here, British rule had been a daily fact of life for longer than most people had been alive. Only those who were well into middle age or older could recall the days when a French officer held court at the governor's house. If Lawrence had not been blinded by hatred and distrust of the Acadians, he might have seen in Annapolis Royal a model for what Nova Scotia could be. The area's deputies had pleaded with Lawrence to understand their unique position. When Fort Anne needed repairs, they had "laboured with all our heart" to complete the work. "Several of us have risked our lives to give information to the government concerning the enemy," they added, proving their trustworthiness and loyalty. The communities coexisted and were also intertwined. British officers and officials had married Acadian women. William Winniett came to Annapolis Royal with Nicholson's forces in 1710, became a wealthy and influential merchant, and married Marie-Madeleine Maisonnat, the daughter of a French officer and an Acadian, Madeleine Bourg. Winslow knew Maisonnat from his time at Annapolis Royal and had fond memories of "the good Old Lady." Three of her daughters married British officers who served on the governor's council at Annapolis Royal. One of them, Elizabeth, was Handfield's wife.

Handfield had been in Nova Scotia for his entire military career. He arrived in 1720, was named to the council a decade later, and built a grand home in Annapolis Royal for Elizabeth and their three children. He was on hand when Governor Philipps convinced the Acadians to swear a conditional oath in 1730 and was behind the walls of Fort Anne with Mascarene when the French attacked in 1744. Now he was under orders to destroy the birthplace of Acadie and send his in-laws into exile. It was, to put it mildly, a "most Disagreable and Troublesome part of the Service," he later confided to Winslow, and one he longed to have behind him.

Keeping the operation a secret within the tight-knit community of Annapolis proved impossible. When a ship arrived in late August to pick up Acadians, Handfield sent a detachment upriver to round up about 100 men and boys to begin the deportation. They found the villages deserted. The inhabitants had fled, taking their bedding with them so they could camp out in the woods. Handfield pleaded with Winslow to send more soldiers as soon as he could, hoping a show of force would convince the residents to return and accept their fate. Winslow had no men to spare—he was about to announce his own deportation order—but within days the residents returned to their homes "and Promised to Submit to the Kings Orders." Within a couple of weeks Winslow and Murray were able to spare about thirty soldiers, who were ordered to collect any Acadians they found on their march down the Annapolis Valley. In late October, once Winslow had loaded most of his Acadians, more of his soldiers were redeployed to Annapolis for a repeat performance.

The Annapolis Acadians endured an agonizing wait. It was mid-November, with the leaves long gone and the brown fields ready for snow, by the time Handfield's allotment of transports sailed into the basin. Seven ships assembled just off Goat Island, within sight of the spot where the Habitation of Champlain and de Monts had stood. Winslow was not on hand to record the scene in his meticulous way. Captain Abraham Adams, a New England officer Winslow sent down from Grand-Pré, would later say little more than he was kept "very busy ... In Embarking the Inhabitants of this River." The scenes of misery and heartache, confusion and destruction were replayed in the place where Acadie was born. Charles Belliveau took his place in the hold of the *Pembroke* with his Melanson relatives, plans for a mutiny no doubt starting to take shape in his mind. No one was spared, not even Louis Robichaux, an Acadian merchant who had been robbed and held captive by the French for helping the British in the last war. All Handfield could do was allow Robichaux to choose his place of exile, which turned out to be Boston. Even Handfield's family was torn apart. While his wife and her mother could stay, he was forced to deport his sister-in-law and assorted nephews, nieces, aunts, uncles, and cousins. The fleet departed on December 8, "Sent off to the great Mortification of Some of our Friends," the understated Adams later told Winslow.

A total of 1,664 Acadians were deported from the Annapolis area. Adams estimated another 300 had bolted into the woods. Tradition holds this group, inhabitants of the village of Belleisle on the northern bank of the Annapolis River, headed inland "with their luggage on their backs, babies in their arms and old people in makeshift carts." They camped for about a month near what is now the community of Aylesford. There was little shelter, only berries and wild game to eat, and many succumbed to dysentery. "With sad hearts they dug their friends' graves in the soft sands of the Aylesford plains ... and their wailings resounded among the trim, straight trunks of the ancient pines," according to a melodramatic account that appeared in a Halifax newspaper in 1889.

As the first snow fell, the group packed up and scaled a high ridge that separated them from the Bay of Fundy, a winding, mile-long climb that would one day challenge Nova Scotia's road builders. They were headed to a place where a creek had spent eons cutting a passage though the sandstone cliffs, affording access to the rock-strewn beach below. The Mi'kmaq had long used the passage as a portage route and the Acadians hoped it might be their escape route. The hills of New Brunswick formed a thin, steel-blue band along the horizon. From this vantage point they watched as ships glided past, carrying the last of their cousins from settlements at the head of the bay. They spent the winter at this desolate spot, huddling in crude shelters fashioned from branches and living off fish, shellfish, seagulls, and anything else they could catch.

The Mi'kmaq, driven into hiding because Lawrence had put a price on their heads, did what they could to help these and other escapees make it through the winter. As few as sixty of the Belleisle group survived. When spring arrived, they built canoes to cross the bay. At least some of them evaded capture and reached Quebec. They left behind heaps of discarded shells, enough to one day make plaster to finish a local church, and a large wooden cross to mark the graves of those who perished. The English named the place Morden, but it is still referred to as French Cross. The wooden cross stood for a century. Today, a replacement fashioned from concrete and rounded beach stones stands in a tiny park at the water's edge, holding a vigil for those who chose death over exile.

It was mid-October before Lawrence summoned the courage to inform the Lords of Trade about the reign of terror he had unleashed. For all Winslow's talk about carrying out "His Majesty's orders and Instructions" when he delivered the bad news to the men and boys of Grand-Pré, this was the first anyone in His Majesty's government would hear about what was afoot in Nova Scotia. Lawrence opened his letter by describing his failed attempts to extract an oath of allegiance. He assured the Lords of Trade that "every means" and "sufficient time" had been devoted to making the Acadians see the error of their ways, yet "nothing would induce them to acquiesce in any measures that were consistent with his Majesty's honor or the security of his province." A copy of the council's minutes setting out the "whole transaction" was enclosed, but his letter glossed over the Acadians' repeated offer to take a qualified oath and the council's refusal to give the deputies and the rest of the population a second chance. The upshot had been the decision to pursue "the speediest, cheapest and easiest method" of removing them from the province. "The embarkation is now in great forwardness," he reported, with the last ship expected to depart at the end of November. He assured his superiors he had pinched every penny, chartering ships at rock-bottom prices and supplying them with food seized from the Acadians and the captured French forts. Assuming the Lords of Trade had recovered from their shock, Lawrence proceeded to outline "the happy effects" of his actions. The expulsion "furnishes us with a large quantity of good land ready for immediate cultivation" and he promised to work over-time to entice New England settlers to fill the void. With the Acadians gone, he was confident Nova Scotia was more secure and the French would be less tempted to try to retake the colony.

Lawrence made it all sound so efficient and so easy: forty-five years of agonizing over how to mold the Acadians into loyal British subjects had been put to rest almost overnight, and the future looked rosy. London's colonial administrators were given no inkling of the misery visited on people King George considered so "useful" that he had refused, only months earlier, to let them leave of their own volition. Lawrence almost forgot to enclose a copy of his circular to the governors of the American colonies. He was no doubt bracing for a backlash from his neighbors for dumping his problems on their doorsteps. "I am in hopes," he ventured somewhat sheepishly, "the provinces will make no difficulties about receiving them."

At some point in the weeks that followed, Secretary of State Thomas Robinson's July 13 letter arrived from England. One can imagine Lawrence's heart skipping a beat when he read the line about using "the greatest Caution and Prudence" in his dealings with the Acadians. Orchestrating an impasse with the Acadians, deporting more than 6,000 of them, and torching their farms—his master plan hardly fit the definition of caution and prudence. Lawrence was back at his desk in his fortified little residence on November 30, crafting a reply. His initial intention, he assured Robinson, had been to deport only the Chignecto Acadians who had defected to the French. "When we found the French Inhabitants who had not deserted their lands enter-tained the same disloyal sentiments with those who had, and positively rejected the Oath of Allegiance," he added, he and his council had "thought it high time" to put the matter to rest and deport the entire population. It was too late to go back now. He assured Robinson that most, if not all, were already headed south.

At least six months passed before a response arrived from the Lords of Trade. Instead of rapping Lawrence for insubordination, the letter of March 25, 1756 was a grudging endorsement of his actions. This was no time to quib-ble with a rogue official on the other side of the Atlantic. War with France was "inevitable," the Lords began, and it was suspected the enemy would marshal most of its forces "to annoy us in North America." With an all-out war on the horizon and memories of Braddock's defeat still raw, no one in London was about to second-guess actions Lawrence had taken in the name of security. If British officials resented Lawrence's methods and lack of candor, it was impossible to turn back the clock—the deed was done and the Acadians were scattered. Lawrence was told that his letter reporting the removal of the Acadians had been forwarded to Robinson. "As you represent it to have been indispensably necessary for the Security and Protection of the Province in the present critical situation of our affairs," the letter concluded, "We doubt not but that your Conduct herein will meet with His Majesty's Approbation." Nothing in the correspondence between Halifax and London suggests the British government appreciated the enormity of what it was approving after the fact. Lawrence's letters made no mention of the number of people rounded up or that entire villages had been obliterated. London named Lawrence governor in July 1756, further signaling its approval of his actions.

To the British authorities, John Bartlet Brebner concluded, the expulsion "was merely an incident in one small campaign in a bitter, dangerous, and expensive war, something already accomplished and therefore beyond useful discussion." And since Lawrence presented it as a closed deal, no one in London thought it prudent or necessary to tell the new governor to stop. Lawrence, on the other hand, considered the summer of 1755 to be the initial engagement in an escalating war on the Acadians. He had his coveted promotion and the green light to take whatever steps he felt necessary to defend his colony. Nothing stood in the way of his mission to rid Nova Scotia of its "inveterate Enemies."

6 Le Grand Dérangement

Far asunder, on separate coasts, the Acadians landed ...
Friendless, homeless, hopeless, they wandered from city to city.

—Henry Wadsworth Longfellow, *Evangeline: A Tale of Acadie*

A half-dozen ships dropped anchor in Boston harbor at the beginning of November 1755, bearing a cargo of human misery. It was a sight that Messrs. Gridley, Hooper, and Otis, investigators sent aboard by the Massachusetts government, would not soon forget. The ships were grossly overloaded and scores of people were lying on the decks. Sickness had broken out on two vessels, food was running low, and some of the water on board was unfit to drink. The captains reckoned they were carrying a total of 1,077 prisoners, Acadians from Grand-Pré and Piziquid. A fierce gale forced the convoy to seek shelter in Boston as they headed to colonies farther south.

The investigators were convinced they would never make it. "The vessels in general are too much crowded," they concluded in their report. "Their allowance of Provisions short being 1 lb. of Beef 5 lb. Flour & 2 lb. Bread per man per week and too small a quantity to that allowance to carry them to the Ports they are bound to especially at this season of the year." Four of the ships exceeded Charles Lawrence's arbitrary two-people-per-ton rule. The worst offender, the *Dolphin* bound for Maryland, was over the limit by forty-seven people. Those passengers were in desperate straits: "Sickly, occasioned by being too much crowded," the investigators noted, with "40 lying on deck." The people aboard another sloop headed for Maryland were also sickly and their water was "very bad." Forty people were found lying on the deck of another crowded ship headed to Virginia, but at least they appeared healthy. Passengers on the least-crowded ship, the *Endeavour*, were in good shape, but did not have enough food to get them to South Carolina. Those on the *Sarah & Molly* needed more water to get them to Virginia. Only the sloop *Three Friends*, carrying sixty-nine people from Piziquid, rated the description "Well in general." The investigators were given permission to bring ashore passengers from the overloaded vessels, but only enough to restore the ratio of two people per ton. There is no record of anything being done about the food shortages and bad water before the ships left with the remaining passengers.

Travel aboard the sailing vessels of the eighteenth century was fraught with peril. Storms, shipwreck, and disease posed a constant threat; bad water, poor food, and seasickness often added to the misery. Conditions belowdecks could be deplorable. One French traveler who crossed the Atlantic in the 1730s complained that men and women were crammed together in a "dark foul place like so many sardines," and the motion of the ship made it "impossible to get into bed without banging our heads and knees twenty times." Disease spread quickly in the crowded holds. An eighteenth-century physician claimed more soldiers were lost to diseases contracted on ships than due to shipwreck, capture, famine, or wounds suffered in battle.

These were the conditions on vessels *intended* to carry people. Most, if not all, of the ships Lawrence pressed into service for the deportation were cargo carriers with few amenities. They were crowded, cold, and poorly ventilated. It was a breeding ground for contagious diseases like smallpox—an often fatal infection accompanied by a high fever—and the Acadians' isolation from the outside world left them with little immunity. Half the Grand-Pré contingent aboard the *Edward Cornwallis*—210 out of 417—died en route to South Carolina. Add to this lethal mix the misery of being tossed around for days in gales like the one that drove the *Dolphin* and its companions into Boston harbor. A violent winter storm blew the *Edward* and the *Experiment*, ships carrying Acadians from the Annapolis area, so far off course that they wound up on the Caribbean island of Antigua, a British possession. Smallpox killed many aboard the *Edward* before the ship finally arrived in Connecticut in May 1756. About thirty of the *Experiment's* 250 passengers were sent to the French island of Martinique and another twenty died before reaching New York the same month.

New York. Boston. Philadelphia. The Acadians were dumped at the commercial, industrial, and political centers of well-established, thriving colonies. The number of people of European extraction in America was approaching two and a half million. Nearly two out of every three Americans was of English ancestry, but there were large German, Scotch-Irish, and Dutch minorities. A fraction of the population, about 50,000, were of French origin, but well on their way to being assimilated into the American melting pot. These Franco-Americans, for the most part, were descendants of Protestant Huguenots who had escaped persecution in France. America offered religious tolerance—there were Anglicans, Puritans, Presbyterians, Quakers, and dissenters of every stripe—but the common denominator was Protestantism. There were fewer than 25,000 Catholics in all of America and most were found in Maryland, which was established as a haven for English Catholics. It was an overwhelmingly agrarian society, where even the tradesmen and merchants of the growing towns and cities pastured cattle or tended their own gardens. "Life in America was profoundly influenced by the nearness of people to the soil," noted one study of the colonial period, "even the largest cities were never very far removed from the back country that supported them, and town dwellers were in close contact with the farmers." The Acadians were people of the soil, but their language and religion made them strangers in what, to them, must have seemed like another world.

Nothing the exiles had done or seen in their lives prepared them for the culture shock of their arrival in America. Consider what awaited the 1,000 or so sent to Charleston, South Carolina. With a population approaching 15,000—half of them slaves—it was considered "perhaps the most urbane of American cities," with a public library, a racetrack, shops stocked with the latest Paris fashions, a symphony orchestra, and "easy mannered men's clubs." Boston and New York, where another 1,400 came ashore, were busy centers of trade and commerce. Boston, the older of the two cities, boasted a mercantile fleet of more than 1,000 ships registered with its harbormaster. A newcomer who strolled the city's streets in the early 1700s remarked that the houses of well-off Bostonians were "neat and handsome ... like their women." The wealthier merchants lived in ornate mansions—on par with the grand homes of London—and imported the finest English furnishings.

America's cities were studded with imposing public buildings that blended rigid Georgian symmetry with classical flourishes like columns and palladium windows. The pre-eminent center in America at the mid-point of the 1700s was Philadelphia. It was the largest city in British North America, the commercial capital of the colonies, and, thanks to the tolerance of its Quaker founders, the gateway for immigrants from Europe. Benjamin Franklin, who arrived from Boston as a teenager, was but one of those who found fortune and fame there. Philadelphia was one of the world's first planned cities; its Quaker founder, William Penn, envisioned a "wholesome ... green country town," with open public spaces and wide streets to avoid the disastrous fires that swept through so many cities of the time. An early eighteenth-century visitor was "astonished beyond measure" to find some 400 brick houses and enough shops to ensure "whatever one wants at any time he can have, for money." By the 1750s the city also featured what was considered the most modern of civic improvements: streetlights.

The colonies were also light-years ahead of Acadian society when it came to culture and learning. America had a vibrant press—Franklin and other early journalists would soon play a prominent role in the lead-up to the revolution—and the larger cities boasted more than one newspaper. There were plenty of readers, since the children of the well-to-do had been attending private schools for more than a century, and free schools were catering to other worthy students. The first institution of higher learning in the colonies, Harvard College, was 119 years old in 1755. A theater was built in Williamsburg, Virginia, in 1718 to stage plays and double as a dance school. In the early 1750s, while Cornwallis and Lawrence were trying to strong-arm the Acadians into taking an oath of allegiance, touring theatrical companies from London were bringing the plays of Shakespeare to New York, Williamsburg, and other cities. There was lower-brow entertainment as well, such as clowns, puppet shows, waxworks, and circuses featuring elephants, lions, camels, and other exotic beasts. There were public lectures on astronomy, physics, and philosophy and demonstrations of optical machines, elaborate music boxes, "electrical fluid," and other scientific wonders of the day. Franklin, who tinkered in a laboratory set up in his home, founded the Philosophical Society in Philadelphia in 1744 to promote scientific inquiry and allow like-minded gentlemen to share their insights into plants, animals, and minerals. In 1752 Franklin conducted his famous and risky kite-flying experiments during thunderstorms to prove his theory that lightning was a form of electricity.

To their new hosts, the impoverished exiles must have seemed as exotic as the circus animals, and as potentially dangerous. The Acadians arrived just as anti-French and anti-Catholic hysteria reached a fever pitch. Braddock's defeat sent shock waves through the colonies. Native war parties attacked homesteads along the American frontier in the fall of 1755, spreading terror and leaving mutilated bodies in their wake. Britain and France were on the verge of war and militias were mobilizing to defend the frontier. There were chilling reports of scalpings and kidnappings, even a lurid tale of a man forced to watch as warriors beheaded his wife and drank the blood of his butchered children. Towns within a day's ride of Philadelphia were raided. A thousand German settlers marched on the capital to demand protection and there was an exodus of terrified people toward the coast. "The roads are full of starved, naked, indigent multitudes," a harried Pennsylvania official wrote in November 1755. Colonial newspapers published reams of propaganda about French plans to conquer and subjugate the American "heretics."

A report appeared in a Philadelphia newspaper only weeks before the exiles arrived in the city, claiming that three Acadians were under arrest for poisoning wells in Halifax. Jonas Green, editor of the *Maryland Gazette*, branded the French in general as "the most ignorant slavish herd of Bigots" and published a letter from Halifax describing the Acadians as "secret Enemies" who "encouraged our Savages to cut our Throats." Then there was Lawrence's circular to the colonial governors, which portrayed the Acadians as disloyal and untrustworthy, traitors and rebels who had helped the Natives kill British settlers in Nova Scotia. It was little wonder, then, that the belea-guered Americans did not welcome them with open arms. New Jersey governor Jonathan Belcher vowed to "crush" any attempt to land Acadians in his colony. "I am truly surprised," he wrote to a fellow governor, "how it could ever enter the thoughts of those who had the ordering of the French Neutrals, or rather Traitors and Rebels to the crown of Great Britain, to direct any of them to these Provinces, where we have already too great a number of foreigners for our own good and safety." He clearly was unaware of his own son's role in the affair.

New Jersey was not on Lawrence's distribution list, but the colonies that were took steps to prevent their unwelcome guests from escaping and wreaking havoc. In the northern and mid-Atlantic colonies, there were fears the Acadians would head for the frontier and join their countrymen. In the south, the genteel citizens of Charleston were said to have "regarded the Acadians as enemy aliens, and rumors spread through the town that they were trying to incite a rebellion of the slaves." Colonial legislatures passed laws scattering the Acadians to different towns, usually to areas farthest from the troubled frontier. They were also barred from traveling, in keeping with Lawrence's request for strict controls to prevent them from trying to assemble or escape. At least one colony, Connecticut, instituted a policy that "no one family of them be separated and sent into two or more towns." But in most instances the divide-and-conquer policy meant families lucky enough to arrive in the same colony were broken up. "Parents were separated from children, husbands from wives, some of whom have not to this day met again," a group of Pennsylvania exiles complained in a 1760s petition. René Le Blanc, the Grand-Pré notary immortalized by Longfellow, was sent to New York with his wife and their 2 youngest children, while his remaining 18 children and 150 grandchildren were sent elsewhere. The couple found only three of their missing children before Le Blanc died in Philadelphia a few years after the deportation. Despite the restrictions on travel, historian Arthur Doughty found evidence that "hundreds of those who were placed under control escaped and wandered, footsore and half clad, from town to town in the hope of meeting their relatives or finding means to return to their former homes."

There were financial reasons to split up the exiles. Acadians who were sick or too old to work—or unable to make a living in their new surroundings— were supported at public expense. Townships and parishes were responsible for maintaining the paupers within their boundaries, so spreading around the

Acadians helped share the burden on the public purse. There were poorhouses for the wretches unable to work, workhouses for those who could. In some colonies recipients of poor relief wore a badge or a large letter "P," in the belief that the stigma and humiliation would spur them to find work and deter others from going on the dole. Indentured servitude was a fact of life in early America—tens of thousands of immigrants eagerly swapped their labor for passage to the New World in the seventeenth and eighteenth centuries. The practice was akin to slavery, but unlike Blacks, who were bought and sold for life, Whites were indentured for specific periods or, in the case of children, until they became adults. The children of families on welfare were routinely "bound out" to employers as laborers and apprentices or to wealthy families as domestics. In a typical newspaper notice of the era, the overseers of the poor in Philadelphia advertised "a boy of about four years of age to be bound out till he is twenty-one," and offered a "young woman's time to be disposed of, for between two and three years."

Colonial officials took the same approach to dealing with the influx of destitute Acadians. Legislators in New York, to cite but one example, ordered all Acadian children under the age of twenty-one to be indentured to "respectable families" as servants. Their Maryland counterparts empowered local magistrates to bind out children to farmers and craftsmen "upon the best terms they can make ... for the ease of the County." Parents endured the heartbreak of seeing their children carted off to homes where their language and religion were unknown—and to almost certain assimilation. Pennsylvania's Acadians resisted attempts to bind out their children, an official noted in 1761, "as they find, by experience, that those few who are in Protestant families, soon become estranged and alienated from their parents."

The hardships the exiles faced—and how they were received—depended on the roll of the dice. A few colonial governments were quick to respond with humanitarian aid; others ignored their uninvited guests or treated them with suspicion and contempt. The Connecticut legislature passed emergency legislation to deal with the exiles when ships arrived in January 1756 with the first of more than 700. The refugees were distributed to various communities, where the sick and elderly were supported at public expense and the able-bodied eked out a living. When the war ended in 1763, virtually every

Acadian in the colony petitioned the French king to transport them to France, which said something about how poorly they fared during their seven-year exile. The request was refused and most of the surviving exiles headed south to the French colony of Saint-Domingue—present-day Haiti— or north to New Brunswick and Quebec.

New York played reluctant host to Acadians from Cape Sable, escapees from Georgia, and a storm-tossed shipload that arrived via the Caribbean. They landed "poor, naked, and destitute of every convenience and support of life ... useless to His Majesty, to themselves, and a burthen to this colony," according to the preamble of a law passed to relieve their suffering. The exiles were scattered among towns on Long Island—well away from the border with New France—and those younger than twenty-one were indentured as servants. One group who refused to be treated like slaves made a desperate bid to escape to Quebec in the summer of 1757. The *New York Mercury* reported that all were captured and the men were imprisoned. After 1763 most of New York's Acadians left for Saint-Domingue.

Exile to Maryland was a death sentence for many Acadians. Four ships carrying 913 Acadians from Piziquid and Grand-Pré, including two of the storm-battered vessels forced to lay over at Boston, arrived in the capital, Annapolis, in late November 1755. Their provisions were exhausted, forcing the city to provide temporary aid until three of the ships were sent to neighboring counties. There were calls for compassion, even in the jingoistic pages of the *Maryland Gazette*. "As the poor people have been deprived of their settlements in Nova Scotia, and sent here for some political reason bare and destitute," the paper noted as the last of 900 exiles arrived in December 1755, "Christian charity, nay, common humanity, calls on every one according to his ability to lend assistance and to help these objects of compassion." Despite the *Gazette's* change of heart, the Acadians received no further public support for the rest of the winter. Refugees sent to Somerset County sought shelter in snow-covered swamps where, it was reported, "they sicken and die." A few kind-hearted souls stepped forward to help. A Baltimore man supported a group of exiles for more than a week until they found places to stay, although the best accommodation some could find was an unfinished house. Henry Callister, a businessman in Oxford, bankrupted himself supplying food and clothing to needy Acadians. "Nobody knows what to do; and few have charity on them," Callister explained to a friend on Christmas Day 1755. "There's a number of them now about me in tears, craving relief for their sick, &c."

The government was forced to take action in April 1756, offering assistance to the needy and requiring the rest to use "their own Labor and Industry to procure a comfortable subsistence for themselves." Those who refused to work faced imprisonment. Some found jobs as sailors or loading ships, but most were still destitute when public assistance was withdrawn in 1758. They were described as living in "Misery, Poverty, and Rags," unable to afford shelter and clothing and reduced to going from house to house to beg for handouts. An outbreak of smallpox in 1757 further thinned their ranks. As soon as they were free to go in 1763, most of the 670 survivors headed to Louisiana.

A more hostile reception awaited the 454 Acadians sent to neighboring Pennsylvania. Louisiana historian Carl Brasseaux has described the eight-year exile in that colony as "one of the bleakest chapters in Acadian history." It was undoubtedly the scene of the worst tensions between the Acadians and their hosts. Faced with frontier raids and anti-French hysteria, the authorities confined the refugees to their transports and posted guards on each ship. "The people here," Governor Robert Hunter Morris observed, "are very uneasy at the thought of having a number of enemy's scattered in the very bowels of the country." He relented and allowed them to disembark on an island off Philadelphia after disease began to sweep through the ships. They came ashore "in great want of blankets, shirts, stockings, and other necessaries." The legislature drew up plans to scatter them among eastern counties, but local officials refused to accept them and the exiles refused to go or allow their children to be bound out. The Acadians considered themselves prisoners of war, entitled to food and shelter and exempt from being forced to work. "We shall never freely consent to settle in this province," they declared in a 1756 petition after the government suspended their meager rations. They demanded food and asked to be returned to Nova Scotia—"our nation," they called it—to save their wives and children from starvation. A commissioner appointed to investigate the complaints discovered no one would employ "the foreigners" and they were trying to make a living carving wooden shoes and recycling rags into new fabric. "Many of them," it was reported, "have had neither meat nor bread for many weeks together, and have been necessitated to pilfer and steal for the support of life."

The Pennsylvania government reintroduced a law to bind out children, in an effort to teach them a trade and to speak English. The Acadians, however, refused to allow their families to be broken up. When the commander in chief of British forces in America, Lord Loudoun, visited Philadelphia in 1757, five Acadian leaders tried to present a petition setting out their grievances. Loudoun ordered the "mutinous" deputies imprisoned for uttering "menacing speeches against his Majesty." The five—Charles LeBlanc, Jean-Baptiste Galerme, Philippe Melancon, Paul Bujaud, and Jean Landry—were shipped to England for trial. They were acquitted of the charges and returned to Philadelphia in 1758. The impasse over binding out children persisted into 1761 when an inquiry recommended that measures be taken "to prevent the ill effects of idleness in their young people." The colony's administrators chafed at being forced to support able-bodied young people as well as "indigent widows, orphans, aged and decrepid persons." As in Maryland, a few citizens stepped forward to help. Anthony Benezet and other Huguenots lodged some of them in a row of houses in Philadelphia that became known as "the Neutral Huts." Smallpox and other diseases killed 250 people—more than half of the original deportees—within five years. "They died heartbroken," an American writer noted a century later, "and the stain of their agony rests on the English name." In 1763 most of the Pennsylvania survivors—their numbers having grown to 383 as children were born in exile—migrated to Louisiana.

South Carolina had been settled by Huguenots who fled persecution in France, and their descendants balked at taking in almost 1,000 of their Catholic enemies. Despite the terrible conditions on board the ships, the exiles were not allowed to land for a month. They were eventually permitted to camp on the beach while officials debated what to do with them. Smallpox and other diseases thinned their numbers. A couple of groups tried to escape inland to French territory and as many as thirty managed to elude search parties. According to a report in the *South Carolina Gazette*, a half-dozen stole guns and money from a plantation and made for Fort Duquesne. South

Carolina's legislators ultimately decided to rid themselves of the Acadians and raised money to buy them two decrepit ships, so they could sail back to Nova Scotia. The leaky ships had to be beached on the coast of Virginia, but the determined passengers bought another ship and continued north. They ran aground in Maryland, repaired and refloated the vessel, and made it to the Saint John River, where some of the men joined Boishébert's forces. Those left behind were scattered along the Carolina coast, where their numbers dwindled as small groups escaped by sea. Some young men were clamped in irons and forcibly removed from their families to work on local plantations as indentured laborers, a status akin to the slaves they worked with in the fields. Only 280 remained in the colony by 1763.

About 400 Acadians were put ashore in Georgia, contrary to Governor John Reynolds's orders barring them from the colony. The government offered minimal support—a week's ration of rice for those too sick to work—and encouraged their efforts to return home. In March 1756 about 200 boarded small vessels and picked their way northward along the coast. Only ninety survived the journey to Massachusetts, where the authorities took them into custody and warned Lawrence of the attempted return. Another group made it as far as New York, where they were detained in the summer of 1756. Lawrence was furious and circulated a letter urging American governors to prevent exiles from returning by land or sea. He also complained to the Lords of Trade, who condemned the government-sanctioned exodus from Georgia and South Carolina as "absurd and blameable." The Acadians left behind in Georgia lived in poverty and many of the young men, like their cousins in South Carolina, were forced to work as indentured plantation hands. In 1763 the survivors headed for Saint-Domingue.

Massachusetts, the colony closest to Nova Scotia—and home to most of the soldiers Lawrence conscripted to round up the Acadians—received more than 1,000 exiles. The Acadians removed from the overcrowded ships in early November were joined by about 900 on four transports. The following year the colony absorbed more deportees from Cape Sable and groups trying to return to Nova Scotia by boat. The government's initial reaction was to demand that Lawrence pay to support them; in the meantime, the exiles were scattered among outlying towns to ease the burden on the welfare system.

Each town's selectmen and overseers of the poor were empowered "to employ, bind out or support" them like any other pauper. Farming and weaving tools were to be provided to help them support themselves, but Acadians were barred from working on fishing boats for fear they would escape. Anyone caught outside the limits of his or her assigned district could be fined or whipped.

The measures created nightmares for many families. The Massachusetts archives contains a stack of petitions from desperate fathers pleading for the return of sons and daughters. In the spring of 1756 the heads of nine families objected to having "our children torn from us, before our eyes .... Had we the power to choose we would prefer to give up our bodies and souls rather than be separated from our children." Joseph Michelle complained about his teenage son being "dragged away" to crew a ship. After Claude Bourgeous retrieved two daughters who were forcibly bound out, the overseers of the poor cut off support to his family. When Augustin Hebert tried to stop one of his children from being taken away, he was beaten so badly he was unable to walk for two weeks. There were other horror stories: elderly parents carted off while gangs restrained their sons, cruel farmers who beat and abused children in their care, workers cheated out of wages. Margaret Dowsett was ill with a fever when she begged for permission to travel to join her brother, "the only relation or Friend she has in this Country." Eleanor Tibaudau, distraught over the recent death of her husband, applied in August 1756 to have her niece brought from another town to help raise her five young children; the request was denied. The government urged local officials to treat the Acadians as humanely as possible and to respect the wishes of parents, but most of the petitions appear to have been ignored.

Living conditions were appalling. Massachusetts petitioners claimed to be near starvation or too sick to work. Two Boudreau children, bound out to care for a farmer's horses, were given "nothing but a few rags" in exchange for three months' work. Hammond Tibido, with four children under the age of nine and another on the way, asked for beds, bedding, and some extra provisions; the selectmen of Dorchester denied the request, noting they already had given him a house and some firewood. One man claimed his wife and children had nothing to eat but acorns. Another described his young family as "almost naked for want of work" and living in a house so drafty the snow drifted onto their beds. When a family complained their house was leaking, an official flippantly suggested they take advantage of the chance to "build a boat and sail in it." Francis Meuse filed a petition that painted a bleak picture of the lodgings the town of Tewkesbury provided to his twelve-member family in the winter of 1757–1758. It was:

> the most miserable House in the world, all the Timber rotten, not one Square of Glass in the House. No Chimney but a few stones piled up to the Height of about six feet; and then a hole opens thro the Top, so that they are smoked to Death; add to this, that at every blast of wind they expect the House to be down upon their Heads, and think it a miracle that it has stood so long ... in short a dolefuller Hole could not be imagined.

The family was moved, but their new house was not much of an improvement. It had been abandoned for a year, Meuse noted, and "Rain, snow, Wind and Storm have a free passage, whenever they come to attack."

Some of the hardier souls risked being whipped as escapees and fled north. Quebec was tantalizingly close, only a two- to three-week hike through the river valleys of New England. Acadian genealogist and historian Bona Arsenault has preserved the story of Joseph Hébert, who walked from Boston to the St. Lawrence River. "Hébert with his meagre savings purchased flint, steel and tinder box, a compass, fish hooks, line, wire for snares, and axe and probably a musket and a tiny stove .... Each night he picked his campsite carefully, built a shelter of boughs, set out his snares and fish lines and slept 'with the Grace of God'." Hébert emerged on the south bank of the river opposite Trois-Rivières, sized up suitable sites for homesteads, and retraced his steps to fetch two of his brothers from Massachusetts.

After the war ended in 1763, large numbers of Acadians assembled in Boston and demanded permission to emigrate to France, Quebec, or Saint-Domingue. They lived "crowded in small apartments," vulnerable to disease and "wanting the necessaries of life," according to a petition appealing for government aid. A December 1764 report described Boston's Acadians as "very sick and others taken daily down," while those still in good health were unable to find work in the city. After the British governor of Quebec agreed to accept exiles who would take the oath of allegiance, two shiploads sailed to Quebec City from Boston in 1766. More followed by sea and by land, but most of the Massachusetts exiles had a new destination in mind—their beloved Acadie.

A flag snapped in the breeze as the schooner glided into the harbor. A French flag. To the haggard men and women emerging from huts along the water's edge, it was more of a vision than a ship. Their nightmare would soon be over. They were saved. It was February 8, 1756, one month to the day since Charles Belliveau steered the *Pembroke* to the mouth of the Saint John River. The mutiny was front-page news in New England, with the *Boston Gazette* reporting that the crew of an unnamed transport had been overpowered "thro' the Treachery" of its "cargo of French Neutrals." The details were sketchy and garbled—the ship supposedly had sailed from Chignecto—but it was obviously the *Pembroke*. The Acadians had taken the precaution of landing the ship's small cannon and setting up a crude battery onshore. The British, they knew, would be scouring the coast for the missing vessel, which lay at anchor. But the schooner bearing down on their ramshackle settlement was friend, not foe. As it drew closer, people gathering along the shoreline could see soldiers in French uniforms lining its deck.

Four Frenchmen came ashore in a boat. They were from Louisbourg, they said. Other ships were on their way to re-establish the fort when the French withdrew the previous summer. One of the Acadians agreed to help guide the schooner to a safe anchorage. The news seemed too good to be true, and it was. The men who came ashore were French deserters, the soldiers on deck were Americans in disguise. The schooner had been sent by Charles Lawrence himself on a reconnaissance mission. Recovering the *Pembroke* and its escapees would be a bonus. But the ruse unraveled as soon as the Acadian pilot was aboard. Somehow—"by accident," Lawrence would note with chagrin—the real identity of the schooner and its crew was discovered. The captain hoisted a British flag and opened fire with his cannon.

Determined to keep the *Pembroke* from being seized, the Acadians set the ship on fire. According to a French account of the attack, the Acadians' little battery of guns "made so lively a fire upon the enemy" that the schooner withdrew, taking the pilot as a prisoner. The Acadians abandoned their camp and headed upriver. Belliveau and his Melanson relatives walked through the wilderness to Quebec.

The battle of the *Pembroke* was the opening skirmish in Lawrence's campaign to capture every Acadian who escaped the initial deportation—"to compleat our design of sending away the French inhabitants," as he explained in an order issued in 1756. Over the next seven years, British forces captured another 5,000 Acadians and sent most of them into exile. Some of those banished in 1755 made epic journeys home by land or by boat, only to be deported a second time or spend years confined in forts and prisons. Hundreds died of starvation, cold, and disease while cowering in the woods or while holed up in squalid refugee camps with little food, clothing, or shelter. The governor of Quebec, Philippe de Rigaud de Vaudreuil, described the condition of more than 1,000 refugees who spent the winter of 1756–1757 at the mouth of New Brunswick's Miramichi River, where Boishébert's forces offered some protection but no comforts. "The misery of the Acadians there is so great that Boishébert has been compelled to reduce their allowance to ten pounds of peas and twelve pounds of meat per month," Vaudreuil wrote, vowing to send a supply ship as soon as the ice receded:

> In a word the Acadian mothers see their babes die at the breast not having wherewith to nourish them. The majority of the people cannot appear abroad for want of clothes to cover their nakedness. Many have died. The number of the sick is considerable, and those convalescent cannot regain their strength on account of the wretched quality of their food, being often under the necessity of eating horse meat extremely lean, sea-cow, and skins of oxen. Such is the state of the Acadians.

About 1,600 escapees fled to Quebec, France's last North American bastion, arriving on ships or after long treks through the woods. Here, misery and death also awaited. Acadians seeking refuge among their French-speaking neighbors faced hardships much like those their deported cousins endured in the American colonies. New France was under constant threat of a British attack and there was not enough food or shelter to handle an influx of destitute people. To make matters worse, the refugees were at the mercy of corrupt officials who "plundered everybody, and the starving Acadians did not escape," according to an account published in the 1920s. "They had managed to bring with them a little money and a few household treasures, of which they were soon robbed. For a time they were each allowed but four ounces of bread a day, and were reduced, it is said, to searching the gutters for food."

The church and concerned citizens stepped forward to help, and resettled the newcomers in parishes along the St. Lawrence River. Between 1757 and 1758 a smallpox epidemic killed 300 exiles in the city of Quebec alone. "Small pox keeps on doing great ravages among the Acadians," a French officer stationed at Quebec noted in December 1757. "In recent days, fifteen and twenty are buried at a time." Charles Belliveau and other *Pembroke* exiles twice escaped the clutches of the British, but they could not escape this latest onslaught. The disease killed Belliveau's uncle, Ambroise Melanson, and Ambroise's wife, Marguerite, within weeks of each other in the summer of 1757. Another elderly uncle, Charles Melanson, died the following month. Belliveau contracted smallpox and died in January 1758, at age sixty.

Lawrence, meanwhile, launched the second wave of deportations in the spring of 1756. He ordered shiploads of New England troops on their way back to Boston to raid and plunder villages in the Cape Sable area. The officer in charge, Major Jedediah Preble, was told to seize as many inhabitants as possible, burn every house, and divide the Acadians' goods and cattle among his troops "as a Reward for the performance of this Service." Anything they could not carry off was to be destroyed. The fishermen of Cape Sable lived in isolated coves at the southern tip of Nova Scotia, cut off from the rest of the colony and were apparently oblivious to the upheaval of 1755. They had not been ordered to take the oath of allegiance and Lawrence was not going to give them a chance. Lawrence, never one to discriminate between good Acadians and bad ones, claimed they "had done us much mischief," but offered no examples. He, on the other hand, sent plenty of mischief their way. Preble's forces captured seventy-two Acadians and burned more than forty houses in the Port La Tour area. The prisoners were taken to Boston, but the Massachusetts government, already up to its neck in unwanted exiles, decided to send them along to North Carolina. The Acadians, however, refused to leave. They camped out on the wharf and demanded to be allowed to settle in Massachusetts, where they could support themselves as fishermen. The authorities relented and resettled them along the coast.

In 1758 Lawrence ordered a more thorough sweep of the area. Inhabitants of the long-settled Pubnico inlet and surrounding villages fled as British forces spent more than a month burning homes and destroying crops along the coast. At Chegoggin, near Yarmouth, soldiers surprised a congregation celebrating mass and took the priest and more than sixty people prisoner. The Acadians were conveyed to Halifax and confined until the spring, when the survivors were expelled to France.

With France and England formally at war, officials in London set aside their initial misgivings about the deportation. Promoting resettlement of vacant Acadian lands was "an object of the utmost importance," they said. But the specter of bitter, determined Acadian escapees roaming the woods made it impossible to attract new settlers. "It is certainly very much to be wished that they could be entirely driven out of the Peninsula," the Lords of Trade told Lawrence in early 1757, "because untill that is done, it will be in their power, by the knowledge they have of the country, however small their numbers, to distress and harass the out-settlements, and even his Majesty's Troops." With reluctance, the Lords of Trade shelved plans for resettlement until Lawrence could put down the rebellion. Acadian and Native raiding parties and privateers like Beausoleil Broussard posed a threat that was real and deadly. They knew every river and hiding place, every secluded road where they could stage an ambush. "Land ruffians, turned Pirates," Lawrence called them. The Acadians and Mi'kmaq, seeking revenge and desperate to seize supplies to feed their wives and children, might have preferred the term "freedom fighters." Both sides were guilty of atrocities that fit the definition of terrorism.

Acadian and Native fighters struck at the heart of the British presence in Nova Scotia. Lawrence claimed they murdered German settlers at Lunenburg, scalped five soldiers at Fort Cumberland, and lurked on the outskirts of Halifax. There were persistent rumors of an attack on Annapolis Royal and in December 1757 at least twenty-five soldiers from the Fort Anne garrison were killed at nearby Bloody Creek, the scene of a similar ambush in 1711. More than a dozen British vessels were seized and plundered. In retaliation Lawrence unleashed a detachment of American Rangers—fighters as skilled at wilderness warfare as the Acadians and Mi'kmaq—and offered a bounty for every Native captured and every scalp they brought back. Since the founding of Halifax, the French had been guilty of using similar bounties to induce the Natives to attack British settlers. There is evidence to suggest that at least some of the scalps brought to British outposts came from the heads of murdered Acadians.

The bloodiest act of British retribution took place on the Saint John River in the winter of 1758–1759. Robert Monckton, named Nova Scotia's lieutenant governor as a reward for his victory at Beauséjour, led a mission to drive the Acadians out of the river valley that served as a gateway to the interior of New Brunswick. Hundreds of Acadians, including survivors of the *Pembroke* and refugees who made their way north from the American colonies, cleared land and built new homes along the river. The largest village, St. Ann's, sprang up at a site destined to become the provincial capital, Fredericton. Monckton's troops burned empty houses and barns as they ascended the river. The British camped for the winter and sent a scouting party to St. Ann's in January 1759 under the command of Lieutenant Moses Hazen. They proceeded to set fire to the church and houses at St. Ann's, but this time, instead of fleeing, the Acadians made a stand. They confronted the outnumbered soldiers and forced them to withdraw. Fearing their camp would be discovered, the retreating soldiers seized every Acadian they could find. Vaudreuil, the governor of Quebec, claimed they killed and scalped two women and four children and carried off two dozen prisoners. French records name the victims—Nastasie Bellefontaine and three of her five children, and Michel Bellefontaine's wife and child. The massacre was not the invention of French propagandists. A year later an American clergyman overheard one of Hazen's soldiers boasting about the murders, and claiming to have personally "split the head of one asunder" as the Acadian begged for mercy. Major-General Jeffrey Amherst, commander in chief of British forces in North

America, was disgusted when he learned the details: "I shall always disapprove of killing women and helpless children," he wrote.

Lawrence kept up the offensive. About 200 Acadians returning from Quebec were found near starvation on the Saint John River in late 1759. Even though they had sworn an oath of allegiance to the British forces occupying Quebec, Lawrence and his council declared them prisoners of war and deported them to England. Cape Sable Acadians who evaded two expulsions sent a message to Boston in late 1758 begging the Massachusetts government to have compassion on "your poor distressed fellow creatures." In desperation they asked to be transported to Boston, promising to pledge allegiance to Britain and support the war against France. The Massachusetts legislature turned down the request, but Governor Thomas Pownall appealed to Lawrence to come to their aid. "If Policy cou'd acquiesce in any measure for their relief," he argued, "Humanity loudly calls for it." Lawrence waited several months before sending a ship to pick them up. All 152 were locked up on Georges Island, the colony's most secure prison, and deported to France at the end of 1759.

The fall of Quebec that year, on the heels of the recapture of Louisbourg the previous summer, broke the back of the resistance in Nova Scotia. With the French making a last stand at Montreal, the Acadians and Natives lost their source of supplies and the will to fight. On a November day in 1759, sentries on guard at Fort Cumberland sounded the alarm as four men approached under a flag of truce and asked to speak to the commandant. The Broussard brothers, Beausoleil and Alexandre, and two other men, leaders of the resistance in the Petitcodiac and Memramcook areas, said their families and followers would starve without help. All 200 would surrender in exchange for food and shelter for the winter. The British commander agreed to allow a third of the ground to winter at the fort and the rest to reoccupy Acadian houses that had escaped destruction. Two days later a delegation from Miramichi and other camps along New Brunswick's northeastern coast turned up to surrender on behalf of another 700 refugees facing starvation. In a rare show of compassion, and despite the armed resistance of the Broussards and their ilk, the council agreed to support the refugees for the winter. Lawrence convinced the council that, come spring, all 900 should be shipped to Europe as prisoners of war. While the government failed to follow through, the episode exposed the depths of Lawrence's ruthless-ness. Even with the Acadians destitute and defeated, his first thought was to banish them from his sight.

Low cliffs of ruddy sandstone line Charlottetown harbor, where only the relentless wind and the odd seagull break the silence of a summer afternoon. A pair of pint-sized lighthouses poke their heads above the scrubby spruce, scanning the horizon in search of boats to warn of the dangers on the rocks below. The church spires and docks of Prince Edward Island's capital city decorate the opposite shore. Rocky Point is off the beaten track for the tourists who flock to this island and its world-famous beaches and golf courses each summer, leaving this million-dollar view to cottagers with homes in town. Beneath a few of those cottages, archeologists suspect, lie the remains of much of Port-la-Joye, a French settlement founded almost three centuries ago on what was then Île Saint-Jean. Digs carried out in the late 1980s in the adjacent fields yielded a wealth of Acadian artifacts and what's left of the home of Michel Haché-Gallant, one of the island's first European settlers. The house burned to the ground in 1745, a fact the archeologists knew before they scraped away the layer of charcoal covering his cellar. They also had a pretty good idea where to look because the British built a fort beside the old Haché-Gallant homestead when they took possession of the island in 1758. Grass-covered mounds and ditches on the crest of a nearby hill are all that remain of the fort's eroded earthworks. It was named Fort Amherst, in honor of a general who proved almost as ruthless as Charles Lawrence when it came to dealing with the Acadians.

The French arrived here in 1720 when a colonizing company brought in 300 farmers, fishermen, and soldiers. A village and garrison were established at Port-la-Joye, overlooking the narrow entrance to the harbor. They were joined by a few families who left the Chignecto settlement of Beaubassin, which was by then under British rule. The company went bust within five years and most of the settlers who stayed were descendants of Haché-Gallant, one of the Acadians from Beaubassin.

Over time, fishermen from France founded small settlements on the island's northern coast. British raiders burned the main village and Haché-Gallant's house after the first siege of Louisbourg in 1745, but both Île Royale and Île Saint-Jean reverted to France three years later. Port-la-Joye was re-established and the French hoped Île Saint-Jean's fertile red soil would produce enough surplus grain and beef to feed the garrison at Louisbourg. But poor harvests and plagues of mice left the inhabitants barely able to support themselves.

A trickle of Acadians arriving from Chignecto and other mainland communities after the founding of Halifax became a torrent in 1755 as families all over Acadie fled their homes to escape deportation. Some 3,000 gathered on the island. The refugees lived in crude huts and had little food, rags for clothing, and no shoes for their children. "Their nakedness, which is almost universal and extreme, affects them sore," a priest wrote in an appeal to the French authorities for aid. "They cannot protect themselves from the cold, either by day or by night." The surrender of Louisbourg in July 1758 left the island's tiny garrison and its penniless Acadians at the mercy of the British. Major-General Jeffrey Amherst, who orchestrated the capture of Louisbourg, ordered the garrison's soldiers and officials shipped to England as prisoners of war. Acadians living in the immediate area of the fortress and the inhabitants of Île Saint-Jean were to be deported to France.

British ships and soldiers under the command of Lieutenant-Colonel Andrew Rollo arrived at Port-la-Joye in August. The commandant, Gabriel Rousseau de Villejouin, surrendered without a fight. Rollo graciously allowed two French priests to carry a petition to Louisbourg from the Acadians, who begged to be allowed to stay on their lands. The British, however, were in no mood for leniency, especially after Rollo's men found scalps in Villejouin's quarters. They suspected Île Saint-Jean had been used as a base for French and Native raiding parties and the scalps undoubtedly came from the heads of British soldiers and settlers murdered in Nova Scotia. The petition was ignored and, at the end of August, Rollo sent 700 Acadians to France via Louisbourg.

The British soon realized they had grossly underestimated the number of Acadians on the island. Admiral Edward Boscawen, commander of the victorious fleet at Louisbourg and a key figure in the deportation of 1755, had expected no more than 500 deportees. He ordered more than a dozen additional transports, furnished with enough provisions to sustain 3,500 prisoners for two months. The fleet was beset by poor weather and did not reach Port-la-Joye until the beginning of October. The ships were loaded and on their way by the first week of November with another 2,150 men, women, and children and two priests who were stationed on the island. Some may have endured their second deportation—a group of exiles who made their way back from the Carolinas had arrived on the island in 1756. There was not enough room on the ships for everyone, forcing the British to leave behind an unspecified number who were "sickly and most of them Women and Children." Others fled to remote areas of the island or made their way to the mainland. Nicolas Gautier—son of Joseph-Nicolas Gautier, the Acadian shipowner declared an outlaw for aiding the French in the 1740s—used his schooners to ferry escapees to Acadian camps on the mainland. Lack of provisions in the Miramichi area forced some to return to face deportation. Out of an estimated population of 4,600, about 1,500 escaped to the mainland and perhaps 100 went into hiding on the island. The remaining 3,000 were deported.

The fleet assembled to carry them to France was ill fated from the start. High winds buffeted the ships as they maneuvered through the narrow strait separating Île Royale from the Nova Scotia mainland. One of the transports ran aground and its passengers had to be transferred to other ships. A second transport carrying fifty Acadians struck the rocks, but was refloated. Once in the open ocean, the ships were beset by gales and heavy seas. One ship was diverted to Portsmouth, England, two days before Christmas, its passengers "in great distress, being in want of fresh Provisions and very Sickly." The largest transport, the *Mary*, carrying 560 people, was leaking badly when it limped into Portsmouth. The captain reported burying at least 250 passengers at sea, most of them children. The survivors were gripped by fever, but fears of an epidemic proved unfounded. A doctor sent on board concluded that their symptoms were "more from want of the Necessaries of Life, than any other thing." He attributed the deaths to lack of food "and their having been so much crowded, and breathing consequently foul Air, and lying Dirty."

Disease wiped out a third of the passengers—as many as 350 people—on five other ships that landed at St. Malo in January 1759. Another 200 died after arrival. The *Ruby*, with 310 Acadians on board, was off course and filling with water when it was run aground in the Azores to prevent it from sinking. A British official stationed on the islands reported that only 120 Acadians were saved. Another ship reputedly was wrecked off the coast of Spain with the loss of all aboard.

The transports *Violet* and *Duke William*, carrying some 700 people between them, sailed from Île Royale at the end of November with the *Ruby* and three other ships. By one account, the *Duke William*'s master, a Captain Nichols, accepted the charter despite misgivings about the condition of his vessel and "the impossibility ... of his arriving safe in Old France at that season of the year." A storm broke up the convoy, and gales and high waves pounded the vessels for days. The *Violet*, with 400 on board, foundered on December 12. There were no survivors. The *Duke William* began taking on water about the same time, and its terrified passengers and crew struggled for three days to keep the ship afloat. They worked the pumps around the clock and men and women formed a bucket brigade to bail out the hold, but the ship settled deeper and deeper in the water. A nineteenth-century writer described what happened next:

> About six o'clock on the fourth morning, the people came to the captain and declared they had done all in their power; that the vessel was full of water; and that it was in vain to pump any more. The captain told them he was convinced that what they said was too true, and complimented them upon their attention and exertion. He then acquainted the priest with their situation, assuring him that every method for saving the ship and the lives of the people had been resorted to in vain, and that they expected the decks would blow up every moment. The priest appeared confused; but immediately went to give his people absolution; and a melancholy scene ensued. Strong, hearty, and healthy men, looking at each other, with tears in their eyes, bewailing their unhappy condition, and preparing for death.

The ship carried two lifeboats with barely enough room for the crew. According to another version of the disaster, the priest gave absolution and the terrified passengers "with one consent, agreed to the master, crew, and priest taking the boats, and themselves to perish with the ship." One of the Acadian men was said to have made for the boats, but was shamed into staying to die with his wife and children. Captain Nichols, thirty-four crewmen, and Father Jacques Girard, on the other hand, had no difficulty saving their own skins and consigning 300 men, women, and children to a watery grave. They cast off and came ashore near Penzance. Girard would claim, rather dubiously, that he abandoned his doomed flock so he could save the souls of the English heretics escaping in the lifeboats. Four Acadian men managed to launch a dinghy as the ship went down and the pressure of the water shattered the deck "like the explosion of a gun, or a loud clap of thunder." They also managed to make it to shore.

The deportation from Île Saint-Jean was a tragedy. At least 1,700 people—more than half of the deportees—perished in shipwrecks or died of disease. The operation was poorly planned, rushed, and carried out at the worst season for transatlantic crossings. It culminated in the sinkings of the *Violet* and the *Duke William*, disasters that rivaled the horrors deportees had faced during the previous three years. The deaths and suffering could have been avoided if Amherst and Boscawen had removed the garrison at Port-la-Joye and left the Acadians where they were. They posed no threat to British forces—they could barely support themselves—and there was little, if any, strategic advantage to be gained from another massive deportation.

The British were now in complete command of the East Coast of North America and poised for the final thrust against Quebec, the key to New France. A few thousand Acadians on Île Saint-Jean were not going to halt the British juggernaut, but by 1758, deporting Acadians had become British policy. The Lords of Trade had come around and were backing Lawrence's effort to round up Acadian stragglers on the mainland. British forces in Nova Scotia were locked in a bitter fight with the Broussards and other partisans. The deportation from Île Saint-Jean was part of a campaign to root out Acadians, wherever they were.

An interpretative center at the Port-la-Joye–Fort Amherst National Historic Site at Rocky Point displays a panel bearing a quotation from

Boscawen, who helped Lawrence set events in motion in 1755. In a mere ten words, it captures the mind-set of the men who decided the fate of the Acadians: "We must," as Boscawen bluntly phrased it, "rid His Majesty's dominion of its French vermin."

7 HOSTAGES TO FATE

Weep sore for him that goeth away: for he shall return no more, nor see his native country.

—*Jeremiah* 22:10

No one knows how many people were at the ball. History records only that the guest of honor, Charles Lawrence, spent a lot of time on the dance floor. It was October 1760 and the governor and the people of Halifax were in a festive mood. British forces had just captured Montreal, signaling the end of French power in North America. That was reason enough to toast the king's health, but Lawrence could think of plenty of others. Most of the Acadians had been deported, and the rest were in prison, being kept alive on government rations, or cowering in the forests. New England settlers were beginning to resettle their lands. His vision for Nova Scotia as a British colony was finally taking shape.

At some point as the music played and the dancers danced, Lawrence took a long drink of water to cool down. No doubt he had been partaking of stronger drinks as well. Within days he was gravely ill with congestion and running a high fever. To the medical thinking of the day, the cold water was such a shock to his system that it triggered the onset of pneumonia. His death in Halifax a week later, on October 19, startled his colleagues. He was only fifty-nine. "I should have taken an annuity on his life as soon as anyone I knew," said a shaken Major-General Jeffrey Amherst.

The local press lamented the loss of "the guide and guardian of our interests" and eulogized him as someone who had "protected the oppressed and relieved the needy." His role in making the province "flourishing and happy" was noted, but not that this was accomplished by oppressing Acadians. His old pal Jonathan Belcher muscled aside the senior councillor, Benjamin Green, and took over the colony's administration. Snubbed in his bid to become governor, Belcher was made lieutenant governor in 1761 and wound up in charge when Lawrence's replacement chose to remain in Britain.

Lawrence's death unleashed a torrent of allegations of patronage and mismanagement; among other things, the late governor was taken to task for diverting Acadian lands to his cronies, helping soldiers evade justice, mismanaging public funds, and operating his own fleet of vessels at public expense. The Lords of Trade ordered an investigation, and handed the task to Belcher, who swept the mess under the rug. "Upon the best examination in the severest charges," he reported in 1762, the allegations were unfounded.

Lawrence was buried, at public expense, after an elaborate funeral procession from his residence to St. Paul's Church. The troops of the garrison and public figures walked behind the coffin, which was draped in black velvet. A choir of orphans sang a hymn as the mourners passed and the citadel's gunners fired off a round every minute to pay their respects. His coffin was lowered beneath the floorboards of St. Paul's Lawrence was the first of at least twenty prominent Halifax citizens who have been interred under Canada's oldest Protestant church.

The office towers of downtown Halifax now encircle the church, where his hatchment—a diamond-shaped board bearing his family coat of arms—hangs from the upper gallery. A display case near the entrance holds church-related memorabilia, including a document Lawrence signed six months before his death. Beside it, a floor plan shows that Lawrence is entombed at the other end of the church, just in front of a row of carved-oak choir benches. He lies in a gloomy crawlspace, his only visitors the repairmen who descend into the church basement from time to time. When Acadians visit, a tour guide confesses, most are delighted to discover they can walk on the grave of the man who caused their ancestors so much misery.

Jonathan Belcher, an old hand at persecuting Acadians, was determined to pick up where Lawrence left off. In February 1761, the chief justice and his council passed a unanimous motion calling for the removal of the roughly 2,000 in custody or still under British control. Since they were considered prisoners of war, though, it was up to Jeffrey Amherst to determine their fate. A year earlier, with the French still ensconced in the interior of North America, the commander in chief supported Lawrence's deportation of the 200 starving exiles who tried to return via Quebec. With New France conquered and the French threat waning, he abruptly changed his course of action. Perhaps he was haunted by the thought of all the innocent people who had perished in shipwrecks after he ordered the rushed deportation from Île Saint-Jean. Whatever his reasons, Amherst turned down Belcher's request. If he thought for one minute that expelling the remaining Acadians would make Nova Scotia safer, he replied from his headquarters in New York, he would do so in an instant. But he cited the cost of transporting and maintaining people who could be put to good use within the colony as laborers. "Under the new circumstances of that Valuable and flourishing Province, I do not see that it can have anything to fear or apprehend from these Acadians," he said, and they should be allowed to stay "under proper regulations and restrictions."

Miffed at being told how to run his province, Belcher appealed to the Lords of Trade, but they declined to intervene. But Belcher still had a free hand to crack down on Acadians outside his borders. At the end of 1761, he ordered Captain Roderick Mackenzie's Highlanders to attack a French privateering base on the Restigouche River in northern New Brunswick, where a large number of Acadian families had gathered. Mackenzie took the Acadians by surprise and carried off 335, which was all he could squeeze onto his small vessels. Another 450 were allowed to stay after promising to turn themselves in when ordered.

Belcher continued to spar with Amherst through the mail, complaining of the Acadians' "high degree of Obstinacy" and lack of gratitude for the "mild Treatment and Indulgencies shewn to those who have surrendered themselves." But for all his bluster, Belcher knew Amherst was right and he needed the Acadians, for now at least. The effort to recruit New England settlers stalled when a powerful storm—perhaps the most destructive in the region's history—struck in November 1759. The wind flattened whole stands of trees and a tidal surge broke though the neglected dikes, drenching the hard-won Acadian marshlands with seawater. At Chignecto, which bore the brunt of the storm's fury, surveyor Charles Morris reported that "the Dykes are universally levell'd and scarcely the Traces of them appear." The British turned to the Acadians to oversee the repairs. Even Belcher had to admit they were "the most skilfull people in the Country" when it came to "the preservation and recovery of the Marsh Lands."

The Acadians demanded high wages for their services, easing the bitterness of restoring their own dikes to enable English settlers to take away their lands. With the end of the fighting and peace with the Mi'kmaq established, Belcher was able to follow through on Lawrence's plans for large-scale immigration. By 1763 about 5,000 settlers had been lured to the colony with promises of 1,000-acre land grants, a ten-year tax holiday, and tolerance for every faith except Catholicism. Settlers from Massachusetts, Connecticut, and Rhode Island snapped up the vacant, ready-to-farm Acadian lands along the Minas Basin. The Grand-Pré area was divided into the townships of Cornwallis and Horton; Piziquid became Newport and Falmouth; the townships of Truro and Onslow—old Cobequid—welcomed Irish immigrants. As Lawrence predicted shortly before his death, the new settlers "have but to see the lands and to be in love with them."

Just as Lawrence's grand plan for a British Nova Scotia was taking shape—and the war seemed won by the British—word reached Halifax in July 1762 that a French squadron had captured St. John's, Newfoundland. Panic swept through Nova Scotia's exposed and scattered new settlements. Belcher and his council were convinced that Halifax would be next. They put Nova Scotia on a war footing—martial law was declared, the militia was called out, and neglected forts were repaired. And when the attack came, they were certain the Mi'kmaq would rejoin their old allies and the Acadians would exact revenge for the deportation.

The Acadians were suspected of having caches of guns and ammunition. It was rumored that Acadians working on the dikes had threatened to cut the throats of the interlopers. Some new arrivals in Horton Township headed home to New England to escape the expected bloodshed. The Nova Scotia assembly—an elected body that Lawrence and Belcher reluctantly established in 1758 to attract democratically minded New Englanders—passed a shrill resolution demanding the deportation of the remaining Acadians. "These people seeing the English daily in possession and enjoyment of the lands forfeited, and formerly occupied by them, will for ever regret their loss," the legislators asserted, "and consequently will lay hold of every favorable opportunity for regaining them, at any, even the most hazardous risk."

Belcher and the council needed little prodding. Militiamen marched about 130 Acadians working on dikes in the Minas area to Halifax, where another 1,000 were confined to a barracks, with armed guards posted to prevent escapes. Whole families were incarcerated on Georges Island, the military prison used to hold Acadian deputies in 1755 and the destination for the Broussards and hundreds of other surrendered and captured resistance fighters. A ship was sent out to collect Acadians who were fishing along the coast. "In this Time of Danger," the council declared at the end of July, "it is absolutely necessary immediately to Transport the said Acadians out of this Province."

In mid-August five ships carrying more than 1,000 Acadians sailed from Halifax to Boston. Amherst, who was not consulted and still believed the Acadians posed little threat, offered his approval after the fact. Amherst needed some of the British troops stationed in Nova Scotia for a counterattack on St. John's—the city was retaken in September—and uprooting the Acadians was a small price to pay to mollify Belcher and his councillors. While officials in Halifax and New York congratulated themselves on their cleverness, folks in Boston were tired of being the dumping ground for Nova Scotia's problems. The Massachusetts legislature refused to allow the refugees to land and they languished on the transports in Boston harbor. Nova Scotia's agent in Boston, Thomas Hancock, one of the merchants who cashed in on the deportation of 1755 by supplying ships and provisions, decided he had no choice but to send them back. The fleet returned to Halifax in September, earning Hancock a stern rebuke and leaving the Nova Scotia council no closer to ridding itself of the Acadians.

In October, Belcher appealed to the Lords of Trade to be "freed from the dangers to be dreaded from so inveterate an Enemy," but to no avail. With the crisis passed and the war with France winding down, their lordships replied, it was no longer "necessary nor politic to remove them." It was time, they advised, to take steps to transform former enemies into useful members of Nova Scotia society. London also believed a new governor was needed to oversee Nova Scotia's transition to peacetime. Belcher's autocratic style—one of his many enemies dismissed him as "unskilled in the Art of Government"— alienated the legislature and Halifax's influential merchants. His mismanagement of the colony's finances, at a time when Nova Scotia was con-sidered a drain on the British treasury, sealed his fate. Montagu Wilmot, a military officer and protégé of veteran colonial administrator Lord Halifax, was sent to replace Belcher as lieutenant governor in 1763 and was named governor the following year. Belcher retreated to the courts, where he presided until he died in 1776 and joined Lawrence under the floorboards of St. Paul's Church. The Lords of Trade, in a final rebuke, decreed that Nova Scotia would never again be ruled by a chief justice.

Wilmot's lackluster performance during his two-year tenure branded him a "man of weak character ... poorly fitted for the post of governor." He inher-ited Belcher's massive public debt as well as the challenge of resettling the Acadians. Under the terms of the Treaty of Paris that ended the war in 1763, Acadians living in exile under British rule were given a year and a half to reset-tle in France or any of its colonies. About 1,800 remained in their homeland, about 1,000 of them in the Halifax area, and the remainder were clustered around the garrisons at Windsor, Annapolis Royal, and Chignecto, subsisting on government rations. Another 300 remained on Île Saint-Jean.

Wilmot and the council were ecstatic when more than 500—including the belligerent Broussard clan and other former resistance fighters locked up on Georges Island—opted to leave at their own expense, using money amassed from repairing dikes. They were headed to the French island of Saint-Domingue, despite reports that the harsh climate was taking its toll on exiles already gathered there. Wilmot had been lobbying the Lords of Trade to deport the lot of them to some distant Caribbean island where, he noted with some satisfaction, the tropical climate was known to be "mortal to the natives of the Northern countries." "The further they are distant," he contended in March 1764, "the greater our safety."

Lord Halifax rejected the idea and directed Wilmot to allow Acadians to resettle in Nova Scotia, but in enclaves scattered around the province—in effect, an internal diaspora to sap their strength and alleviate the security threat. The Acadians were no longer prisoners of war and those who agreed to take an oath of allegiance were to be treated like any other Catholic subject of the British Crown. With reluctance, Wilmot and his council drafted a suitable oath in the fall of 1764 and earmarked lands for the Acadians "at the back of the Settlements" and as far as possible from France's remaining North American possessions, the islands of St. Pierre and Miquelon south of Newfoundland. Acadians who wanted to remain in Nova Scotia and those trickling in from exile swore the oath and received small grants of land. In the late 1760s the Township of Clare, an empty and exposed stretch of coastline along St. Mary's Bay, facing New England, was set aside for resettlement. Nine years after it began, the deportation of the Acadians was officially over.

Throngs of people lined the streets of Bristol, hoping to catch a glimpse of the parade of newcomers. Constables were called out, by one report, "to keep the Mob in order, which was very numerous." The objects of curiosity were about 300 people, newly arrived on the *Virginian Packet*. They came from the colony of Virginia, but they were not Americans—they were French captives from the other side of the Atlantic. There was a camp at Bristol to hold French soldiers and sailors, but it was clear to the rubberneckers in the crowd that these were no ordinary prisoners of war. Women, children, and old people outnumbered the men and there was not a uniform in sight.

This group of Acadian exiles, 1,044 of them on four ships, arrived in England without warning. Louis Guigner, a commissioner with the Sick and Hurt Board of the British Admiralty, was called to Bristol on June 24, 1756 to meet the first shipload, which arrived two days later. Virginia's governor, Robert Dinwiddie, was outraged when he read Lawrence's letter thanking him in advance for taking the Acadians off his hands. "We can have but a very poor Prospect of their being either good Subjects or useful people," he griped in a missive to London. It was, he added, "very disagreeable to the People" of Virginia to have them show up at a time when the French "are now murder'g and scalp'g our Frontier Settlers." Dinwiddie maintained them over the winter, and sent them to England on the first available ships in the spring. British officials did not realize they were coming until a Bristol trading firm contacted the Admiralty to say one of its ships was about to land with "Neutral French on board." Within weeks other shiploads arrived in Liverpool, Falmouth, and Southampton.

Guigner swung into action. He tried to arrange lodgings in private houses for the Bristol group, but found "a very strong aversion among all the inhabitants to take these poor wretches in." City officials also rejected them at first, fearing they would wind up on the dole. After Guigner promised the government would pay the bills, he was given approval to rent several large warehouses, "built round an airy and spacious court," on "a back street at the extreme end of the town." He ordered straw for bedding and arranged for the Acadians' belongings to be carted over from the ship. They were on the same footing as prisoners of war when it came to food, which was supplied at no cost. Each person was entitled to an allowance of sixpence a day (threepence for children under the age of seven) to buy clothing and extras.

The Acadians in Bristol and other ports had some freedom of movement within their neighborhoods. Guigner imposed two rules: the Acadians were "not to be found drunken" and were to be in their quarters by eight each evening. "They promised to behave well," he noted. The 293 Acadians sent to Southampton were housed at first in "a very bad barn where there is hardly a chimney and no water to be had," according to a letter of complaint several of the men filed with the Admiralty. "There are a great number of sick persons and also young people of both sexes all together in a lodging where there is neither separation nor distinction of rooms." The group was moved to a building formerly used as a powder magazine that apparently addressed their concerns.

Some of the Acadians who landed at Bristol were ill as well. At first Guigner and Admiralty doctors attributed the symptoms to colds or seasickness, but within a week the first case of smallpox was confirmed. A makeshift hospital, set up in a house attached to a tavern, was soon filled with the sick and there were several deaths. Smallpox broke out among the exiles in other port cities and by August 9 it was reported that 200 were sick. At least five deaths were confirmed in Liverpool, but records are scanty and the number of victims was much higher, perhaps as many as 250. There were only 741 Acadians left in England at the end of 1762, and almost a quarter were children born during and after the deportation.

Word of the epidemic spread almost as quickly as the disease, and by September 1756 the French government filed a protest claiming the Acadians were being neglected and mistreated. (Louis XV's government was oblivious, it appears, to the plight of Acadians in Nova Scotia and the American colonies—no complaint was ever lodged in response to their mistreatment there.) With England's reputation at stake, Secretary of State Charles Fox ordered the Admiralty to do all it could to alleviate the suffering, "sparing no expense that may contribute to their recovery and well-being." An investigator sent to Bristol found the refugees living in filthy conditions and accused the attending doctors of neglect. The Admiralty sacked the surgeon in charge at Bristol for failing to contain the outbreak.

In November, once the disease had run its course, Guigner appealed to his superiors for warm clothing to comfort the survivors during the winter months. They were "real objects of compassion," in need of shoes and stockings and other clothing, he wrote. War-related shortages and the rising price of wheat prompted the Admiralty to trim the food allowance. The local agent responsible for the Acadians and prisoners of war began to withhold reports and falsify records in an ill-advised bid to cushion the blow. He was caught in 1757 and fired. His replacement was "found guilty of the greatest mismanagement" and let go within a year.

Admiralty records are silent on how these upheavals affected the Acadians' living conditions. The exiles were almost completely dependent on the government for support. Most of the men were barred from working because local laborers objected to the competition. Some children were apprenticed to tradesmen and, it was noted with some alarm, were learning English and adopting English ways. Acadian women in Bristol wove and sold coarse cloth, described as "very serviceable." Others were not so lucky. There was a report that welfare payments to the Falmouth exiles were cut off in 1762, and "those without a trade lived by borrowing, the widows and orphans begged."

In 1763, with peace negotiations underway, British officials asked the Bristol exiles where they wanted to be sent when the war ended. They received a detailed reply that speaks to the Acadians' political savvy. Their first wish was to be returned to Nova Scotia, compensated for their losses, and allowed to practise their religion. In exchange, they would submit to an oath of allegiance, but, stubborn to a fault, they insisted on taking an oath that would not bind them "to bear Arms against any warlike Nation whatso-ever." After enduring so much disruption and hardship, these Acadians desired most to be left in peace. It would be "an essential Point of happiness," they wrote, if forts were never again built in their midst. And should there be another war, "We desire ... that we may be permitted to retire where we may think proper."

The groups at Southampton and Liverpool backed those demands at first. But another plan was afoot, one with all the trappings of a spy novel—international intrigue, a secret letter, even a secret agent. Normand Duplessis, a French sailor being held at Liverpool, suggested the Acadians there smuggle a letter to the French government appealing for help. An Irishman named Turney, married to one of the Acadian women, was recruited as the courier and carried the letter to London. So it was that two people who had never seen Nova Scotia determined the fate of the Acadians in England.

The letter was delivered to Louis Jules Barbon Mancini Mazarini, Duc de Nivernois, a French nobleman who was in London to take part in the peace negotiations. Nivernois, a soldier-turned-diplomat, was intrigued and asked his secretary to find out more. The secretary, known to history only as Monsieur de la Rochette, went undercover and visited each group of exiles at the beginning of 1763 to gauge their interest in being moved to France. La Rochette was not always warmly received; he detected a defiant attitude among the Acadians and some suspected he was a British spy. But they had been living in limbo for more than six years, cooped up in British camps, and to most of the exiles it seemed as though salvation was at hand. La Rochette described the Liverpool group as overcome with joy when he spoke to them at a clandestine meeting in their quarters. "All men, women and children were weeping for joy and muttering in their cries, God bless our good King," he reported. "Many seemed beside themselves; they clapped their hands, raised them to Heaven, struck them against the walls, and sobbed like children."

Nivernois sold the plan to the French foreign minister, Etienne-François, Duc de Choiseul, and made the Acadians an offer too good to refuse. They were promised land, tools, building materials, and livestock. The French government threw in an exemption from taxes for fifty years and offered to pay any debts they had incurred while living in England. After Nivernois negotiated a clause in the Treaty of Paris giving Acadians under British rule eighteen months to resettle in France or any of its colonies, similar promises of support were extended to Acadians in the American colonies and Nova Scotia. It was a ray of hope to people who had known only suffering and neglect. "Communicate this letter to your brethren," La Rochette urged the Liverpool group in March 1763. "Tell them of their coming liberation."

Governors along the eastern seaboard soon were besieged with requests for permission to emigrate to France. Acadians exchanged letters with their far-flung kin throughout the exile, employing a networking system that was remarkable for the time. Port cities were clearinghouses for news and mail in the Age of Sail, and most of the exiles were stuck in or near some of the world's busiest seaports. Those who could not read and write enlisted supporters in their temporary homes to help draft letters and petitions. Even after more than a decade in exile, a group of Acadians in France was able to pinpoint the locations of hundreds of relatives in America, Quebec, the West Indies, and Louisiana. Few families, however, were reunited in France. The British colonies, while eager to be rid of their Acadians, refused to pay their passage across the Atlantic. The French, for their part, were willing to transport only those in England, and few, if any, of the others could afford to accept Nivernois's offer.

Nivernois had his own reasons for reaching out to the Acadians; he expected to resettle a good number of the heavily subsidized exiles on his estates in France. Choiseul had his own agenda as well. France had lost much of its overseas empire at the negotiating table, and the foreign minister was determined to hold on to its remaining possessions. To him the Acadians, while "a race sluggish by nature," were a hardy stock of loyal subjects who could tame the jungles of Guiana and Saint-Domingue. They were "very ingenious and good farmers," he noted, "in general fitted for all things, because in their own country they were obliged to make all things."

For all their self-interest, Nivernois and Choiseul seem to have had a genuine desire to rescue and help people they believed had sacrificed everything for their faith and for their king. They viewed the Acadians as lost countrymen who would become loyal, model citizens. But the Acadians had little in common with the peasants of France, and, for all their ingenuity, they were ill suited for life in the tropics. Every man, woman, and child had been born either in Acadie or in exile. They considered themselves to be a distinct people—they often referred to themselves as a "nation" in their petitions— and they were a distinct people. France would prove as foreign to them as the American colonies and the port cities of southern England. Saint-Domingue and Guiana would cost many of them their lives.

The mission to rescue the Acadians in England seemed doomed from the start. The ships sent to bring them across the English Channel were as crowded and unhealthy as those Lawrence had used to cast them into exile. They landed at St. Malo and Morlaix, ports on the Brittany coast, where the French authorities housed them in temporary barracks while they debated where to settle them. Smallpox, their old enemy, broke out, killing an unknown number. There were by now about 3,400 Acadians in France—the newcomers from England, the survivors of the deportation from Île Saint-Jean in 1758, and others who had been deported to France or had made their own way there since 1755. They lived on a small daily allowance from the government and were parked in towns along the north coast as officials considered resettlement proposals. Any number of "unscrupulous merchants and land sharks," as one writer has described them, were eager to turn the

Acadians loose on their estates in exchange for taxes and tithes. One promoter offered to put them to work in his mines. Nivernois failed to follow though on his pledges, and a plan to settle some of them on his private island off the coast of France never materialized.

Choiseul, meanwhile, was recruiting colonists to settle Guiana, a French possession on South America's Caribbean coast. Even though the region's hot and unhealthy climate was notorious, thousands of people succumbed to promises of free land, generous subsidies, and the potential to grow two crops a year. Several hundred Acadian refugees, tired of living in limbo in France, joined the French and German peasants who sailed for South America. Conditions on arrival were appalling: there was not enough money or supplies to deal with the influx, and the corrupt governor squandered what was available on banquets for his friends. Colonists endured months in crowded, unsanitary camps awaiting boats to take them to settlement sites. Food was in short supply and hundreds became sick, far more than could be accommodated in what passed for a hospital. Over 2,000 newcomers were diverted to Devil's Island—later to become a notorious penal colony—where, by one account, they fell prey to "fevers, scurvy, malnutrition, and dehydration" and "died like flies." The survivors, including almost all of the Acadians still alive, returned to France in 1765.

Choiseul's effort to populate Saint-Domingue doomed hundreds of other Acadians desperate for a fresh start. The French offered free passage to the Caribbean island and, in 1764, the local governor promised the newcomers "land and sustenance until they became self-sufficient." Three hundred exiles in Massachusetts answered the call, despite Governor Francis Bernard's warnings that the heat and tropical diseases would bring their "certain destruction." Groups from New York, Connecticut, Pennsylvania, Georgia, and South Carolina also converged on the island. A new life under French rule in the Caribbean, no matter how perilous, offered more hope than a life of poverty and humiliation in America.

The promises proved hollow and the island was akin to a prison camp. The governor's real goal was to recruit laborers to build a naval base in the jungle at Môle Saint-Nicolas. The refugees received food and old clothing, but worked for no pay other than the promise of land of their own once the base was completed. Conditions were as bad as any in exile, if not worse. Rations were inadequate and the drinking water was poor; yellow fever, malaria, and scurvy claimed many lives, with children the hardest hit. At least a third of the 938 Acadians dispatched to Môle Saint-Nicolas in 1764 died within a year. One visiting French official found "some men bewildered, without shelter, dying under bushes," unable to bear the tropical heat and too sick to eat the rations available. "The worst criminal would prefer the galleys and the torture associated with that punishment rather than stay in this horrible place," he lamented. "Only constraint keeps the residents there."

A few were granted permission to leave and some deserted, but most had no choice but to tough it out. The survivors adapted to the tropical climate and carved out a livelihood as farmers and craftsmen or found work on the island's sugar and coffee plantations. Many became refugees once again in the 1790s when a slave revolt forced European settlers and freed Blacks to flee for their lives. The initial wave, like the Acadian deportees of 1755, dispersed to ports along the eastern seaboard of the United States. Acadian exiles and their descendants were among a later exodus from the island, arriving in New Orleans via Cuba in 1809.

The most remote destination for the exiles—and rivaling Guiana as the bleakest—was the Falklands, a group of scattered and windswept islands 300 miles off the tip of South America. Located deep in the South Atlantic and uncomfortably close to Antarctica, the islands were a treeless barren of craggy mountains and dark-brown peat bogs that offered little shelter from the gales and storms that churned the surrounding waters. The early scouting reports should have been enough to deter visitors, let alone year-round residents. One eighteenth-century observer described it as a place "thrown aside from human use, stormy in winter, barren in summer ... which not even the southern savages had dignified with habitation." The French explorer Louis Antoine de Bougainville—the first Frenchman to circumnavigate the globe, but perhaps best known for lending his name to the bougainvillea, a bright-blooming shrub native to South America—acknowledged it was "a countryside lifeless for want of inhabitants," with "everywhere a weird and melancholy uniformity." Which makes it all the more remarkable that Bougainville undertook a mission, at his own expense, to colonize the islands for Louis XV.

Nine Acadians signed on for Bougainville's first mission, which sailed from St. Malo in the late summer of 1763. When they arrived more than four months later, their leader christened the islands the Malouines in honor of their port of origin (transformed into Las Islas Malvinas by the Argentinians, whose long-standing claim to the area erupted into war with the islands' British landlords in 1982). A fort was established and the settlers tended live-stock brought over from South America. The Malouines may have been cold and bleak, but at least they were free of the tropical diseases that were mow-ing down exiles in the Caribbean and Guiana. Promises of a year's provisions and continuation of the daily dole enabled Bougainville to recruit about 160 more Acadians, who were established by 1766.

Even on these remote specks of rock, the Acadians were buffeted by the forces of imperial rivalry. The strategic value of the islands—the gateway to Cape Horn, the only passage between the Atlantic and the Pacific—encour-aged rival Spanish and British claims. The British, who already referred to them as the Falklands, sent in a naval expedition that claimed the islands in 1765, oblivious to the presence of Bougainville's settlers. A British surveying party stumbled upon the colonists the following year and ordered them to leave. Help arrived in the form of the Spanish, who struck a deal to assume con-trol of the islands after reimbursing Bougainville for his investment. After the handover in 1767, just under 100 Acadians opted to stay on under Spanish rule. They eked out a living in "this miserable desert"—the blunt assessment of one Spanish newcomer—raising cattle, struggling to grow corn, and hunting seals. The harsh conditions wore down most, if not all, of the Acadians and, like sol-diers defeated in battle, they retreated to France in the early 1770s. The fate of those who left and any who remained has been lost to history.

As the overseas ventures collapsed, a plan finally emerged to resettle Acadians within France. The unlikely site was Belle-Île-en-Mer, a craggy, almost treeless island about 15 miles off the coast of Brittany. Seven miles long and about 5 miles across at its widest point, the island had been a British naval base during the last years of the war and was ceded to France in 1763. A delegation of Acadians scouted the island, but had misgivings about the poor soil and its exposure to the weather and to the British. The last thing they wanted was to settle on land with strategic value. "In all probability we would find ourselves in a similar position to the one that has placed us today in such painful straits," the deputies reported.

To overcome these misgivings, the French government turned to a ghost from the Acadians' past, Abbé Le Loutre, the priest whose blandishments and warmongering had gone far toward sealing their fate in 1755. Le Loutre escaped from Fort Beauséjour before it fell to Monckton's troops, but was captured on his way to France and spent the rest of the war in a British prison. Freed in 1763, he made his way to France and fell in with the exiles waiting for the land they were promised. Out of guilt for having contributed to their plight, or perhaps just out of pity, Le Loutre became their champion. "My poor Acadians," he called them. He convinced about eighty families to settle on Belle-Île-en-Mer in 1765, among them Trahans, Aucoins, Doucets, Richards, and LeBlancs. They were offered homes, barns, cattle, and tools. Le Loutre is said to have taken a shovel in hand to break ground for the foundation of the first house. The Acadians wanted to be settled as a group, but were distributed among the island's four parishes. The farmers and fishermen already on the island, the *bellilois*, as they called themselves, had their own language and customs and "did not wish to give up their villages to strangers," noted the governor. Six years of drought ravaged crops and an outbreak of hoof-and-mouth disease decimated livestock. The taxman did the rest. The settlers had been promised a five-year break from taxes, but payment was demanded early. Le Loutre bickered with French bureaucrats, but could not delay the levy. With no income and no prospects, most of the Acadians had retreated to the mainland by 1772.

Belle-Île-en-Mer was the first of a string of debacles. A scheme to establish 550 exiles on the islands of St. Pierre and Miquelon in 1767 also collapsed and most were back in France within months. In 1771 the Acadians as a group rejected a plan to send them to Corsica, complaining that the soil was poor and the rents were high. The Acadians were mired in poverty, most of them relegated to the slums of French seaports. The government was growing weary of trying to accommodate their guests, who were becoming a serious drain on the treasury. "They can be looked upon in no other light than as a chaos of indolence stupidity and nastiness," wrote one exasperated official. "They seem to resent being treated as peasants," noted another.

The deadlock was broken in 1772 when a delegation of Acadians made a direct appeal to Louis XVI to fulfill the promises his grandfather, Louis XV, had made when they came to France. After hearing their long list of grievances, the king rapped his ministers for their inaction and decreed that a new attempt be made to establish them as farmers on French soil.

Acadians were offered 2,500 acres on an estate belonging to a cash-strapped French nobleman in the Poitou area, near the city of Poitiers and inland from the ports of Nantes and La Rochelle. The ancestors of many Acadians emigrated from the region in the mid-1600s. The colony became known as Grand Ligne for the government-built houses that lined a dead-straight section of road through its heart. About 1,500 people signed on, but there were not enough houses to go around and most had to be quartered in a nearby town.

The area was dry and barren and the sandy soil proved impossible to farm. Crops withered and died two years in a row. The Acadians could no longer turn to Le Loutre for help—he died in 1772 while inspecting the area on their behalf—and abandoned the project in droves. By 1776 only 160 people were still trying to tough it out. The rest headed for Bordeaux, Nantes, Rouen, and other ports in search of work. The collapse of the Grand Ligne project left the Acadians in "a state of idleness, discouragement, and uncertainty," noted Oscar Winzerling, author of (*Acadian Odyssey*) the definitive account of their bitter sojourn in France. A few families defected to England; others defied a ban on emigration and made their way to Île Saint-Jean and Halifax.

About twenty families won permission in 1777 to emigrate to Spanish-held Louisiana, where Acadians from the American colonies were building new lives. Rifts emerged within the Acadian community. A vocal group of younger people demanded permission to move to Louisiana, while others backed a revived proposal to settle on Corsica. Another faction advocated a wait-and-see approach, predicting the American Revolution would drive the British from Nova Scotia and allow them to reclaim their homeland. Permission to emigrate was denied, the second Corsican plan evaporated, and Nova Scotia not only remained British, it became a haven for tens of thousands of Loyalist Americans at the end of the Revolutionary War.

By 1783 the 2,400 Acadians in France were deeply in debt and mired in poverty. Failed settlement schemes and broken promises left them little hope for the future. "After twenty-eight years, after the loss of our property," their delegates lamented that year in a petition to the French government, "we find ourselves in poverty and misery. The landlords daily refuse to house us, and without His Majesty's pay we cannot live. We are grieved that we are a burden."

As the French gave up on the Acadians, as their Acadian guests were about to give up on themselves, a man showed up in Nantes after a seven-year absence in Louisiana. His name was Henri Peyroux de La Coudrenière and he had an idea.

8 LOUISIANA REFUGE

It was a band of exiles: a raft, as it were, from the shipwrecked
Nation, scattered along the coast, now floating together ...
Men and women and children, who,
guided by hope or by hearsay,
Sought for their kith and their kin among the few-acred farmers,
On the Acadian coast, and the prairies of fair Opelousas.

—Henry Wadsworth Longfellow, *Evangeline: A Tale of Acadie*

In the fall a sweet, smoky aroma fills the air in Loreauville, a village of fewer than 1,000 souls in southern Louisiana. This is the heart of sugar country and tall rows of sugarcane, each bamboo-like stalk topped with a green crown of spiky leaves, stand at attention in the fields fanning out from the murky Bayou Teche. Early November is harvesttime, and this close to the Gulf of Mexico, it is warm enough to rate as a perfect summer's day in Nova Scotia. Trucks and tractors pulling hoppers filled with chunks of cane hog the roads, and clouds of brownish smoke engulf houses and fields as farmers burn off the stubble left behind. In a region where sugarcane has been king for a century and a half, it is the sweet smell of success.

Teche is derived from a Native word for "snake," and the 130-mile, tree-lined river lives up to its name here, making a U-shaped loop to sideswipe Loreauville as it flows toward the urban sprawl of nearby New Iberia. The Teche is surprisingly narrow—the village's lone drawbridge is not much longer than a tractor-trailer rig—but the riverfront supports three boatyards.

The facade of St. Joseph's Catholic Church, with its white portico and Greek columns, dominates the heart of the village and stands on land donated by the Loreau who gave the village its name. There are a couple of diners, two banks, and a sports bar, and the locals have their pick of two dance schools. An Internet site touts the village and its businesses, but otherwise the forces of time and change seem to move as slowly in Loreauville as the dark waters of the bayou. The grocery store opened by Charles Broussard in 1935 is still in business. The streets were unpaved until 1960. One of the biggest stories to hit the local weekly paper, *The Magnolia Tymes*, was the decision of Forbus Mestayer Sr. not to run in the fall 2004 election. The eighty-four-year-old Democrat and former awning salesman had been the village's mayor since 1956.

This quiet rural community, bypassed by the main roads and overlooked on some highway maps, is the cradle of New Acadia, the new land that exile-weary Acadians carved out of the swamps and prairies of south Louisiana. Somewhere under Loreauville's tree-lined streets and the fields of sugarcane, perhaps in the shade of one of the oaks that dot the landscape, lie the bones of Beausoleil Broussard, one of the first Acadians to set foot on Louisiana soil.

Released from prison on Georges Island after the war ended in 1763, Broussard collected his extended family and followers and prepared to move to Saint-Domingue. But before the group left Halifax, letters arrived from Acadians warning of the nightmarish conditions there. The resourceful Broussard devised a new and more ambitious plan. His group would stop at Saint-Domingue, pick up Acadians there, and together they would travel up the Mississippi and settle in Illinois country, far from the British. Broussard chartered a ship and, in November 1764, left Halifax with about 200 Acadians. By the time the ship reached Saint-Domingue, though, Broussard's Acadian contacts were either dead or too ill to travel. The Halifax group continued to the Mississippi and 193 arrived in New Orleans in February 1765. To their surprise, Louisiana was no longer a French colony. Under the Treaty of Paris, Spain and Britain divvied up the territory stretching from the Gulf of Mexico to the headwaters of the Mississippi River. The British took possession of lands to the east of the river, while points west remained in the hands of French officials until the Spanish took official control.

New Orleans was the capital and trading center of the colony, 100 miles from the river mouth and perched on a narrow ribbon of land backing on the inland sea of Lake Pontchartrain. Broussard and his clan found a sympathetic welcome—the acting French governor, Charles Philippe Aubry, had encountered Acadian exiles while a prisoner in New England during the war. The Acadians abandoned the idea of continuing up the Mississippi and Aubry offered them homesteads in the area of Poste des Attakapas, a hamlet on Bayou Teche. Eleven years after being stripped of their homes and possessions, they were handed an expanse of fertile land that was treeless and ready for farming.

For Broussard and other transplants from the Chignecto region, the prairies along Bayou Teche must have brought back memories of the marshlands along the Bay of Fundy. And as at Chignecto, cattle became the mainstay of many farms. In April 1765 Broussard, his son Vincent, his brother Alexandre, and the heads of five other families signed a contract with a wealthy landowner, Antoine Bernard Dautrieve, which amounted to a sharecropping deal for cattle. The Acadians agreed to tend Dautrieve's herds in exchange for cattle and grants of land from Dautrieve's holdings along the Teche. Assuming the herd grew under their care, after six years the Acadians would be entitled to keep half of the additional cattle.

Within days after signing the cattle contract, Aubry commissioned Beausoleil as a captain of the militia and "Commandant of the Acadians" at Attakapas, the latter honor an official recognition of his long leadership role. The Broussard group established a camp on the Teche in an area known as Fausse Pointe, present-day Loreauville. An epidemic broke out, possibly yellow fever picked up during the stopover on Saint-Domingue. At least thirty-nine died between July and November, including Beausoleil and Alexandre. There is a tragic irony in their sudden deaths. The Broussard brothers had dodged bullets and the noose for more than a decade; they had fought to free their families and friends from British rule, only to succumb to disease far from their homeland just as they were about to establish a new one. Beausoleil was sixty-three years old; Alexandre was sixty-six. Their grave sites and even the precise dates of their deaths remain a mystery.

The rest of Broussard's extended clan scattered to escape the epidemic. Most appear to have survived and their numbers were soon bolstered by new arrivals from the American colonies. A Spanish governor finally arrived in 1766, Antonio de Ulloa, a scholar and naturalist unsuited for colonial middle management. Within a couple of years, Ulloa managed to antagonize the Creoles—Louisiana-born residents of French and Spanish descent—as well as the Acadian newcomers.

At first, though, he saw the Acadians as the ideal settlers to secure Louisiana against the threat of a British invasion. Britain was busy establishing forts and Native alliances along the Mississippi, leaving Louisiana with a vast, undefended eastern border. Thousands of Acadians in the American colonies, Ulloa was convinced, would flock to Louisiana if given free passage, land, and provisions. "They would rather expose themselves to mortal dangers while searching for the desired freedom of religion and civil treatment than remain ... under English rule," he assured Spain's colonial minister in May 1766.

Ulloa had nothing but praise for the Acadians, describing them as "naturally good, quiet, hard-working, and industrious ... without vices and able farmers" who would work themselves to death to provide for their families. More important, from a military standpoint, many were good marksmen, very loyal to family and friends, and harbored an intense hatred of the British. The king of Spain, he predicted, could count on them to be "good vassals who, when the time comes, will gladly take up arms and sacrifice themselves to his royal service, in defence of his domains."

For now, the Acadians were more interested in spreading the word to their brethren that Louisiana was a land of promise and freedom. Some pioneers asked Ulloa's permission to contact relatives in the American colonies and invite them to emigrate. When the governor asked for time to consult his superiors, they displayed a typically Acadian disregard for authority and sent the letters anyway. Three groups arrived by ship from Maryland between September 1766 and February 1768. Among them were Isabelle Brasseux, a widow, and three other Acadians who had successfully petitioned a justice of the peace in their Maryland county to cover their passage. Word of the exodus spread to Pennsylvania and, during 1766 and 1767, as many as 200 exiles fled that colony for Louisiana on merchant ships. By Ulloa's account, many arrived in New Orleans "consumed by wretchedness and in the greatest possible need."

Smallpox and other diseases came along for the journey, as they had during the original deportations. The arrivals received fresh bread and biscuits, and when Ulloa gave an ox and calf to a group desperate for food, they slaughtered the animals on the spot and ate the meat raw.

The first Maryland refugees, a group of 224, settled along the banks of the Mississippi below present-day Baton Rouge, an area that came to be known as the Acadian Coast. Another 210 arrived in the summer of 1767 and were established farther upriver, at Fort St. Gabriel, where the wooden church they built in the 1770s still stands as a modest monument to their tenacity. The final shipload of 150 exiles was dispatched to Fort San Luis de Natchez, hundreds of miles inland.

Dispersing the colonists along the Mississippi served Ulloa's defensive strategy, but it put him at loggerheads with the Acadians and their desire to regroup and replicate their close-knit homeland. The contingent assigned to Fort St. Gabriel demanded land closer to their kinsmen, but relented when Ulloa threatened to expel them from the colony.

The last group of 150 Maryland arrivals was mostly one extended family, the Brauds. Its leaders, brothers Honoré and Alexis Braud, had been deported from Piziquid in 1755; they were adamant they would not be separated from their countrymen a second time. Ulloa dug in his heels, cutting off Honoré Braud's rations and then ordered him to be deported. The Braud brothers jumped ship to avoid arrest and went into hiding. The rest of the group departed for San Luis de Natchez as ordered, but in the months that followed, they bombarded Spanish officials with demands to relocate among relatives downriver. Their grievances were valid—the lands around the outpost were poor for farming and exposed to attack by tribes allied with the British. An exasperated Ulloa, echoing every French and British governor who had tried to rule the unruly Acadians, complained of their insubordination, their "sense of liberty and independence, and the little regard they show for the advantages which they have just received under the protection of His Majesty."

The Acadians' honeymoon with the Spanish was over. The French and Creole merchants of New Orleans were also chafing under the Spanish administration. Louisiana's elite had opposed Spanish rule—an eleventh-hour appeal to the king of France to halt the takeover had failed—and was fed up with Ulloa for restricting trade with France, particularly imports of French wine. In October 1768 they organized a coup. Hundreds of settlers, including as many as 300 Acadians, descended on New Orleans where they were armed with muskets and fortified with wine. Ulloa, with only a handful of soldiers at his disposal, fled without a fight. He retreated to a ship moored in the Mississippi River and escaped to Cuba, never to return.

It was more of an early Mardi Gras than a rebellion, with boozy rebels roaming the streets and celebrating their victory with shouts of *"Vive le roi"* and *"Vive le bon vin de Bordeaux."* The rebellion's leaders set up a provisional government, but were ousted the following summer when the Spanish returned with a large army under the command of Alexander O'Reilly, an Irish mercenary. Alejandro O'Reilly, as he styled himself, was named governor and patched up relations with the Acadians. After reviewing the Brauds' grievances, O'Reilly agreed to allow the settlers at San Luis de Natchez to relocate closer to existing Acadian settlements.

Political upheaval and a lingering distrust of the Spanish halted the first wave of Acadian immigration to Louisiana. The last large group to arrive in the 1760s endured a harrowing, ten-month journey. In January 1769 about 100 Maryland Acadians boarded the *Britain*, an unfortunate name for a schooner hired as their one-way ticket from British rule. When the ship arrived at the mouth of the Mississippi River about six weeks later, high winds drove it westward to the Texas coast. Provisions ran out and, by one account, passengers "subsisted on the rats, cats and even all the shoes and leather on the vessel." When they came ashore in search of food—a horse grazing near the beach quickly became that day's meal—Spanish authorities seized the vessel and jailed the passengers and crew as smugglers. Some of the prisoners worked at hard labor before they were released.

After walking hundreds of miles to Natchitoches, a fort deep in the Louisiana wilderness—and after evading the local commandant's attempts to keep them as settlers—the Acadians paddled canoes down the Red and Mississippi Rivers to New Orleans, finally arriving in early November. The group was granted land along the Mississippi River the following spring.

Refugees continued to arrive from the American colonies in dribs and drabs in the 1770s, coming by ship or taking overland routes through the wilderness. About 1,000 Acadians were carving out new homesteads and adjusting to the heat of the Louisiana summer by the time the Revolutionary War broke out in 1776. The war gave the transplanted Acadians something they had dreamed of for a long time—a chance to even the score with the British. When Spain joined the war on the American side in 1779, Louisiana governor Bernardo de Gálvez seized the opportunity to drive the British from the east bank of the Mississippi and reclaim the Florida Panhandle. A call went out for volunteers, and older Acadian men, who had endured the humiliation of the deportation, joined sons born in exile and eagerly signed up. Among them, not surprisingly, were two of Beausoleil Broussard's sons, Amand and Claude, and three of their Broussard cousins. The desertions that had hobbled the defense of Fort Beauséjour were a thing of the past. With Acadians accounting for half of his regiments, Gálvez overran forts at Manchac, Baton Rouge, Natchez, Mobile, and Pensacola, driving the British from the region.

No exile seems to have been itching to fight the British more than Michel Trahan. His parents, Jean Baptiste and Madeleine, were among the Acadians barred from landing in Virginia in 1755. Sent to England, where they were married in Liverpool in 1757, they relocated to France after the Treaty of Paris. Michel was born in Morlaix in August 1764 and the family was among those who tried to make a go of it on Belle-Île-en-Mer. Michel was just fifteen when he came to America in 1779 with the Marquis de Lafayette's armies to support the rebel colonists. According to a newspaper article published after his death at the age of 100, Trahan was present when Lord Cornwallis surrendered at Yorktown, Virginia in 1781. Thanks to the forces of time and coincidence, an exiled Acadian savored the spectacle of a British general—the nephew of the founder of Halifax, no less—humbled on the soil of the very colony that had rejected his parents.

Olivier Terrio was working in his cobbler's shop in Nantes one day in 1783 when a talkative gentleman arrived, looking for someone to repair his wife's shoes. His name, he said, was Henri Peyroux de La Coudrenière. A druggist by trade, he was back in his native Nantes to visit relatives after spending seven years in Louisiana. Louisiana—did Terrio know of it, that veritable paradise where so many Acadians had gathered? For Terrio and other exiles living in limbo in the slums of French seaports like Nantes, the word had become synonymous with hope and freedom. Peyroux did his best to feign surprise when Terrio offered that he, was an Acadian, deported to France from Nova Scotia with his family in the late 1750s while just a boy. Now thirty-one, Terrio was outraged at the French government's treatment of the exiles who had washed up on its shores. "So poor," he would later write, "with many children and no schools, eaten up with despair and the constant deception of false promises ... of our receiving lands as the reward of faithful attachment to France." Many had gravitated to this medieval city at the mouth of the Loire River. While the merchants of Nantes grew rich by building and chartering ships for the slave trade, the Acadians subsisted on a daily dole and found what work they could. Terrio and his Acadian wife, Marie Aucoin, wanted better for their three young children.

Peyroux's visit was no coincidence. Invariably described in the history books as a "soldier of fortune," he was a slick promoter who had lost a bundle in Louisiana. His latest get-rich-quick scheme was to resettle France's disgruntled Acadians in Louisiana. Spain desperately needed people on the ground to prevent Louisiana from being gobbled up in the westward expansion of the newly independent American colonies.

The Acadians desperately wanted to get out of France and reunite with their long-lost cousins. Peyroux would act as the middleman and earn fat commissions from a grateful Spanish government. The Spanish ambassador to France, the Count de Aranda, and his secretary, Ignacio Heredia, were already onside. But Peyroux knew the Acadians would be wary; the French had turned down repeated requests to emigrate to Louisiana, and too many resettlement schemes had failed. He needed a front man to sell the idea, an Acadian with passion and credibility. Terrio had both and was literate to boot, having studied Latin for three years as a teenager before abandoning plans to enter the priesthood. A deal was done. Peyroux would work out the arrangements with the Spanish and French governments and Terrio would sell the idea of a mass exodus to the Acadians. Terrio would receive "honorable and lucrative" compensation for his efforts and, in the event of failure, Peyroux promised to "share his last morsel of bread" with his partner.

Terrio stopped repairing soles and threw himself into the work of saving souls. He wrote letters and lobbied Acadians in Nantes and surrounding cities, but, at first, there was little enthusiasm for the scheme. By July he could convince only four other Acadians to sign a petition seeking Spain's permission to emigrate to Louisiana and rejoin family and friends. Despite the meager show of support, the petition was forwarded to Madrid. Timing is everything and, as it happened, Louisiana governor Bernardo de Gálvez was in town and endorsed the scheme. The Spanish monarch, Charles III, assented in October 1783 and, more important, agreed that his government would cover the costs of transporting and resettling the Acadians.

Peyroux, who was on the verge of giving up, was ecstatic at the news. He urged Terrio to redouble his efforts to recruit settlers and headed for Brittany to spread the word. Their zeal almost scuttled the project. The Spanish had yet to approach their counterparts in Paris, and the French government learned of the scheme in March 1784 when a group of skeptical Acadians confronted officials in Nantes to find out if they were free to leave. Heredia, the Spanish ambassador's secretary, managed to avert a diplomatic incident by coming clean and admitting his government had been in contact with the Acadians. Spain followed up with a formal request to the king of France to remove the Acadians, supported by a new petition from Terrio bearing thirty-five names. Louis XVI approved the Louisiana resettlement plan in May, but not before the authorities in Nantes issued arrest warrants for Peyroux and Terrio, accusing them of being illegal foreign agents. Peyroux was thrown in prison, but Terrio managed to find refuge in the home of a sympathetic judge until the warrants were rescinded and Peyroux was released.

Recruitment could be conducted openly. Terrio, billing himself as "Spain's official agent," encountered resistance. Some Acadians saw the venture as a ploy to cut off the dole they received from the French government. Terrio complained that Acadians in Nantes cursed and insulted him, and one even threatened to kill him. An uglier incident awaited him at an inn in another seaport. A heated debate with three Acadians who opposed emigration turned violent. As Terrio recalled, one of the men "assaulted me like a desperado, struck me several times, and would undoubtedly have killed me if some friendly Acadians, who took his knife away, had not intervened." Despite such setbacks, about 1,500 Acadians—more than two-thirds of the exiles in France—signed on.

It took months for Aranda's officials to negotiate contracts with shipowners, bumping the departure date into 1785. There would be no repeat of the appalling conditions Acadians had endured aboard the deportation ships. Spanish officials ensured their new citizens would be as comfortable as possible on a voyage that could take up to three months. There was plenty of food and water, coal and firewood for cooking, room for trunks and furniture, and a doctor was assigned to each ship. Great care was taken to send extended families and friends on the same ship.

The first vessel, *Le Bon Papa*, arrived at New Orleans in July 1785 with 156 Acadians and the loss of only one passenger, a child who died at sea. Terrio and his family were among the 273 passengers on *La Bergère*, which arrived in mid-August. Six elderly passengers died, but seven children were born during the voyage. A speedy frigate, *Le Beaumont*, brought Peyroux and his wife and about 170 other people. As it became clear the Spanish meant business, Acadians who had been hedging their bets clamored for space on the ships. The *St. Rémy* sailed from France on June 20 with the largest group, more than 320 men, women, and children and 16 stowaways. It was more people than the ship could comfortably accommodate and smallpox broke out, killing a dozen children at sea and sixteen more passengers after the ship landed at New Orleans.

Sickness and death dogged the remaining ships—*La Amistad* lost 6 of its 270 passengers, and about 10 percent of the 300 people aboard *La Ville d'Arcangel* fell ill during the voyage. *La Caroline*, the last ship, sailed from Nantes in October.

Then the French government withdrew its support for the exodus, stranding the remaining Acadians in France regardless of whether they wanted to stay or go. Those left behind could only wonder how their lives would have been different in Louisiana. When Oscar Winzerling visited Nantes shortly after the Second World War while researching a book on the Acadians in France, an elderly Acadian descendant showed him the street where Olivier

Terrio once repaired shoes. "What a mistake my great grandfather made in not accepting Terrio's advice to go to Louisiana," the man lamented. "See, Sir, how poor I am today." In all, 1,624 Acadians set out for Louisiana in what was said to be the largest single project to colonize North America.

The Acadians found the Spanish were as good as their word. There were hospitals for the sick and a compound of tents and barracks where immigrants could recuperate for a month. The local administrator, Martin Navarro, welcomed each shipload, and was so popular, he was named godfather of countless Acadian children born at sea. According to one account, there were joyful celebrations as young couples who had met during the voyages were married in the Acadian camps, their new lives symbolizing the rebirth of a culture in a new land.

Four of the seven shiploads chose homesteads along Bayou Lafourche, a river that runs roughly parallel to the Mississippi River and spills into the Gulf of Mexico south of New Orleans. Two groups settled in the Baton Rouge area. The passengers on *La Ville d'Archangel* had the misfortune of selecting land along the Bayou des Ecores, which was devastated by a hurricane in 1794. The arrivals from France marked the end of large-scale Acadian immigration to Louisiana. A final group of nineteen stragglers arrived in 1788 from the island of St. Pierre, the only Acadians to arrive directly from the neighborhood of Acadie. They brought to more than 2,600 the number of exiles to seek refuge in Louisiana.

As for Peyroux and Terrio, the partnership forged in the Nantes cobbler's shop did not last long. Peyroux snubbed Terrio as they prepared to leave France in May 1785, rejecting the Acadian's plea for money to settle up with his creditors. Peyroux, who had no further use for a middleman, was said to have "offered only insults" and refused Terrio's plea for a letter informing the Spanish of his recruitment efforts. Terrio's fellow Acadians chipped in to settle his debts so he could leave, and chose him to serve as their representative or "chief" aboard *La Bergère*.

In New Orleans, Terrio again confronted Peyroux and demanded the rewards he had been offered two years earlier. "I have promised you nothing," was Peyroux's haughty reply. Terrio filed a formal complaint against Peyroux with the Louisiana governor in 1792, but was never compensated.

He gave up and focused on his farm on Bayou Lafourche, where he and Marie raised their three children and four more born in Louisiana. Terrio died in 1829, forgotten by the French and Spanish governments, but hailed as a hero among the Acadians of Louisiana.

Peyroux, in contrast, has been condemned as an opportunist who was more interested in his own advancement than the welfare of the Acadians. He arrived in New Orleans with a fat salary from the Spanish government as an immigration agent. Commissions as a captain in the Spanish army and as commandant of a territorial post in present-day Missouri followed in 1786. He was still in office at the time of the Louisiana Purchase of 1803. If Terrio had bothered to follow Peyroux's subsequent career, he would have derived some satisfaction when his old partner became the victim of broken promises. The Louisiana government sent Peyroux on a mission to recruit settlers in the United States, but when he returned in 1794, refused to pay his wages and travel expenses.

Carl Brasseaux dubs the exercise "Colonial Survivor," a classroom version of the reality television craze. Students in his Cajun history classes at the University of Louisiana Lafayette pretend they have been issued the same tools and supplies that the Spanish offered Beausoleil Broussard and his followers in 1765. There are four saws for every 200 people, four families share an ax, and so on. Some of those goods, meager as they are, will be confiscated by greedy Spanish commandants. Each would-be settler consults a topographical map of the Bayou Teche area and chooses a site for a homestead. In this version of "Survivor," though, no one is voted off the bayou. Survival in the Louisiana wilderness in the mid-eighteenth century was a matter of making good choices and plenty of good luck.

"Those who make mistakes die," as Brasseaux bluntly puts it. It is the same for his students, who are asked to move to the side of the classroom as bad decisions take their toll. Even the ones who make the right choices may find themselves among those felled by epidemics or tropical diseases. One by one, students succumb to cholera, dysentery, malaria, and unspecified fevers, just like Broussard and many of his followers. By the end of the exercise the walls of the classroom are lined with students and Brasseaux has made a vivid point about the brutal odds the Acadian immigrants faced.

"If you were a refugee today, would the Amazon Basin be your first choice?" Brasseaux asks in his snug corner office atop the university's library in Lafayette. "That was exactly the way the world viewed Louisiana at the time. And with good reason, because this was an extremely unhealthy area. It was relatively primitive."

Brasseaux, arguably, has done more than any other scholar to clear up the muddied waters of Louisiana history and separate fact from fiction. The fifty-three-year-old director of the university's Center for Louisiana Studies has written the definitive books on the century-long transformation of Acadian exiles into Louisiana Cajuns. His titles—professor of history, director of the Center for Cultural Studies and Eco-Tourism, editor of both the state's histori-cal newsletter and its historical journal—almost outnumber his prodigious publications. When not writing, studying, or teaching history, this undisputed authority on the Acadians and their descendants in Louisiana somehow finds time to publish fiction and poetry under the pseudonym Antoine Bourque. Even though his desk is piled high with books and files that scream for attention, he's never too busy to share his insights into Cajun history and culture.

"It's been an odyssey of self-discovery," he says, his salt-and-pepper mus-tache stretching in either direction when he breaks into a wide grin, which is often. Brasseaux's ancestors, Cosme and Isabelle Brasseux, were deported from Grand-Pré in 1755 and endured the deprivations of exile in Maryland. Cosme died sometime before 1763, leaving his widow to do anything she could—"from begging door-to-door to prostitution," he suspects—to sup-port her young children. Also known as Élisabeth, she was the woman who boldly petitioned a Maryland justice of the peace for passage to Louisiana. She settled with her children in 1767 at Fort St. Gabriel. But like Beausoleil Broussard and so many of Brasseaux's students, she did not last long in the tropical wilderness. While burial records for those early years are spotty, he's convinced she died sometime before 1773. The children survived and his grandfather, who scratched out a living growing 10 acres of cotton north of Lafayette, added the extra letter "a" to the surname.

Brasseaux knew none of this family history until he pursued graduate studies at the University of Lafayette in the 1970s. In his day Louisiana children encountered their state's history in grade eight, and the textbook contained just two paragraphs about the Acadians-turned-Cajuns. The first was a summary of Longfellow's *Evangeline*. "And the second," he recalls with a chuckle, "announced the demise of the culture." Few Acadian descendants knew their history, assuming that their forebears must have been from France—most of them still spoke French as their first language, after all. Few people made a connection between the fiction of *Evangeline* and their heritage, and those who did were happy to let the past remain in the past. "This was a society that had been universally denigrated for a century," Brasseaux explains.

He got serious about history just as Cajuns embarked on the cultural renaissance that has made their lively music and spicy cooking known worldwide. The Spanish archives were opened after General Franco's death in the mid-1970s, making millions of pages of Louisiana's colonial records available to scholars. Brasseaux began studying a minor French colonial official and wound up unearthing an incredible story of Acadian survival.

The Acadians who arrived between 1766 and 1788 were thrust into an alien world. Alligators and snakes stalked the steamy swamps and bayous, beasts the newcomers must have found more fanciful than menacing. Wispy strands of gray-green Spanish moss cascaded from the cypress and oak trees. The oaks stayed green year-round, with fresh leaves constantly replacing the old and earning them the name live oaks. If the strange flora and fauna did not jolt the Acadians into realizing they were in a new land, the climate soon did. Temperatures in mid-summer topped 90°F and rarely dipped below 40°F in the depths of winter. It snows in southern Louisiana roughly once every fifteen years. Brasseaux's oldest son is pushing thirty and has seen it snow twice, and only once was there enough to make a decent snowball.

The seasons are the mirror image of those in Acadie: eight months of steamy summer weather and four of cool, rainy winter, versus the short summers and snowy deep-freeze of most winters along the Bay of Fundy. Visit southern Louisiana in early November and expect to hear the locals comment on the chilly weather, even though daytime highs drift into the upper seventies. What Louisiana lacks in snow and cold it makes up for in unbearably humid summers, heavy downpours, and the odd scrape with a tropical storm or hurricane blowing in from the Gulf of Mexico. The climate came as a shock to the new arrivals. "The heavy rains, the harsh sun, and the great fickleness of the weather has been the cause of some sickness among the Acadians," the commandant of Fort St. Gabriel noted in 1767. There was one annoying constant—mosquitoes, which were plentiful enough to merit a word unique to the Cajun lexicon, *maringouin*.

The Acadians adapted to their new surroundings with resourcefulness and survival skills honed in exile. Wheat, barley, and oats would not grow well in the hot, wet weather, so farmers along the Mississippi and the bayous switched to corn. Flax was also hard to grow and wool was too hot to wear, so the Acadians planted and spun cotton to make clothing. Wooden shoes were suited to working in wet fields, but the mild weather allowed people to go barefoot much of the time. Homemade palmetto hats and wide-brimmed bonnets offered protection from the sun. Okra, an African vegetable brought to Louisiana by slaves, was absorbed into the Acadian diet in soups and eventually became the basis for the spicy gumbos that are synonymous with Cajun cuisine.

Families again established orchards, but the long growing season—up to 300 days in some regions—meant that apples gave way to peaches, figs, apricots, and grapes. The prairies stretching west of Bayou Teche to the Texas border offered open grassland for raising cattle. Horses were more abundant than in Acadie and the prairie Acadians became the first American cowboys, carving out large ranches and driving herds of longhorns overland to the slaughterhouses of New Orleans. By the early 1800s, the average Acadian ranch or *vacherie* boasted 125 head of cattle. The Acadians had to adapt their dwellings as well. Early homes preserved in Louisiana parks look much like their counterparts in Maritime Canada, with a couple of rooms and a few rustic furnishings. But thatched roofs and other features designed to retain heat were out, and plenty of windows to circulate the air and wide verandas to provide protection from the sun and rain were in. Acadian homes in Louisiana were raised above the ground on pilings to protect against periodic floods and termites. Despite the ravages of disease and the heat, Louisiana truly became the Acadians' promised land. "Within ten years," Brasseaux writes in his book

The Founding of New Acadia, "most of the exiles attained a standard of living at least equal to that of predispersal Nova Scotia."

As in Acadie, the extended family was the center of Acadian life. The Spanish relented on their policy of spreading out settlers, and most newcomers congregated in family-dominated settlements as they had in their homeland. In Louisiana, the Acadians proved as prolific as ever and their population rose to about 4,000 by 1800. Families of six to ten children were common, which soon put pressure on the original settlements. Land grants were laid out in long ribbons stretching back from the riverfronts, affording access to the outside world and sharing the burden of building levees to hold back floodwaters. But under Spanish succession laws, when the head of a family died, the farm was carved up among the children in equal portions. After a single generation, Brasseaux points out, much of the land was subdivided into narrow strips that were almost impossible to farm.

The development of a method to granulate sugar and the influx of American entrepreneurs and their money after the Louisiana Purchase rapidly transformed the economy. Huge tracts of land were needed to produce sugarcane, and large numbers of slaves were pressed into the unending work of tending and cutting cane. Americans bought out most of the small Acadian farms along the lower Mississippi and consolidated them into sprawling plantations, with the grand, colonnaded homes that became a southern icon and the rundown slave shacks that became a southern disgrace. The displacement was so thorough that Acadian names are scarce on the oversized, pre–Civil War map of Mississippi plantations that dominates one wall of Brasseaux's office. The Acadians headed west to unoccupied lands on the prairies, to hunt and trap in the cypress swamps of the broad Atchafalaya Basin, to fish the gulf of Mexico, or to establish their own sugarcane operations along the bayous. American writer William Faulkner Rushton likened the exodus to a second expulsion, albeit a voluntary one rooted in economics rather than imperial rivalry.

Relations between the Acadians and their neighbors were tense in the early years. Louisiana had been a French colony for more than a half-century before the Acadians showed up, complete with its own social structure. The Creoles saw the Acadians as perfect candidates to occupy the bottom tier of Louisiana's White society, peasant farmers who were one rung above freed

Blacks and well below "their betters," the aristocracy of European-born and Creole planters and merchants. This social pressure-cooker erupted into disputes over cattle and property lines that often turned violent. One Acadian hothead, Basile Préjean, broke into a commandant's office to attack a Creole neighbor who was in the process of swearing a complaint alleging an earlier assault at Préjean's hands. The Acadians kept to themselves, a visitor noted in 1804, and "had little to do with the families who are pretentious."

The Acadians displayed the same zest for life that had worried their priests in Acadie. Horseracing and billiards became passions for the men, and everyone, from grandparents to children, gathered to kick up their heels at spirited *bals de maison*, a precursor of the rural dance halls that still dot Cajun country. Fiddlers were the stars of the show, playing music that evoked memories of the carefree days before the deportation. There was plenty of gumbo and, to wash it down, rum distilled from sugarcane. The dances and *joie de vivre* reflected a blend of old and new that gradually forged a new Cajun identity as zesty as the food and as exotic as its near-tropical setting, yet retaining its strong Acadian undertones.

Brasseaux says a distinct Cajun identity emerged by 1812, the year Louisiana achieved statehood. In the decades that followed, the trappings that most people associate with Cajun culture appeared. Shrimp, crawfish, and rice became staples, and hot-pepper sauce became the seasoning of choice. Cajun musicians borrowed from the country swing of Texas and the Caribbean-inspired zydeco rhythms of their Black neighbors to produce a new sound track for a new land. A distinctive dialect, with centuries-old roots in France, emerged in isolation from both France and Acadian cousins establishing new communities in Maritime Canada. *Pleuvoir* may mean "to rain" in France and Acadie, but to a Cajun it's *mouillier*. There were no raccoons in France, so the Cajuns adapted a native word, *chaoui*. The French put the words for bull and frog together into the unwieldly term *grenouille taureau*; Cajuns mimicked the *wah-wah-rawn* of the bullfrog's croak to create their own word for the pond dwellers, *ouaouaron*.

It is unsettling to discover that the Acadians' experiences as an oppressed and exploited people in exile did not prevent them from embracing slavery. Louisiana's Acadians began buying slaves to help work their farms as early as the 1770s. Within four decades a majority of households in most Acadian parishes owned at least one slave, and by 1860 forty-nine Acadians could boast of owning more than fifty slaves apiece. Slavery marked a major break with the Acadians' egalitarian leanings and long tradition of live and let live. Brasseaux sees several factors at work—the need to exploit slave labor to compete with other farmers, the prestige it brought within slave-owning Creole society, and the need to close ranks with other Whites to protect themselves from runaway slaves. He suspects the Acadians' fear of Mi'kmaq reprisals in the years before the deportation may have been projected on the Blacks they encountered in Louisiana. While some Acadian descendants joined the vigilante groups that terrorized Blacks and Whites alike just before and after the Civil War, the notorious Ku Klux Klan never gained a toehold in southern Louisiana—the Klan was anti-Catholic as well as anti-Black.

The Acadians never wavered from their Catholic faith in exile, but Acadian men scorned the priests imported from France and French Canada to staff Louisiana's churches. Stories abound of men escorting their wives and children to church, retiring under the shade of a nearby tree to smoke and swap jokes during the sermon, then filing into the back of the church in time to take communion. It was apparently an improvement over an earlier practice of smoking and swapping jokes on the church steps. There are less credible tales of priests ducking outside in mid-sermon to stop the more exuberant members of their flock from racing horses around the church.

There's a kernel of truth in such tales that Brasseaux says reflects the Acadians' ingrained stubbornness and resistance to authority. "These are people who survived on the basis of wits and their ability to stand up to challenges and to adapt to challenges," he says, leaning back in his chair as he ponders Acadian resilience in the face of unimaginable adversity. "The reason that they survived here, I think, is because of those two traits: they're pragmatic and they're also as stubborn as hell." Stubbornness is a wonderful survival mechanism as well as a double-edged sword—remember the steadfast refusal to swear an oath of allegiance that landed the Acadians in exile. There's an old saying, Brasseaux adds, that does the rounds in the ranching country west of Lafayette: "You can tell a Cajun a mile off, but you can't tell him a damn thing up close."

James Akers is a walking encyclopedia of Louisiana's Acadian history. The sixty-three-year-old retired department-store employee and guide at the Acadian Memorial in St. Martinville is also a flesh-and-blood example of the melting pot of cultures and ethnic backgrounds that have fused to create today's Cajuns. "We're all a mixture now," he explains, the breast pocket of his navy T-shirt bulging with a pack of smokes eager to be pressed into service at his next break. "There are very few people who are pure Acadian in Louisiana now."

In the case of this laid-back southern gentleman with the gentle drawl and gray goatee, that's an understatement. The branches of his extensive family tree spread out like the limbs of a live oak, embracing ancestors who were English, Scottish, Irish, German, and what he calls "French of the lesser nobility of France." And Acadians—lots of them, including the famous Beausoleil Broussard. In the memorial's courtyard, overlooking the sluggish Bayou Teche and a replica of the deportation cross at Grand-Pré, frescos preserve the coats of arms of nineteen families who settled in Louisiana. Akers is related to a dozen of them and rattles off a few of the names: Trahan, Breaux, LeBlanc, Cormier, Dugas, Blanchard, Thibodeaux. Some insist that, with his pedigree, his surname must have been anglicized from the French word for acres of land. "To many people," he says, having set the stage for a well-worn punch line, "I'm Jean Arpent."

And to some folks in St. Martinville, Akers is a traitor and a heretic because he insists on telling visitors the truth—there never was an Evangeline or a Gabriel. "It's just a story," he says, repeating his heresy. "Those two people never existed."

St. Martinville is a city built around Longfellow's tragic heroine, who has been clothed in a new name and a new mythology for the New Acadia. A section of the poem *Evangeline* is set in "the Eden of Louisiana ... the region where reigns perpetual summer," and makes specific reference to the town of St. Martin on "the banks of the Têche." In his one-man mission to preserve some aspects of Acadian history and distort the rest, Longfellow portrayed Evangeline and a band of exiles rafting down the Mississippi in search of refuge, even though virtually all Acadians arrived by ship through New Orleans.

Evangeline, of course, is still looking for her lost Gabriel. Somewhere in the expanse of the Atchafalaya swamps, the lovers pass like ships in the night. Gabriel, headed to the backcountry with a band of trappers, paddles past Evangeline and her exhausted rafters as they slumber on an island, concealed from view by a screen of fan like palmettos. The next day the southbound Evangeline finds Gabriel's father, Basil, the blacksmith, who has been transformed into the sombrero-wearing, cattle-herding Basil, the cowboy. Gabriel, she discovers, has been pining for his lost love, and Basil, hoping to cheer him up, has just sent him north on a mission to trade for horses. After Basil assures the heartbroken Evangeline she can easily overtake her northbound lover and the couple will be reunited at last, Acadian neighbors and a fiddler come out of the woodwork for a joyful reunion party.

Basil welcomes his lost cousins to "a home, that is better perchance than the old one," where he boasts that "no hungry winter congeals our blood like the rivers" and grass grows "more in a single night than a whole Canadian summer." Best of all, "No King George of England shall drive you away from your homesteads," he assures the newcomers, "burning your dwellings and barns, and stealing your farms and your cattle." Evangeline, unaware that Longfellow's plotline has condemned her to find Gabriel on his deathbed many years in the future, drifts away from the revelers and wanders into Basil's garden. Standing "beneath the brown shade of the oak-trees," she surveys the Louisiana prairie and wonders how many times Gabriel has stood on this very spot and thought of her.

It's not hard to find an Evangeline oak in St. Martinville. No fewer than three broad-limbed live oaks have held the title since the turn of the last century, and a fourth is growing in the wings. Akers is happy to provide a genealogy of these revered trees. The first stood on the bank of the Teche a short distance below the Acadian Memorial. It was not the one where Evangeline stood as she yearned for Gabriel—these are fictional characters, after all—but it is the tree where local women gathered each week to do their washing. Tradition holds the tree was destroyed long ago when a campfire under a laundry tub set it ablaze. The spot is now a boat ramp. Oak number two is slightly closer to the memorial and stands in the backyard of a heritage building that once lodged steamboat travelers. The tree is still there, but since it's on private property—and a magnet for tourists and Acadian pilgrims seeking branches and acorns as souvenirs—a gnarled oak on the riverbank has served as the Evangeline Oak since the 1920s. It claims the title of the world's most photographed tree. Conveniently located next door to the memorial, the moss-covered oak is old enough to have been here in the days when St. Martinville was Poste des Attakapas and Acadians were settling along the Teche. And like the Acadians, it has survived more than its share of adversity. A spotlight installed in the branches fell off in a storm a dozen years ago, sparking a fire that blackened one side of the trunk. The damage is still visible and Akers points out the concrete pillar inserted, like a tooth filling, to shore up its base after floodwaters weakened the roots. One of the tree's offspring stands beside it, ready to take on the job of Evangeline Oak when the time comes.

In the shadow of this ailing and aging giant, a metal plaque proclaims this "the legendary meeting place of Emmeline Labiche and Louis Arceneaux, the counterparts of Evangeline and Gabriel." This is where the new mythology begins. Felix Voorhies, a Louisiana judge and one of St. Martinville's native sons, published a book in 1907 purporting to tell the "true" story of Evangeline, as related by his Acadian grandmother. In his version of the tale, the heroine, Emmeline, was engaged to Louis when they were whisked from Grand-Pré in separate ships. They meet again years later under a towering oak tree in St. Martinville, but the ending is just as tragic as in Longfellow's version. When she discovers that Louis gave up hope of ever seeing her again and has married another, Emmeline is driven to madness.

The impact of Voorhies's book rivaled Longfellow's poem in Louisiana. The city fathers of St. Martinville, eager to attract tourists to replace business lost after the railroad bypassed the community, embraced the myth. "The whole town became a promotion of Evangeline," says Akers. The first oak was designated to mark the site of the bittersweet reunion. A crocheted handbag purporting to have belonged to Emmeline was put on display. The name Evangeline was soon plastered across South Louisiana—on storefronts, consumer products, and streets signs—just like in Nova Scotia, only it is pronounced *ee-van-ge-lyn* in these parts. The Lafayette phonebook lists more than two dozen businesses and organizations using the Evangeline name, including a bakery, an art gallery, a racetrack, a steakhouse, an animal hospital, and a Boy Scout troop. Writer William Faulkner Rushton has dubbed her "the reigning superstar of Acadian folklore and mythology."

Acadians from Canada began making pilgrimages to St. Martinville. Couples from all over the world, their heads full of Acadian romance, flocked to the city to be married under the oak. In one of his first books, Carl Brasseaux presented convincing proof that Voorhies's "true" story was a falsehood. There was a real Louis Arceneaux in Louisiana, but he was born after the deportation. And, as Akers points out, Labiche is not even an Acadian name. But Voorhies was a pillar of the community and since the story was good for business, his tall tale was accepted as gospel, and still is in some quarters. Hollywood moguls came to St. Martinville in 1929 to film a movie version of *Evangeline* starring the Mexican actress Dolores Del Rio in the lead role. Del Rio was so touched by the story that she paid half the cost of erecting a statue of Evangeline beside the city's historic St. Martin de Tours Church, and graciously agreed to serve as the sculptor's model. A plaque at its base describes the image as "the prototype of the Acadian maiden." When tourists ask for directions to Evangeline's statue, Akers feels compelled to bring them back to reality. "There's no Evangeline," he says for the umpteenth time. "That's the statue of a Mexican actress."

The Acadian Memorial opened in the mid-1990s to separate the facts of Louisiana history from the fiction. The main hall, once the city's market, is dominated by a 360-square-foot mural of a band of forty-five Acadians arriving in Louisiana. Present-day descendants of these pioneers posed for many of the faces, which flicker with smiles of hope and relief. Beausoleil Broussard stands front and center, flanked by Élisabeth Brasseux and Olivier Terrio. A push of a button launches a narration that relates their removal from Grand-Pré, the misery that awaited them in the American colonies and France, and the founding of New Acadia. A spotlight illuminates Broussard, Brasseux, and Terrio as they take turns describing their journeys to Louisiana.

A bronze plaque covers the opposite wall, recording in raised type the names of close to 3,000 of the original Acadian settlers, many of them children. "It's a blessed place, as far as I'm concerned," says Brenda Comeaux Trahan, the petite bundle of energy who serves as the memorial's curator and director. "It's a place where we can look at and touch the people who suffered to get here, who were separated from their loved ones." It is also a place where Acadian descendants can trace their families and get the hard facts on their history using the memorial's library and on-line genealogical database. "Longfellow's poem was not enough. It did not tell us who we are and why we're the way we are," she adds. The memorial attracts fewer than 2,000 visitors a year, a victim of a tourism slowdown in the wake of the 9–11 terror attacks and overlooked by tens of thousands of visitors who never make it beyond the Evangeline Oak. Those who drop in are exposed to a painful past that older generations of Louisiana Acadians thought was best forgotten. Comeaux Trahan remembers learning the bare-bones story of the deportation in school and asking her mother why she was never told about it. Her answer was *laissez ça tranquille*—leave that alone. It was a common attitude, one Comeaux Trahan suspects grew out of a lingering stigma that, somehow, the Acadians deserved to be banished from their homeland.

Carl Brasseaux says the trauma of the deportation is only part of the reason most Louisiana Acadians turned their backs on their history. "The Acadians here are a doubly defeated people," he points out. Most Acadians managed to make a better life for themselves in Louisiana, only to have their hard work wiped out during the Civil War. While some joined the ranks of the wealthy plantation class in antebellum Louisiana, most were small farmers who kept to themselves.

The Louisiana Purchase of 1803 and statehood in 1812 attracted English-speaking settlers and fortune-seekers from the United States. To the Acadians the newcomers were *les américains*, foreigners who went about their business in a world set apart by language and culture. The Acadians eagerly defended New Orleans against the hated British during the War of 1812, but had little interest in fighting for the Confederate cause in the 1860s. Even though many owned slaves, they did not see the Civil War as their war. Most resented being conscripted to fight for the rebel cause and deserted in droves. Union forces invaded southern Louisiana twice during the war, ravaging the countryside. Louisiana went from being the most prosperous state in the South to the nation's poorest one by 1870. The Acadians became dirt-poor subsistence farmers or hunters and trappers in a state where almost everyone was now dirt-poor.

The collapse of the class structure and intermarriage transformed the Acadians into the Cajuns, a polyglot that became the region's dominant culture. In a rare example of reverse assimilation, the Cajuns absorbed peoples of other backgrounds—Spanish, Germans, even the American interlopers—to create people like James Akers with their diverse backgrounds. It became common to find people with surnames like Walker, Lopez, Hymel, and McGee whose first or only language was French. A popular myth arose that the letter X was added to surnames like Comeaux, Boudreaux, and Thibodeaux because the backward Cajuns had to sign their names with an X. While illiteracy was the norm and compulsory schooling was not imposed until the twentieth century, Brasseaux has put that myth to rest. His painstaking research has shown that a judge who oversaw a census in 1820 arbitrarily added an X to surnames that ended in -*eau*, which is the proper way to pluralize such endings in French.

Cajun country was seen as a backwater, the quaint language and customs of its people the subject of ridicule. After the Civil War, a succession of Yankee journalists toured southern Louisiana and filed articles portraying the Cajuns as backward, lazy, and ignorant. An article describing them as "industrious and prosperous" in 1875 was an exception to an avalanche of bad press. A correspondent for the influential *Harper's Weekly* stereotyped the Cajuns in 1866 as "primitive people"—poor, inbred, and "grossly" ignorant. Another dismissed them in 1873 as "the least intelligent of the Creole population," with no ambition other than to "digest well by day and sleep well at night." An 1879 article in the widely read *Scribner's Monthly* provided a slightly more balanced view. R.L. Daniels looked down his nose at the Cajuns for their lack of education and ambition, not to mention their lives of "simple pleasures and easy work," but he acknowledged their hospitality and willingness to help a neighbor in need. This faint praise gave way to his damning conclusion that the Cajuns displayed none of "the enterprise, strength of character, or intellect" of other French emigrés. *Harper's* took a second look at Cajun country in 1887 and suggested the Acadians had been fortunate to exchange the "bleak meadows" of Grand-Pré for the "sunny, genial and fertile lands" they occupied in Louisiana. "Nowhere else on the continent *could* they so well have preserved their primitive habits, or found climate and soil so suited to their humor."

Dismissed as White trash, their culture denigrated and ridiculed, Cajuns desperate to climb the social ladder embraced the legends of Evangeline and Emmeline. The legends took hold, celebrating the past while obscuring the truth. The Acadian Memorial is a monument to the truth about one of Louisiana's founding peoples, but it struggles to have its voice heard above the din of Evangeline and her namesake oak.

One of Comeaux Trahan's first jobs out of college was assessing the mental health of the elderly, and she always asked those of Acadian descent what they knew about their past. Most had heard of *Evangeline*, but few made a connection to their own families. Because French was their first language, they thought their ancestors must have come from France. Yet not one of the scores of men and women in their seventies, eighties, and nineties she interviewed had learned of their Nova Scotia roots from their parents. For generations, the subject was taboo. An eternal flame burns in the memorial's courtyard and an inscription chiseled into its granite base reads, "*Un peuple sans passé est un peuple sans futur*"—a people without a past is a people without a future.

Carl Brasseaux has supplied the hard evidence of Louisiana's Acadian story. James Akers is trying to correct the historical record, one visitor at a time. "Our mission," Comeaux Trahan says of the memorial, "is to help people get interested in their genealogy and their ancestry, and to be able to say, 'I'm proud to be a Cajun today.'

"Because there was a time," she adds, "when we were not proud."

9 THE SURVIVAL OF A PEOPLE

Let sleeping bears lie ... especially the one asleep on your own
doorstep. And that's why, when Acadie wrenched itself out of
exile at the end of the eighteenth century, it quit its crib so
quiet, with never a wail nor a shout, without even clapping its
hands. It came home by the back door, and on tiptoe. And when
the world got round to noticing, it was too late; Acadie already
had springs in its shanks and its nose in the wind.

—Antonine Maillet, *Pélagie: The Return to Acadie/Pélagie-la-Charrette*

Église Saint-Bernard emerges in all its Gothic splendor from the fog blowing
off Baie Sainte-Marie, as if conjured up by magic. Twin steeples of gray
granite rise seven storeys high and dwarf the houses and scrubby spruce
trees along Highway 1 as it snakes through the village of Saint-Bernard. The
walls of this fortress of faith are over 3 feet thick at the base and contain
more than 8,000 rectangular blocks of stone. Inside, a vaulted ceiling soars
upward, creating a million square feet of enclosed space and emulating the
great cathedrals of Europe. The wooden pews will accommodate 1,012 people, which means there's just about room for everyone in Saint-Bernard and
three of the neighboring villages.

This building, which defies its humble surroundings, is a monument not
only to the glory of God, but to the unshakeable faith and steely resolve of the
Acadian people. The farmers, fishermen, and lumbermen of the area built it
with their bare hands and their boundless ingenuity. Teams of oxen hauled the
stones over a gravel road from a railroad siding 2 miles away. Each one was cut

and dressed with hand chisels; every inch of woodwork was fashioned with hand tools. The plaster coating the soaring ceiling—all 96 tons of it—was hoisted upward on pulleys one bucket at a time. They began this Herculean task in 1910 and kept at it, year in and year out, through the First World War and the Great Depression and into the opening years of the Second World War. In 1942, after thirty-two years of toil, they were done. The project was managed from start to finish by Isaïe Belliveau, a local farmer described in the press as having "little knowledge of carpentry." Belliveau, who received a gold cross from the Pope in recognition of his dedication, took on the job at age forty-three and lived to burn the last mortgage on the building in 1950, when he was eighty-two.

Saint-Bernard and its imposing church mark the beginning of the Municipality of Clare in southwestern Nova Scotia, the province's largest Acadian community. Older residents call the area *la ville française* and their English neighbors call it the French Shore. Acadians freed from exile gravitated to this rocky shore when they "came home by the back door, and on tiptoe," as Antonine Maillet put it in her novel *Pélagie-la-Charrette*. The inspiration for her tale, in which a determined widow leads a caravan of ox-carts filled with exiles on a ten-year trek from the American colonies to Acadie, was the exodus of some 800 people from Massachusetts to Nova Scotia in the 1760s. Acadian writer Edouard Richard recounted the story in 1895 as he claimed to have heard it from descendants of those who trekked across Maine and New Brunswick:

> On foot, and almost without provisions, these pilgrims braved the perils and fatigues of a return by land, marching up the coast of the Bay of Fundy ... across six hundred miles of forest and uninhabited mountains ... dragging the slender baggage of misery .... How many died on the way, children, women and even men? How many breathed their last, overpowered by weariness, suffering from hunger, sitting down to be forgotten forever in some wild path, without priest, without consolation, without friends?

Some of the survivors settled in new Acadian communities being built in southern New Brunswick. About fifty families forged ahead to Nova Scotia, only to find their old villages renamed and their old lands occupied. These "ghosts come back from a past age," as Richard imagined them, pressed on through the lush farmland of the Annapolis Valley and kept going until they reached the shores of Baie Sainte-Marie.

Other communities sprang up in remote areas along the Nova Scotia coast, in keeping with governor Montagu Wilmot's plan to scatter the returning Acadians and keep them away from the coloney's new British settlers. Exiles from the Cape Sable area were able to reclaim some of their former lands, with the first families returning to the Pubnico area in 1766. Acadians who were held in Halifax during the war were allowed to settle in Chezzetcook, an uninhabited stretch of coast east of the city. The villages of Tracadie, Pomquet, and Harve Boucher along the shores of the Gulf of St. Lawrence were settled after 1772. Isle Madame at the base of Cape Breton Island, home to a few Acadian settlements before the deportation, became the focus of a thriving community of escapees and returning exiles.

The Chéticamp area along the mountainous northern coast of Cape Breton, first settled in 1782, was the last piece of the puzzle. Charles Robin, a merchant based in the Channel Islands, recruited Acadians to work at fishing stations he had established there, at Isle Madame, and on the Bay of Chaleur separating northern New Brunswick from Quebec. Acadians also returned to the Saint John River and the Petitcodiac and Memramcook valleys in the southern part of the province, where in the 1780s they took a backseat to a new wave of refugees—Loyalists fleeing the American Revolution.

On Prince Edward Island, the British name for Île Saint-Jean, Acadians resettled the western end of the island, opposite the New Brunswick mainland. The population grew rapidly. There were about 1,500 Acadians in the three colonies in 1771 and almost 9,000 thirty years later. By the 1880s the population was closing in on 120,000; about half were living in New Brunswick, where they formed a majority in three counties.

The Acadians were back, but, as Catholics, they endured second-class status. When Nova Scotia's legislature was established in 1758, the first laws passed wiped out Acadian claims to their confiscated lands and declared that no "papist" could own property. The law forbidding ownership remained on the books until 1783, but in practice Acadians were given title to their grants if they swore an oath of allegiance and cleared the land. It was illegal to publicly celebrate mass until the 1780s, and for decades it was illegal for Catholics to set up schools.

Acadians were also political outsiders. Catholics could not vote in Nova Scotia until 1789 and Acadians in New Brunswick and Prince Edward Island waited another twenty years for the right to cast a ballot. Catholics were barred from running for political office unless they swore an oath that renounced some of their core beliefs as "superstition and idolatry," as one oath phrased it. Thomas Chandler Haliburton, the writer and judge whose criticism of the deportation inspired Longfellow, led the fight to extend political rights to the Acadians. Nova Scotia finally abolished the oath in 1827 and the first Acadian members of any legislature in the Maritimes, Simon d'Entremont from Pubnico and Frédéric Armand Robichaud of Clare, were elected a decade later.

But old habits and prejudices died hard. When d'Entremont was sworn in, he was asked to sign the old oath, ostensibly to prove his loyalty to the British Crown. D'Entremont, a self-made man fluent in English and French, was defiant: "I would rather swallow a dogfish tail first, than swear to that," he replied, forcing the lieutenant governor to relent and administer the oath in its new form. Britain granted full political rights to Catholics in all colonies in 1830, paving the way for the election of the first Acadian member of the New Brunswick legislature in 1846. Prince Edward Island voters elected their first Acadian representative in 1854.

The Acadians became a people apart. The English majority in all three Maritime provinces dismissed the Acadians as backward, lazy, and inferior— "a half-way house between the Indians and the white people," a Protestant minister sniffed in the early 1800s. The expulsion left a legacy of animosity and distrust. A century after the deportation, one observer noted that Prince Edward Island's Acadians were compelled to avoid their neighbors "by the remembrances of the sufferings their fathers endured at the time of the conquest of these provinces by the English, and subsequently." Until the mid-1800s, Acadian historian Jean Daigle has noted, an outsider would scarcely have noticed that the Acadians had returned. Exclusion from mainstream society, he added, enabled Acadians to build new communities "where cherished values could be preserved: the Catholic religion, family and French language."

Freedom from outside interference—the freedom their ancestors craved when their homeland was a battleground—came at a cost. The Acadians were relegated to the poorest lands in the remotest areas. They farmed as best they could or turned to fishing, lumbering, and shipbuilding to feed their families. The church remained the center of the community, but decades passed before many areas were large enough to warrant their own priest or develop their own schools. By the beginning of the nineteenth century, the head of only one out of every five families could read and write.

A century after the deportations, though, Acadians had the numbers, leadership, and confidence needed to assert their identity. They found a heroine when Longfellow's *Evangeline* was translated into French, validating the stories of injustice and hardship handed down within Acadian families. A Quebec priest, Father Camille Lefebvre, founded Collège Saint-Joseph in Memramcook in the 1860s to educate an elite of professionals and clergymen. The first French-language newspaper, *Le Moniteur Acadien*, began publishing in 1867 in New Brunswick. A weekly paper, the aptly named *L'Evangéline*, rolled off the press twenty years later to serve Nova Scotia's Acadians.

In July 1881, 5,000 Acadians gathered at the Memramcook college for the first in a series of "national" conventions that laid the foundations for modern Acadie. The first order of business was to choose the trappings of a nation. While Acadians maintained close ties with their francophone counterparts in Quebec, history and distance gave them a distinct identity. The idea of adopting the Québécois patron, Saint John the Baptist, was rejected in favor of distinct Acadian symbols honoring the Virgin Mary. At the initial meeting in Memramcook, the Feast of the Assumption of Mary, August 15, was selected as the Acadian national day. Three years later, at a convention in the Prince Edward Island village of Miscouche, a flag and national anthem were chosen; the song was "Ave Maris Stella," a popular Catholic hymn dating to the ninth century. The flag was the red, white, and blue *tricouleur* of France with a five-pointed yellow star—the *stella maris*, or star of the sea—applied to the top corner of the blue band. The star, recognizing Mary as the patron of mariners, was an appropriate symbol for a people who survived a stormy voyage through exile and, once the storm cleared, steered a course for home.

Driving along the French Shore at the height of the Congrès mondial acadien 2004, there was no escaping this symbol of Acadian pride. The flag snapped in the stiff breeze on almost every flagpole along the highway from Saint-Bernard to Rivière-aux-Saumons. Smaller versions sprouted from lawns and mailboxes or flanked doorways. Red, white, and blue stripes decorated with a yellow star were splashed on garages, boulders, lobster traps, picnic tables, and, in one front yard, on a pair of driftwood stumps. A few miles along the shore from Saint-Bernard, in Pointe-de-l'Église, stands a seaside church as impressive, in its own way, as the one that took a generation to build. The 185-foot-high steeple of Église Sainte-Marie makes it the tallest wooden church in North America. Pointe-de-l'Église—Church Point, in English—is also home to l'Université Sainte-Anne, established in 1890 and Nova Scotia's only francophone institution of higher learning.

In August 2004 the university was the site of a symposium, held in conjunction with the *congrès*, that brought together Acadian scholars, writers, artists, politicians, and other movers and shakers to discuss the future of Acadie. Billed as Vision 20/20, the symposium examined an array of subjects, from promoting tourism and the challenges of conducting business on-line, to the role of education in preserving Acadian language and culture in the new millennium. The keynote speaker on the opening day, Maurice Basque, director of the Centre for Acadian Studies at l'Université de Moncton in New Brunswick, tackled the question, What is an Acadian?

The question seemed straightforward, but Basque's answer was controversial. Three million people around the world can trace their heritage to Acadie, but in Basque's view that does not make all of them Acadians. An Acadian, he asserted, is someone who lives within Atlantic Canada, an area that incorporates the traditional boundaries of Acadie, and speaks French on a daily basis. "There are Acadians in many places," he noted, "but there is only one Acadie." Madonna may have Acadian roots, but in his view the pop star should move to eastern Canada and sing in French before she can claim to be an Acadian.

But even as Basque advanced a narrow definition of what makes someone an Acadian, he called on his fellow Acadians to be more inclusive and to look beyond the founding families who reunite for each *congrès*. The modern Acadie that has risen from the old includes francophones with English surnames and French-speaking immigrants from Africa and Asia. The time has come, he said, to recognize the changing face of contemporary Acadian society. "Acadie now is more than this loose constellation of these pioneering families," he explained later to reporters. "It's very limiting [as a definition] and it gives the idea of a society that is of the past ... a society that is nostalgic for what it was."

Clive Doucet, an Ottawa city councillor with Chéticamp roots and the author of two books on what it means to be Acadian, took exception to the idea of imposing geographic limits on a people and its culture. Doucet speaks French, but would not meet Basque's criteria of what makes an Acadian because he lives in Ontario. Acadie has been "a place without borders since 1755," he responded in a radio interview, and the deportation created "a world community of Acadians." When a Halifax newspaper asked readers during the *congrès* to define what it means to be an Acadian, Roseline LeBlanc of West Pubnico replied that "Acadie has no specific boundaries, but wherever there is an Acadian, there is Acadie."

There was no dispute over Basque's contention that language is fundamental to being Acadian. The French language "is why there are still Acadians today," he told his audience at l'Université Sainte-Anne. "This is the common denominator. This is what cements us, this is our foundation." By that measure, Acadians now account for just 4 percent of the population of Nova Scotia. The 2001 census found that French is the mother tongue of 34,000 Nova Scotians, with a third of all francophones living in the province's largest city, Halifax. The French Shore, home to 6,300 Acadians, is the next largest community, with the Pubnico area and Cape Breton each having about 6,000 francophones. Just 5,600 residents of Prince Edward Island claimed French as their first language in 2001.

The use of French at home is a truer measure of the health of the language and on that front, Acadians in Nova Scotia and Prince Edward Island are losing ground in the battle against assimilation. As of 2001, only 19,000 of Nova Scotia's Acadians spoke French at home on a regular basis, down from 27,000 in 1971. Less than half of Prince Edward Island's francophones still use French at home, a sharp drop from the number thirty years earlier.

Canada's Acadian stronghold is New Brunswick, where 235,000 people—a third of the population—speak French as their mother tongue. It is the language almost all of them use every day because, in New Brunswick, French is one of the languages of everyday life. Canada is officially bilingual, offering federal government services in both languages to accommodate Quebec's francophone majority, the significant French-speaking minorities in Ontario and Manitoba, and the Acadians. But New Brunswick is Canada's only officially bilingual province (French is the only official language of Quebec) and has been since 1969 when Acadians won equal rights and access to provincial services in French. The first Acadian elected premier of the province, Louis Robichaud, made French an official language and also established l'Université de Moncton in the early 1960s. The university and its law school were the engine of a political and cultural resurgence, producing Acadian scholars and business and political leaders. Minority language and educational rights, enshrined in the Canadian constitution in 1982 through the Charter of Rights and Freedoms, have benefited Acadians in all three Maritime provinces.

Acadians emerged from the internal exile of the nineteenth century to join the mainstream of Canadian life. Acadian politicians, judges, artists, writers, and business leaders have made their mark across the country and on the world stage. Bands with names like 1755 and Grand Dérangement have put Acadian music on the map, merging rock-and-roll or bluegrass with traditional fiddle tunes. New Brunswick–born writer Antonine Maillet created a sage Acadian cleaning woman named La Sagouine and brought Acadian storytelling and the rhythms of Acadian French to an international audience.

But economic forces and assimilation are chipping away at this vibrant new Acadie. Many Acadians, particularly those in northern New Brunswick, remain dependent on seasonal work in fish plants or in the forests to make their living. These have long been industries in decline, and in the last century tens of thousands of Acadians have been forced to seek jobs in other parts of

Canada or in New England. There are about 1 million Acadians or Acadian descendants in Quebec, 200,000 in Ontario, and an estimated 400,000 in the northeastern United States. There are success stories, from the Acadian businessmen who have muscled their way to the top in the fishing and shipbuilding industries to the Nova Scotia–based company that is a world leader in finding ways to use the nutrients in seaweed. Moncton, an officially bilingual city located at the geographical heart of the Maritime provinces, has become a booming commercial center and the unofficial capital of the Acadian world, an irony since the city of 117,000 was named for Lieutenant-Colonel Robert Monckton, the British officer who launched the deportation of 1755.

Nova Scotia's small Acadian minority faces an uphill battle to preserve the language of its ancestors. The province's communities are islands in an English sea and lack the numbers needed to demand the language rights that New Brunswick's Acadians have won. Hosting the 2004 Congrès mondial acadien brought new attention to the Acadian communities on the fringes of the original Acadie, and prompted the Nova Scotia government to introduce legislation to provide more services in French. But the long-term prospects for survival received a major boost a few years earlier when a group of Acadian parents took the provincial Department of Education to court to demand more French-language schools. A judge of the Nova Scotia Supreme Court sided with the parents in June 2000, ruling that under the provisions of the Charter of Rights and Freedoms, there were sufficient Acadian students to justify building schools in five areas—Clare, Pubnico, the Annapolis Valley, Isle Madame, and Chéticamp. The judge also ordered provincial officials to return to court on a regular basis with updates on construction, an aspect of the ruling that took on national significance and carved out new powers for Canada's judges. In 2003 the Supreme Court of Canada upheld the reporting requirement and gave judges the power to ensure that governments comply with court orders issued in an "urgent context of ongoing cultural erosion," as was the case for Nova Scotia's Acadians. The judge behind the groundbreaking decision was Arthur LeBlanc, an Acadian born on Isle Madame who was appointed to the province's Supreme Court in 1998. Jonathan Belcher, the court's first chief justice and an architect of the deportation, surely must have spun in his grave.

"Have y'all tried *lou-wheez-eanna* coffee?" Jim Bradshaw asks his northern visitors as he pulls up a chair at his favorite diner on Jefferson Street, the main drag that arcs through downtown Lafayette. "It's a little thicker." Cajuns like their coffee as strong as their accents and as black as blackened redfish, the signature Cajun dish that, it turns out, is not a traditional Cajun dish at all. "When my grandma burned a fish," Bradshaw deadpans, "she threw it out."

Separating the facts of Cajun culture from the fiction is as tough as stripping away the layers of mythology that coat Louisiana's Acadian history. Bradshaw, a lanky and garrulous career newsman who finds it hard to resist a good joke, pleads guilty to fueling a few of the misconceptions. A week ago, he admits, while eating at a local Cajun restaurant, he pretended to drench his food in hot sauce for the benefit of the horrified Japanese tourists at the next table. Another time, when city officials placed the cupola from a demolished orphanage in a nearby park, Bradshaw suggested they make up a story claiming it was the steeple of the Little Church of the Acadians, hauled to the site by devout exiles two centuries ago. When Bradshaw visited the park a few months later, he met a woman from New Jersey who was taking photos of the cupola. To his amazement, she recounted his tall tale almost word for word. He assured her the story was false, but she would have none of it. "That's the trouble with you people," she said, glaring at him over her sunglasses. "You don't know your own heritage."

Bradshaw loves telling that one. He lets out a hearty laugh that dissolves into the din of the breakfast rush at Dwyer's, a local institution where the eggs come with biscuits or grits on the side. Despite his weakness for making mischief, Bradshaw has worked hard to spread the truth about Cajun history and bring the work of Carl Brasseaux and other scholars to a general audience. For three years he immersed himself in the history of southern Louisiana, driving the back roads with a photographer in search of old-timers and their stories. Once a month, back at his desk in a darkened corner of the newsroom of the Lafayette *Daily Advertiser*, he pumped out a 30,000-word tabloid insert chronicling the history of the Acadians and their transformation into Cajuns. Many of the stories were republished in a coffee table book. Now sixty—"going on twenty-seven," he insists, a claim his snowy hair and beard expose as yet another tall tale—Bradshaw is the paper's regional editor and still writes a daily column of historical nuggets under the fitting title "C'est Vrai."

What's true about Bradshaw is that, like so many other Louisianians with English surnames, he's as much a Cajun as any Babin or Landry. In fact, he's related to both of those families. "There's three ways you can become a Cajun: by the blood, by the ring or by the back door," he observes. By those criteria, it is estimated that more than a half-million people in southern Louisiana and eastern Texas trace their lineage to the Acadian refugees of the late 1700s. Bradshaw is a Cajun by the blood and grew up speaking French to a grandmother who could not speak English. His Acadian ancestors, Joseph and Marguerite Vincent, were deported from Grand-Pré with their two young children. Smallpox felled scores of passengers after their ship was barred from landing in Virginia. They were diverted to England, where Joseph Vincent died in Southampton. His widow and children were shipped in 1763 to France, where they endured the poverty and failed resettlement schemes of the next two decades. Marguerite Vincent died at Belle-Île-en-Mer. Their son Pierre, who was only seven at the time of the deportation, was among the exiles who boarded *Le Beaumont* and sailed for Louisiana in 1785. He settled on the Vermillion River just south of Lafayette.

That's how Bradshaw became a Cajun. But what exactly is a Cajun? The image of swamp-dwelling good-old-boys, Bradshaw admits, is hard to shake. Never at a loss for a good story, he relates how a CNN reporter came to town a few years back and asked to be introduced to a real Cajun. At that moment one of Bradshaw's many acquaintances emerged from the building across the street, a multimillionaire businessman "as Cajun as they come," wearing a three-piece suit and headed to a meeting of directors of a local bank. Bradshaw tried to flag him down. "No, no, no," the reporter protested. "I want a Cajun." What she wanted, Bradshaw says, was a Cajun who fit the stereotype—barefoot, clad in bib overalls, and ready to wrestle a 'gator at the drop of a straw hat.

Cajuns have been some of the worst offenders when it comes to promoting the stereotype because, these days, Cajun is cool. Cajun cooking and

Cajun music went mainstream a couple of decades ago when Americans discovered an exotic, laid-back culture in their midst and companies inside Louisiana and beyond cashed in on the craze. Fitting the preconceived mold was good for business, and combination dance hall–restaurants sprang up to serve visitors helpings of old-style fiddle and accordian music along with the crawfish *etouffée* and jambalaya. Lafayette, a city of 120,000 hit hard when Louisiana's Post-Second World War oil boom went bust in the 1980s, emerged as the capital of Acadiana, as Cajun country came to be called. "We began to kind of mimic ourselves," Bradshaw acknowledges. Worse, authentic Cajun culture was forced to compete with pretenders like the Scandinavian band Cajun du Nord and spicy Cajun foods and sauces concocted in places like Buffalo, New York, and Eugene, Oregon.

So, what makes something truly Cajun? "There is a somethingness. It's hard to define," he says. There are "the basic things you can see and feel"—the music and the food—"then there's a certain character," like close-knit families, self-reliance, and a self-deprecating sense of humor. A zest for life captured in the phrase *"laissez les bons temps rouler."* Being Cajun is about ancestry, Bradshaw says, but it's also a state of mind, a thought that prompts him to add a fourth qualification for membership in the club: "You're Cajun by the culture."

It is now a culture under fire. "The genial Cajuns," *National Geographic* magazine proclaimed in 1990, "may be the country's prime example of an ethnic group that celebrates its own distinctiveness while remaining comfortably a part of 20th-century America." Cajuns still revel in their distinctiveness, but the party is over. In 2001 the New Orleans *Times-Picayune* published a three-part series, "Culture at a Crossroads," exploring the challenges facing Cajun culture in the new millennium. "Amid the vibrant burst of cultural pride," it warned, "there are worries about just how long the distinctive old ways can survive the pressures of the modern world." The culprits are the same as those threatening every other culture on the planet—television, the Internet, globalization, and, worst of all, commercialization. Stand in front of Lafayette's Mall of Acadiana and look in any direction, Bradshaw says, and the suburban low-rises and the forest of signs that meet the eye betray no hint that this is the center of Cajun culture. "If you go out into the countryside, you still find some French speakers and you still find some of the old traditions, but we've become so Americanized," he laments. "Lafayette is becoming Anyplace, USA, just another off-ramp."

To find out how Cajun culture reached this crossroads—and its prospects for survival—drive south on Route 90 for about twenty minutes and take the off-ramp at New Iberia. The patchwork of sugarcane fields and oilfield depots along the highway gives way to a broad marsh where only cattle compete against the ubiquitous cane. Avery Island soon rises above the horizon, a wooded ridge that covers the top of an immense dome of salt left behind when a prehistoric sea evaporated. Avery is an island in name only, ringed by marshes and cypress swamps and still some distance from the Gulf Coast.

A sharp, vinegary aroma fills the nostrils, drifting from a line of brick buildings on the lush grounds of a plantation at the island's edge. Inside, workers are bottling a blend of vinegar, salt, and barrel-aged red peppers that has become the most famous icon of Cajun culture. The McIlhenney family has been making its fiery Tabasco on Avery Island since just after the Civil War, when ex-banker Edmund McIlhenney stumbled on the recipe for the world's most famous hot-pepper sauce, "the ultimate Cajun Country product," according to one tourist guide. While the McIlhenneys are of Scotch-Irish extraction, most of their 200 employees are Cajuns. One, a thirty-seven-year-old pop-culture historian named Shane Bernard, is an authority on the forces that are reshaping what it means to be Cajun.

Bernard is the McIlhenney Company's in-house historian and curator. When not ensconced at the firm's headquarters, an antebellum-style mansion on the plantation grounds, he's putting the finishing touches on a museum in New Orleans that will pay homage to McIlhenney's history and its products, which now include such novelties as Tabasco-flavored ice cream and jelly beans. He's editor of the on-line *Encyclopaedia of Cajun Culture* and author of a newly published book on the Americanization of his fellow Cajuns.

Six decades ago, Bernard argues, Cajun society was transformed by an event as traumatic as the Civil War and the deportation. The Second World War ripped Cajuns from their insular existence and thrust them into mainstream America. The search for oil to fuel the war effort and the construction of military bases brought Americans and their values to southern Louisiana.

Thousands of Cajuns fought in the Pacific and in Europe, where a few proved invaluable as interpreters when American forces swept across France after D-Day. Learning to speak English became a matter of life and death on the battlefield. Soldiers and sailors went to war as Cajuns, but came home infused with the same patriotism and outlook as *les américains* they had kept at a distance for so long. They furthered their education on the GI Bill, in most cases becoming the first in their families to attend college. An entire generation turned its back on the old ways and embraced the suburban lifestyle with its modern conveniences. Owning a brick house became a measure of wealth and success and, to some Cajuns, it still is. "Everything changed," Bernard says after retreating to a quiet corner of McIlhenney's head office. "They were buying into the American dream."

Americanization nearly sounded the death-knell for the French language in Louisiana. It was already hurtling toward extinction, thanks to First World War–era laws mandating that all Louisiana children be schooled in English. It was a two-pronged attack—a 1916 statute made education compulsory and a 1921 amendment to the state constitution made English the language of instruction. As late as the 1950s, pupils whose first language was French were punished for speaking French in class or on school grounds. Teachers lined up offending students against trees at recess or forced them to stay after school to write "I am an American. I must speak English" on the blackboard.

"It was worse to speak French in school than it is, today, to smoke marijuana," says Loubert Trahan, a retired accountant from the Lafayette area who attended school during the Depression. Dale Broussard has bitter memories of being punished in school and later, when he went to college, having a professor suggest his accent was some form of speech impediment. "They made me feel uneducated, cheap, low class," recalls Broussard, now an official of the U.S. Department of Agriculture.

English-only schooling created linguistic generation gaps within families. Parents of postwar baby boomers, determined to spare their children from suffering the same abuse, continued to talk to each other in French, but spoke only English to the kids. But their own parents had grown up speaking only French, leaving many grandparents unable to communicate with their grandchildren. Cajun French was under siege, and the impact was devastating. Two-thirds of

Cajun children born before the Second World War spoke French as their first language. Within a decade the proportion had dipped below 40 percent and by 1970, just 12 percent of children grew up speaking French at home.

In a bid to save the language from extinction, in 1968 state legislators created the Council for the Development of French in Louisiana (CODOFIL), with a mandate to reintroduce French-language instruction in the schools. The initiative was almost as destructive as the schoolyard humiliations of earlier eras. CODOFIL imported teachers from France, Belgium, and Canada who had little appreciation for Cajun culture and no knowledge of the local dialect. Cajun French, frowned upon as the language of hicks and hayseeds, was again banned from the classroom in favor of "proper" French. Officials eventually recognized their folly, began hiring local teachers, and introduced French-immersion programs that included Cajun words and phrases, but the damage was done; just 3 percent of Cajuns born after 1980 speak French as their first language.

For thirty-somethings like Shane Bernard, it was too late. His young daughter has just started French immersion and already knows as many French words as he does. Visitors to southern Louisiana can spot traces of French, from bilingual street signs in Lafayette, to the sheriff's car that whizzes by on a country road bearing the slogan "À votre service," but fewer and fewer of the locals can read the signs or speak the language.

With their language and culture on the ropes, Cajuns were swept up in the revival of ethnic pride among Blacks, Hispanics, and other American minorities in the late 1960s. Acadiana, a name a radio station coined as a marketing gimmick, was officially adopted in 1971 to designate the twenty-two Cajun parishes of southern Louisiana that stretch from the Mississippi River to the Texas border. Lafayette professor Thomas Arceneaux, descendant of the Louis Arceneaux made famous by Judge Voorhies, designed a flag for the new "country." It is laden with symbols that honor the diverse origins of Cajun culture: the *fleur-de-lis* of France, a castle symbolizing Spain, and the yellow *stella maris* for the Acadians. Activists adopted the Black Power salute—an upraised fist—as the symbol of Cajun Power. Edwin Edwards, the first Acadian descendant to reach the governor's office in modern times, adopted "Cajun Power" as his winning campaign slogan in 1972.

The three Congrès mondial acadien held since 1994 have helped re-awaken Louisianians' interest in their past, none more so than the 1999 gathering hosted in the state. Cajuns also mounted an attack against the offensive term "coonass," which most still regard as a racial slur on par with the N-word. There are various theories about the origin of the epithet; most point a finger at Texas, where there is a sizable Cajun enclave on the eastern border with Louisiana. Jim Bradshaw shrugs it off with a laugh: "A lot of people think it's because we used to call the Texans horses' asses," he says, "and they called us coons' asses." But the term was no joke to James Roach, an oil industry engineer who was fired after he objected to his superiors calling him a "coonass." Roach sued and in 1980 a federal judge recognized Cajuns as an ethnic minority protected under U.S. employment equity laws. A year later the Louisiana legislature passed a resolution condemning the term as "offensive, vulgar, and obscene."

Cajun culture went from square to hip almost overnight. Festivals featuring old-time music attracted thousands of fans and propelled some Cajun musicians to international stardom. Chef Paul Prudhomme from Opelousas brought his version of the traditional cooking to New Orleans and put Cajun cuisine on the world's menus. The 1987 movie *The Big Easy*, in which actor Dennis Quaid portrayed a womanizing, bad-boy New Orleans cop, showcased Cajun culture—Hollywood's version of it, at least. Bernard gives it two thumbs down. "A horrible movie," he says with disgust. "The whole thing was just stupid." He saw it at a Lafayette theater years ago and remembers people in the audience snickering at the bad accents and the idea of rural Cajuns living in the midst of New Orleans. It perpetuated the misconception that New Orleans, not Lafayette, is the center of Cajun culture, a sore spot for the local tourism industry. Bernard found it as realistic as a movie shot in Paris with all the actors dressed up in mime outfits.

The Big Easy was the most visible of a string of movies and television dramas of the 1980s and 1990s that perpetuated cultural stereotypes, many of them unflattering. Bernard has detected a common thread: "Even if the Cajun is the good guy, he tends to be this mysterious lone figure who walks a fine line between good and evil. He'll bend the law to his needs in order to do something good." Bernard bristles at how the media sometimes perpetuate the stereotype, dubbing a terrorist who once lived in Baton Rouge the "Cajun Taliban" and a local serial killer the "Cajun Slasher" when neither had Cajun roots. Then again, former governor Edwin Edwards became an exception who proved the rule when he was driven from office and convicted in 2001 of extorting money from applicants for casino licences.

For all the distortions and imitators, Cajun culture seems as vibrant as ever. The real question is whether the culture can survive without its distinctive language. For Acadians in Canada, the survival of the language is considered essential to the survival of the culture. "This is another world," cautions University of Louisiana historian Carl Brasseaux. "Language has never been politicized here and it's not viewed as being the same lynchpin of culture." Cajuns, Bernard says, must acknowledge that their language will soon be a museum piece, as likely to be heard outside a college classroom as Old Norse. Brenda Comeaux Trahan, at the Acadian Memorial in St. Martinville, is fighting a rearguard action and hosts weekly classes to teach Cajun French. But preserving the language is a losing battle—just over 2,000 students were enrolled in French-immersion programs statewide in 2001, far below the critical mass needed to ensure a language will survive. "I suspect someone, somewhere will always speak Cajun French," says Bernard, "but increasingly it may be confined to college campuses and not to the local country store."

Bernard subscribes to the theory that what really matters is whether people consider themselves to belong to an ethnic group. Irish-Americans, after all, chug green beer and celebrate their heritage on St. Patrick's Day without speaking a word of their ancient language, just as closet Cajuns come out of the woodwork for Mardi Gras. Bernard is convinced Cajun culture will stagger along for at least a few more generations much as it has since the Second World War, under siege but never quite succumbing to the forces of assimilation. "The Cajuns a hundred years from now may find it as hard to recognize the Cajuns of today as the Cajuns of today find it hard to recognize the ones from a hundred years ago, who wore overalls and no shoes and straw hats and rode around on donkeys," he says. "We may not speak French, but I don't think we're going anywhere."

Brasseaux shares Bernard's optimism that a people who survived the genocide of the deportation and exile can survive the onslaught of popular culture.

"The community here has reinvented itself about a dozen times since it arrived in the 1760s," Brasseaux notes. "I think what you're seeing now is the latest installment in that process."

Naomi Griffiths has vivid memories of what it's like to be caught in a battle between superpowers. She grew up in southern England and was just six when the Second World War broke out. As London burned during the Blitz, she could see the flames and smoke from her home 60 miles away. She heard the drone of German bombers heading for their targets and remembers aircraft plowing into the surrounding hills as the Battle of Britain raged overhead. When she attended the University of London in the early 1950s, she learned of a people who were caught in a war zone two centuries earlier. She became friends with Acadian students from Canada, among them Roméo LeBlanc, a New Brunswicker who went on to become a powerful federal minister and Canada's first governor-general of Acadian descent.

It was the first she had ever heard of the Acadians and their saga of suffering and exile, and she was fascinated with their remarkable survival. When she came to Canada in the late 1950s to pursue graduate studies at the University of New Brunswick in Fredericton, her master's thesis analyzed existing literature on Acadian history. "It isn't the Acadians at all," this kindly, patient woman of seventy explains when asked what prompted her to devote a lifetime to the study of Acadian history. "It was the setting."

Griffiths is in Halifax on a fall day in 2004 to deliver the keynote address at a symposium that will explore current trends in Acadian history. Despite the passage of so much time and the millions of words written on the subject, scholars are still fine-tuning our understanding of the Acadians and why they were condemned to expulsion. When Griffiths began her work almost a half-century ago, the Acadians were still regarded as misguided peasants who fell victim to forces they could neither understand nor control. She began teaching history at Carleton University in Ottawa in 1962 and quickly became the favorite professor of a succession of students. An appointment in 1979 as dean of arts at Carleton—the first woman dean of arts anywhere in English Canada—

cemented her reputation as academic trailblazer. But she is best known for the breadth and depth of her Acadian scholarship, which includes several books and numerous articles that have revolutionized the way we think about the Acadians. One of her books was dedicated jointly to her sister, her thesis adviser and, tongue-in-cheek, to "the Acadian who remarked nastily that my ancestors deported his and I now make my living from the crime."

Now retired and a visiting research fellow at l'Université de Moncton, she is about to publish her long-awaited opus, a 700-page account of Acadian history from 1604 to the day Lawrence and his council ordered the expulsion. To Griffiths, the Acadians were a pragmatic, politically sophisticated people with a common heritage and world view that compelled them to go toe to toe with their British rulers. They were, in essence, a nation long before the horrors of the deportation and exile forged a sense of community and belonging. "The deportation neither created nor destroyed the Acadians," she wrote more than three decades ago. "In 1755 the Acadians already had their own identity."

It is surprising to discover that, in some quarters, the Acadians are seen as a French splinter group that emerged as a distinct people long after Lawrence drove them into exile. Hogwash, Griffiths says. "The Acadians were not created by the deportation," she insists in a voice tinged with a trace of a Welsh accent, warming up for her address later in the day. "I do not think the Acadians could have survived the deportation without the strong societal links in place before 1755." It is this sense of belonging to a wider community that drew Griffiths, the daughter of a Welsh pacifist and the granddaughter of an Indian colonel, to the study of a people who managed to preserve their identity in the face of overwhelming odds.

The Acadians have survived despite the diaspora and despite having never existed as an autonomous political entity. "What fascinates me is how people define membership in a community and how the community decides that it will continue to exist," she explains. The resilience of the Acadians, she believes, holds valuable lessons as modern society struggles to accommodate a plethora of cultures and nationalities. They provide a sobering example of the destructiveness of intolerance and, at the same time, an example of a people that has survived without resorting to violence. "Unless we can understand the crucial importance of community identities, we aren't going to build a very peaceful world," Griffiths argues. "And if we don't, there won't be very many of us left."

Historians and commentators were debating the lessons of the deportation long before Griffiths came on the scene. Despite the scale of the deportation, there was little contemporary discussion of what occurred. The sufferings of a few thousand Acadians in a colonial backwater did not matter much in a world plunged into war. Edmund Burke, the great British statesman and reformer, ventured the opinion in 1780 that his country had "most inhumanely and upon pretenses that, in the eyes of an honest man are not worth a farthing, root[ed] out this poor, innocent, deserving people, whom our utter inability to govern, or to reconcile, gave us no sort of right to extirpate." Burke, a critic of discrimination against Catholics in general, was likely a voice in the wilderness inside Britain.

Writing in 1766, with thousands of Acadians still wandering in exile, French cleric Guillaume Thomas Raynal blamed their misfortunes on "national jealousies" and the "greed of government which devours men and country." It was well into the nineteenth century before historians began to explore the expulsion and its origins. George Bancroft, a renowned American historian of the mid-nineteenth century, doubted that "the annals of the human species have preserved the memory of woes inflicted with so much complacency, cruelty and persistence."

In Thomas Chandler Haliburton, Nova Scotia's first literary star, described the deportation as cruel, unnecessary, and "a stain on the Provincial Councils." As a judge, he could not resist pointing out that it was "totally irreconcilable with the idea, as at this day entertained of justice" that the innocent should be punished along with the guilty. Yet Haliburton felt Lawrence had few options and he ultimately blamed the French for seducing the "misguided" Acadians and leaving them to their ruin. Other English writers took up the blame-the-French refrain, condemning Abbé Le Loutre and French governors in Quebec and Louisbourg for using the Acadians as pawns. Thomas Beamish Akins, who compiled and sanitized Nova Scotia's official documents on the deportation for publication in 1869, later scoffed at the Acadians' professed neutrality and wrote that their "poverty and ignorance placed them completely under the control of a few designing emissaries of the French Governor at Quebec."

Other writers advanced the defense of necessity. In *The History of Acadia*, published in 1879, New Brunswick historian James Hannay described the expulsion as "a necessary measure of self-preservation on the part of the English authorities in Nova Scotia." In the "death-struggle" that erupted into the Seven Years War, he added, "it was evident that there was no room for half-way measures." Hannay praised the leniency and forbearance the British had shown in the face of Acadian obstinacy and was full of praise for Lawrence, whose "strong, resolute character was an excellent guarantee of [Nova Scotia's] safety in any emergency that might arise." As for the fact that innocent men, women, and children had suffered the same fate as the few guilty of treason, Hannay rationalized that the innocent always suffer: "I have never heard that given as a reason why the guilty should go unpunished."

Francis Parkman, another Lawrence apologist, wrote in the closing years of the 1800s that the Acadians refused to take the oath "in full view of the consequences" and that the lieutenant governor and his council acted "in manifest good faith"—gross distortions, since the deputies were not told that refusal meant deportation. Parkman, too, contended that the expulsion was pursued only as a last resort after "every resource of patience and persuasion had been tried and failed."

French-speaking writers objected to this self-serving revision of history. Among the most strident was Acadian descendant Edouard Richard, a former Canadian parliamentarian who grew up in Quebec hearing deportation stories from relatives. In his 1895 book *Acadia: Missing Links of a Lost Chapter in American History*, Richard accused Parkman and Hannay of distortion and ignoring evidence. The Acadians "were deported like cattle, they were hunted like wild beasts," he fumed, in an "act of barbarity that has left upon the civilized world an impression of ineradicable and unassuageable pain." Lawrence, he asserted, was a man "totally devoid of moral sense and utterly heartless." After poring over Lawrence's letters, Richard claimed he could not find "a single line that might hint at the semblance of any feeling of delicacy."

The debate continued into the twentieth century, the venom of writers like Richard tempered by more balanced assessments. "The more [the deportation] is investigated, the more indefensible it appears," David Allison, a retired professor of classics, observed in a three-volume history of Nova Scotia published during the First World War. Even though he was a grandson of settlers who snapped up vacant Acadian lands, Allison concluded there had been no military crisis to avert and Lawrence had "disregarded his instructions and transcended his authority." In a book published a couple of years later, Quebec historian and literary critic Henri Beaudé condemned the deportation as "an attack against humanity ... the most formidable one yet perpetrated and noted in history."

The sad truth is human history has witnessed worse acts of barbarity, and Beaudé's assertion is typical of the shrill rhetoric and shaky evidence he brought to bear on the subject. He saw the deportation as the culmination of a long-running conspiracy to rid Nova Scotia of the Acadians. In the 1920s John Bartlet Brebner, employing the dispassion and discipline of a Columbia University scholar, concluded the deportation was the product of a host of factors—"neglect, expediency, ignorance, the rivalries of empires and religions, eagerness for economic advantage, inertia"—that "triumphed over common sense and humanity." To Brebner, Acadie in 1755 was an accident waiting to happen and the study of the "irresistible" forces leading up to the deportation was akin to watching a train wreck in slow motion.

Opinions about the deportation and its causes have tended to split along linguistic lines. French writers have been quick to condemn, and English writers have been prone to cite mitigating circumstances. When it comes to assigning blame, though, there is universal agreement that Lawrence should stand front and center in the prisoners' dock. He choreographed the showdown with the Acadians, redeployed New England soldiers to round up civilians, and micromanaged their shipment into exile. "Charles Lawrence was the man needed to carry out such a monstrous crime," Beaudé thundered.

But there was plenty of blame to spread around. Admirals Boscawen and Mostyn lent their timely support. The governor's council—Benjamin Green, John Rous, John Collier, and William Cotterell—backed the scheme as co-conspirators. Jonathan Belcher is usually lumped in with the other councillors or attacked for his vindictive attempt to send Acadian prisoners to Boston late in the war; many writers overlook his key role in backing the initial deportation. Boscawen and Major-General Jeffrey Amherst condemned to death 1,700 Acadians from Île Saint-Jean. There is ample evidence to convict all these men in the court of public opinion.

Suspicions have lingered that the British government approved or even engineered the whole affair. There have been allegations that incriminating documents were destroyed, a "pure canard," says Griffiths, who has detected no serious gaps in the paper trail after a thorough review of the archival record. One rumor, worthy of any modern-day conspiracy theorist, held that Boscawen arrived in Halifax with secret orders from England authorizing the deportation. But Brebner believed the letters of the Lords of Trade and the secretary of state "completely exonerate" the British, and it is clear from the correspondence that Lawrence was on a frolic of his own.

William Shirley's name sits high on most lists of culprits. Adams Archibald, a retired Nova Scotia politician eager to shift blame away from his native province, pointed out that the Massachusetts governor "devised the scheme" and Massachusetts soldiers and ships were used to carry it out. If the expulsion was a black mark on Nova Scotia's reputation, he argued in an 1880s speech to the provincial historical society, "it is a stain from which Massachusetts ... cannot claim to be free." Shirley was also at the throttle of the train Brebner saw hurtling toward the deportation. Brebner argued that Lawrence was merely "the agent of the removal" and its root causes could be found in the "expanding energies of New England."

A Canadian historian, George Rawlyk, has jumped to Shirley's defense, offering convincing evidence that the Massachusetts governor learned of the deportation only after the fact. While Shirley advocated a general expulsion in the 1740s, when Nova Scotia's fate hung in the balance, he was soon arguing against such a policy. His letters to London and Lawrence on the subject in early 1755, before he headed to the frontier to play soldier, show that he contemplated the relocation of Chignecto's rebellious Acadians, nothing more. Shirley was out of the loop when the deportation was set into motion and had an ironclad alibi. He spent the summer of 1755 camped on Lake Ontario, gearing up for an attack on the French stronghold at Niagara. After learning of Braddock's defeat, and to avoid a similar fate, he decided to stay put and build a fort in case the French attacked first. The commander of his Nova Scotia expedition, John Winslow, reported in August 1755 that all Acadians, including those "not Equally Guilty of open Violence," were to be deported, but Shirley was not in Boston to receive the letter. When he did return, he could barely conceal his anger when he discovered that his soldiers had been used to round up civilians. In a blunt letter to Lawrence in February 1756, he complained that the troops should have been used to drive the French out of the Saint John River Valley, in keeping with the original plan to secure the Massachusetts sea coast.

The notion that the Acadians somehow deserved to be deported continues to surface. Less than a decade ago, Charles D. Mahaffie Jr., an American lawyer who turned to writing history in retirement, published a finely researched history of events leading up to the deportation. He acknowledged the shortcomings of British rule, then added: "In many ways the Acadians brought it on themselves. They would not adapt. They would not even make a show of accepting the rule that began in 1710."

His conclusion begs some questions: Adapt to what? Haphazard British rule? A succession of governors sending mixed signals? There is no doubt the Acadians' ingrained stubbornness contributed to their downfall; it is equally clear that British distrust and inflexibility, stoked by Lawrence's posturing and scheming, sealed their fate. Time and objectivity have tended to produce a more balanced view of the deportation. Modern historians have concluded that the removal of the Acadians was not inevitable, and a population of innocent civilians did not deserve to be banished from their homeland. Despite the efforts of Belcher and historians like Parkman to magnify the scale of Acadian cooperation with Britain's enemies, Griffiths has taken a good long look at the historical record and found "no evidence of a major rejection of British rule throughout the Acadian settlements."

John Reid, who teaches at Saint Mary's University in Halifax, has brought a fresh perspective to many aspects of Acadian history. Writing on the deportation in 1987—a reinterpretation Griffiths has praised as "brilliant" and "perceptive"—Reid argued the endgame played out in 1755 was far from inevitable. "It depended," he concluded, "on a particular interpretation of the military interests of Great Britain." Rejecting the temptation to demonize Lawrence and his councillors, Reid stressed that deportation was never the sole option; the Lords of Trade and past governors had recognized the Acadians as industrious settlers. The ascendancy of Lawrence and his get-tough policy at a crucial juncture may have been the driving force behind the deportation, but the outcome was never carved in stone.

The symposium Griffiths has come to Halifax to attend has been convened in honor of Reid's election as a fellow of the prestigious Royal Society of Canada, a sort of academic hall of fame. As she prepares to discuss the people she has devoted her academic career to rescuing from obscurity, Griffiths agrees that the expulsion that devastated yet ironically preserved the Acadians and their culture was not preordained. It was the product of a moment in history and the attitudes and prejudices of Lawrence and the others in charge at that pivotal moment. "The British fear of French strength was hysterical and unfounded but it was there, and it was part of their politics," she notes. But for the deportation not to have been inevitable, "you would have had to have had men of a very different temper. And much less fear of the French."

Another petite woman, this one with sandy-blonde curls and lively eyes, takes the podium to a round of warm applause. She steps onto a makeshift plywood platform to boost her height—so she can have a better view of the audience, she jokes, not the other way around—but Antonine Maillet is a giant of Acadian culture. She's the first writer outside France to win the Prix Goncourt, joining the illustrious ranks of writers like Marcel Proust. The honor was bestowed for the 1979 novel *Pélagie-la-Charrette*, about the return from exile. She has been invited to speak at the Vision 20/20 symposium at l'Université Sainte-Anne and a small lecture theater is packed with people eager to hear the woman who, like Longfellow, has brought Acadian history and their culture to the world's attention. Unlike Longfellow, who never set foot in the land he immortalized in verse, Maillet is among her people and at home. The day before, she strolled through the grounds at Grand-Pré, perhaps seeking inspiration for this talk. Her subject is "Acadie and the Global Village—*L'Acadie face au monde.*"

For the next forty minutes Maillet reflects on the history of her people and their place in today's world. A born storyteller, she's still a lively, forceful speaker at seventy-five. Her words tumble out in her native language in a cascade of passion and wry humor, triggering laughter and insights in equal measure. Since 2004 is the 400th anniversary of French settlement in North America, she offers a century-by-century review of Acadie's triumphs and tragedies. For the first 100 years after 1604, she notes, Acadians "were pretty well alone" and the world "forgot about us." Left largely to their own devices, the Acadians developed "the first true republic in the modern world," a nascent democracy overseen by elected deputies at a time when Europe was mired in the feudal past. Acadie changed hands many times as the French and English jockeyed for position in North America, she acknowledges, but "we didn't know anything about that. We didn't know who we belonged to. We thought we belonged to ourselves."

That changed, and changed dramatically, over the course of Acadie's turbulent second century. After 1713, Acadie belonged to the English. "It was back to reality," she says. "We were reduced as a people." The Acadians possessed the era's most valuable commodity—land. "We were the first, so we chose the best land. You should never do that," Maillet cautions her audience with a sly smile, "because other people will be jealous." She ignores the endless debate over oaths of allegiance taken or refused, and cuts to the chase. The term *le grand dérangement*, she says, is a euphemism because Acadians "never call things by their real name." It is a way of soft-selling the horrible events of 1755 and the years that followed. She prefers a term that is far stronger and more accurate: quasi-genocide.

But the deportation failed to wipe out the Acadians, or Acadie, for that matter. "The strongest came back," she notes, establishing new communities on the fringes of their homeland. The Acadians were like salmon battling their way through river currents to return to the place of their birth. Once back, they had to be as sly as the fox, keeping a low profile in the hope that their English neighbors would again forget about them. "We were foxes. A wolf is able to defend himself—he bites," she says. "The Acadians were not strong enough to fight, so they had to defend themselves with their smarts." The third century, the 1800s, was the century of revival. The winter nights were long and "we made lots of people," she quips. The scattered communities discovered one another and adopted the trappings of a nation—an anthem, a flag, a patron saint. "And now we're a people," a people forged by injustice and exile and survival. "No one saved Acadie, except for Acadians," she declares to a burst of applause.

The twentieth century brought new battles to keep the Acadians' language, culture, and history alive in the face of the relentless forces of assimilation. This university, this *congrès*, this homecoming of Acadians is proof that many of those battles have been won. Maillet tackles the question Maurice Basque posed to kick off the symposium: What is an Acadian? To her, it is someone with a powerful will to survive. "It's a person who wants to live. We didn't die because we wanted to live ... as long as there is one living Acadian, Acadie will go on."

What lies ahead for Acadie and its people? "The world is taking note of who we are. Acadians around the world are waking up," Maillet insists. She sees the Acadians as a model for the rest of the world, a model of survival and what people can accomplish if they work together and remain true to their identity. And there's one more lesson for the world. Maillet spoke at an international francophone summit held in Moncton in 1999, where the Acadians in attendance were the only French-speaking peoples without a leader or a head of state—or a state, for that matter. A provincial political party, the Parti-Acadien, espoused turning northern New Brunswick into a separate Acadian province in the 1970s, but failed to gain much support at the polls. In today's Acadie, as in the Acadie of her ancestors, Maillet says proudly, "the people are sovereign."

Acadie long ago vanished from official maps, yet it exists in "the genius of the people," the unique outlook of Acadian artists and writers. The Acadians, she says, can be an inspiration to the rest of the world. They have proven that human beings can survive and fulfill their destinies, no matter what adversities they may face. "We were, we are," she concludes to a standing ovation, "and we will be."

10 SEEKING JUSTICE

They were spared no barbarity: The dismemberment of families,
the perils of the sea, the hunger of concentration camps, the
making of slaves of children snatched from the arms of parents,
the deaths from grief and epidemics, the scattering of a whole
people throughout nearly every continent of the globe.
We submit that, in a time of peace, there has never been
a tragedy with more human suffering.

—Petition, *Warren A. Perrin et al. versus Great Britain et al.*, January 1990

Louisiana's only copy of the Royal Proclamation concerning the wrongs
inflicted on the Acadians hangs in a gold frame on the wall of a lawyer's
office in the little town of Erath. A local boy made good named Warren
Perrin, the only lawyer this town and its 3,000 potential clients have ever
had, uses the office one afternoon a week when friends and relatives drop
by seeking legal advice or just to say hello. There is no receptionist and no
need for one. Everybody in Erath knows the office and its distinguished
document can be found at the back of the Acadian Museum, a former bank
building jammed from floor to ceiling with artifacts and photographs that
record four centuries of Acadian and Cajun history. Perrin, who has built
a busy personal-injury practice in Lafayette, worked out of a room adjoin-
ing a gas station when he first hung out his shingle in Erath thirty years
ago. A room at the back of a museum with a drop-leaf table as a desk, he
jokes, is a step up. The rest of the week, the office door is left open and the

proclamation he extracted from the British monarchy takes its place among the museum's exhibits.

To understand how this polite, fifty-eight-year-old descendant of Beausoleil Broussard had the temerity to take on Her Majesty Queen Elizabeth II, consider a couple of episodes from his past. Perrin was drawn to competitive weightlifting in his youth. When he was fifteen, he passed out while training with his cousin. He weighed maybe 120 pounds and was hoisting a 140-pound barbell over his head when he collapsed. He broke both wrists, leaving his arms in a cast, from fingertip to shoulder, for two months. As soon as the casts were off, he was lifting again as if nothing had happened. "Athletics in general, and weightlifting in particular, taught me I could be the best," he says. He went on to lead the University of Southwestern Louisiana's weightlifting team to three national titles in four years. Another display of Perrin's steely determination came in the early 1970s. Fresh out of law school, he took on petroleum giant Texaco, which operated the largest natural gas-processing plant in the United States on part of his family's farm. Texaco was paying a pittance in royalties and Perrin used his new skills to sue and win a fair settlement. "When Warren wants something," his mother, Ella Mae, once noted, "he gets it."

In the late 1980s, with his practice chugging along, Perrin found a new target for his stubbornness. He read a children's book about the Acadians to his son Bruce, who was eight or nine at the time. Perrin mentioned that their ancestor, Beausoleil, had fought the British and had captained a privateering ship after the deportation. His son, of course, was intrigued to discover a distant relative had been a pirate, and it struck Perrin that Acadians and Cajuns still bore the stigma of disloyalty. "I realized that we were viewed as people who deserved the treatment that was inflicted on us," he recalls after seeing to a handful of clients at the Erath office. "And that wasn't true."

To find the truth, he devoured every book he could find on the deportation and its causes. It is what any lawyer would do—find the facts, build a case. He became convinced that a grave injustice had occurred in 1755 and it was high time the British Crown owned up to the misdeeds of Charles Lawrence and its other Nova Scotia agents. He delivered a petition to the British government in January 1990 seeking an apology for the way the

Acadians were "cruelly banished from their country and plunged overnight into the most abject poverty." He was prepared to file a class-action suit on behalf of all Acadians and Cajuns, if necessary, to force a response.

Perrin's petition recited Acadie's seesaw history of conquest under the French regime, taking careful note of the royal edicts granting Acadians the right to remain in Nova Scotia as British subjects. Details of oaths of allegiance taken and retaken were carefully recorded, sprinkled with the verdicts of historians who have condemned the deportation. Perrin's boast that "there never was any people more noble, more devoted to duty and more faithful to their oaths" was a bit of a stretch, given the Acadians' proud tradition of answering to neither the British nor the French. He was on firmer ground when he recounted the hardships inflicted on his ancestors—stripped of their lands and possessions, separated from family and friends, exposed to hunger, disease, and shipwreck, the virtual enslavement of their children. "We submit that, in a time of peace, there has never been a tragedy with more human suffering," he asserted.

The bottom line was a demand for an impartial inquiry into the deportation, an admission that the exile was an illegal act, and restoration of the Acadians to the status of French neutrals to underscore the injustices they suffered. Perrin sought no restitution or compensation, even though more strident supporters of the petition suggested he demand a billion-dollar settlement. His goal was to right an injustice and erase the stigma of the deportation. "We still labor as an exiled people, labeled as criminals, malefactors and ruffians," Perrin told a reporter shortly after filing the petition. "To take a culture and try to get rid of it is called genocide, and that is not a pretty term."

Perrin made his case in an accompanying legal brief. Lawrence's order was issued on July 28, 1755, almost ten months before war was declared. "Accordingly, under international law, the Acadians' property could not be confiscated as it might have been during a time of war." While true for the majority of Acadians, those uprooted from Nova Scotia in 1755, this position would not apply to the thousands deported from Île Saint-Jean and other regions in the years that followed. But all Acadians enjoyed the rights and protections of British subjects—or should have. Since Chief Justice Jonathan Belcher and other local officials considered the Acadians to be British subjects,

Perrin pointed out, they were entitled to due process and could be exiled or deported only where stipulated by law or by the sentence of a court. British common law also rejects the concept of guilt by association: "There was no law in effect, then or today, which allows a government to punish an entire people for the misdeeds of a few," he argued. "That's natural law."

Even if Beausoleil Broussard and other Acadian resisters committed acts of treason, the law did not permit "the confiscation of the properties of a father of a family, or the punishment of his wife and children, for an offense that could have been committed by the father." Perrin also attacked the validity of the deportation order. Lawrence, a lieutenant governor, lacked the authority to order the deportation without the authorization of his superiors. He certainly had no power or right to ride roughshod over the royal promises made by Queen Anne and King George, which Perrin insisted "must be viewed as an abuse of power by Lawrence." Despite convincing evidence that no one in London ordered the deportation—and, indeed, advised against it— Perrin argued that the British government remained liable for the actions of officials on the ground in Nova Scotia.

Regardless of whether the deportation could be justified in law, Perrin claimed the hardships and deaths it caused were crimes in their own right. Genocide is the systematic destruction of a national or ethnic group, and the definition fit the horrors inflicted on the Acadians. "By systematically dividing the Acadians into small groups, forcing them to the thirteen Anglo-American colonies and refusing to allow them to travel, the British engaged in genocide," he contended. He cited the United Nations convention on human rights, which prohibits the "collective expulsion of aliens" and affords due process to anyone who faces expulsion but is legally resident in a country. Perrin also accused the British of duplicity in the outright murder of Acadians "scalped and killed by the orders of Lawrence."

Perrin gave the British thirty days to respond. It was a big risk, and he knew it. If the British chose to ignore him, "I'd be seen as a kook or a joke and be printed up in the offbeat column of the newspaper," he later confessed. He would still have the option of taking the complaint to court, but the proper forum for such a claim was unclear. The International Court of Justice in The Hague and the European Court of Human Rights were possibilities. Failing that, he could file a lawsuit in a United States court, but the British were sure to object on jurisdictional grounds, stalling the case for years. With days to go before the deadline, the British embassy in Washington contacted Perrin and asked him to hold off. A day he later he received a call from a Texas law firm, which had been retained by the British consulate in Houston to respond to the petition.

Publicly, at least, British officials downplayed the petition or referred the issue to the Canadian government. In June 1990, six months after the petition was filed, an official of the British embassy in Washington told the New Orleans *Times-Picayune* that his government saw "little value in resurrecting debate on an issue which is best seen in an historical perspective." That position was unchanged eight years later, when the British consul in Dallas insisted the petition was "a matter for historians, not governments." Helen Mann, Britain's vice-consul in Houston, scoffed at Perrin's suggestion that the deportation order remained in effect. "I don't see how you could possibly describe a contemporary Cajun as living in exile," she told the *Los Angeles Times Magazine* in 1994. "To say that a Cajun who travels to Nova Scotia is breaking the law is a real stretch." Even the royal family was not amused. Lyse Doucet, a London-based television anchor with the BBC who grew up in the Acadian bastion of northern New Brunswick, took advantage of a social encounter with Prince Charles to mention the Acadians' request for an apology from his mother. The heir to the throne barely missed a beat and replied: "History can be *so* cruel."

The British may not have been taking Perrin seriously, but the media was. Perrin estimates the petition spawned some 300 newspaper and magazine articles in the United States, Canada, Britain, and France. He was interviewed on the major U.S. television networks and on the BBC. *The Times of Acadiana*, a weekly newspaper in Lafayette, was onside from the start, declaring in a February 1990 article that the petition tackled "an injustice that has never been acknowledged, a crime never punished, a wrong never righted." The *Los Angeles Times Magazine* dubbed Perrin a "one man Acadian liberation front." The *Atlanta Constitution* ran a story under the headline "Rematch: A Cajun vs. the Brits." A few journalists framed his quest as a David-and-Goliath battle— the wiry, 5'10" courtroom scrapper taking on Her Majesty. A writer for *The*

Observer of London condemned the deportation as "a brutal stain on the history of empire." *The Economist* weighed in with a description of the deportation as "an old British crime" that had been "undeniably cruel." Montreal's influential French-language newspaper, *Le Devoir*, called for an apology and published a cartoon poking fun at Britain's refusal to respond to the petition. "Apologies?!" the queen cries out in frustration. "They should thank us for deporting them to a warm country where the taxes are lower."

Perrin took advantage of every opportunity to promote the petition and to turn up the heat on the British. He represented the United States at an international human rights conference in France in 1993 and gave a presentation explaining the petition. His campaign won the endorsement of the Louisiana legislature in 1993 and the following year he spoke about the petition at the inaugural Congrès mondial acadien in Moncton. Perrin's reputation as a rising star in the Cajun firmament was cemented in 1994 when the state government named him president of CODOFIL. When the world's Acadians gathered for a second time in Louisiana in 1999, the American Bar Association and local lawyers staged a mock trial based on the petition. After hearing arguments in French, a panel of more than a dozen judges—including retired district court judge Allen M. Babineaux, a pioneer in the struggle to preserve Cajun language and culture—unanimously ruled that the Acadians' claims were legally valid and should proceed.

In the real world, though, negotiations proceeded at a glacial pace. Perrin hoped to unveil an apology at the 1994 *congrès*, then set his sights on having it in hand for the follow-up gathering in Louisiana. As the years went by, he took heart from a string of national *mea culpas* issued as Britain and other countries owned up to dark episodes in their pasts. The queen apologized in 1992 for the deadly firebombing of the German city of Dresden during the Second World War and, three years later, to the Maoris of New Zealand for taking away their lands in the mid-nineteenth century. Prime Minister Tony Blair apologized to the Irish people in 1997 for Britain's failure to alleviate the suffering of victims of the potato famine, a human disaster almost as old as the deportation. A year later U.S. President Bill Clinton apologized to descendants of the victims of slavery at about the same time as his Russian counterpart, Boris Yeltsin, expressed regret for the sins of communism.

In Canada a member of Parliament from Halifax, Howard Crosby, was an early supporter of the Acadian petition and wrote a 1990 report urging the federal government to remove "this cloud over Nova Scotia." But Acadians north of the border did not share Perrin's enthusiasm. "There was universal support [in Louisiana] here but not in Canada," he recalled in a newspaper interview. "In Canada, I was rattling cages. I was viewed as a Louisiana lawyer doing it for publicity." He credits the *congrès* and other gatherings for forging a better relationship between Cajuns and Acadians and overcoming suspicions about his motives. Acadian lawyers in Nova Scotia and New Brunswick began to throw their support behind the petition. "They realized this wasn't going to be a passing fad," he noted.

The battleground shifted to Canada and the fight became political. Stéphane Bergeron, a member of Parliament for the Bloc Québécois, took the issue to the floor of the House of Commons in Ottawa. In March 2001 he put forward a motion calling on the Canadian government to ask the queen to apologize for the wrongs done to the Acadian people. Bergeron was shocked to discover that the deportation was forgotten or misunderstood. A subcommittee that reviewed his motion demanded historical evidence to back up his assertions. "I even had colleagues who doubted that such an event could have taken place in Canada," he told a Quebec newspaper.

In Parliament, Bergeron appealed to the Liberal government of Prime Minister Jean Chrétien to back the resolution and officially recognize that the tragedy had occurred. "Acknowledging the facts and presenting an apology would be the least the British Crown could do to make amends, in view of the abuse committed on its behalf against the Acadian people," he asserted when the motion came up for debate.

Bergeron was a legitimate champion of the cause—his Acadian ancestors escaped the deportation and made their way to Quebec—but the Bloc's motives were suspect. The party is committed to making Quebec an independent state and Bergeron was accused of using Perrin's petition to embarrass two of the Bloc's favorite targets, the Canadian government and the monarchy. Jeannot Castonguay, a Liberal member of Parliament from northern New Brunswick, accused the Bloc of failing to consult the Acadian community and displaying an "offensive, insulting and hurtful paternalistic attitude" to francophone minorities outside Quebec. Other opposition parties backed Bergeron—Yvon Godin, an Acadian MP from New Brunswick, said the motion would "right a terrible wrong"—but government members defeated the motion.

The issue, however, was on the political agenda in Canada. The Quebec legislature passed a resolution in 2002 calling for an apology, with separatist premier Bernard Landry—an Acadian descendant and not one to pass up a chance to make the monarchy squirm—asserting the events of the deportation "amounted to a crime against humanity." Bergeron tried several times to introduce reworded motions asking the House of Commons to formally recognize the deportation and the harm it caused, but none came to a vote. The New Brunswick–based Société nationale de l'Acadie, which represents Acadians throughout Atlantic Canada, took the lead and sent a letter to Buckingham Palace in June 2002 asking the queen for a formal recognition that the deportation was wrong.

There was speculation that Queen Elizabeth might break her silence during a day-long visit to Moncton in October 2002, part of a Commonwealth tour to mark her Golden Jubilee. Bergeron flew to Moncton in anticipation of an announcement, and at one stop a woman standing a few feet from the monarch waved an Acadian flag and shouted: "Give me back the land you stole from my ancestors in 1755." The queen officially opened a new terminal at the international airport in neighboring Dieppe, a fast-growing Acadian community, but offered no apology. Buckingham Palace sat on the SNA's request and a year passed before the queen's secretary, Stuart Shilson, wrote back in June 2003 to say that Her Majesty would seek the advice of her Canadian ministers.

Stéphane Dion, Canada's minister of intergovernmental affairs, sent a formal request to London asking the queen to formally acknowledge "the great sufferings and hardships experienced by the Acadian people as a result of their tragic expulsion from the British colonies." It was, he added, a matter "of immense symbolic importance, not only for Acadians but also for their fellow Canadians."

Behind the scenes, bureaucrats were grappling with the legal and political implications of acknowledging the harm inflicted by the deportation. The government was involved in delicate negotiations with Aboriginal groups seeking redress for abuse in church-run residential schools and other wrongs.

And there was an expensive precedent—the Canadian government apologized in 1988 for interning thousands of Japanese-Canadians during the Second World War, and paid out $377 million in compensation and restitution for seized property. That settlement prompted the descendants of other Canadians who had suffered wartime internment—Germans, Italians, and Ukrainians—or discriminatory immigration policies—Sikhs, Jews, the Chinese—to demand similar redress. The result was a 1994 policy refusing to make further compensation and committing the government to ensuring that the rights of all citizens were respected in future. Briefing notes prepared for federal ministers cautioned that a formal recognition of the suffering of the Acadians was likely to prompt renewed demands from other cultural groups. "The Acadian file ... cannot be looked at in a vacuum, as any statement made in the support [of it] is likely to prompt other communities to ask for a similar statement," one memo advised. "Although no Acadian group has indicated its desire to ask for compensation up to now," noted another, "this still must be considered as a potential financial risk."

The queen's words would have to be chosen carefully. In a long memorandum drawn up for Chrétien and his cabinet sometime in 2003, government lawyers warned that a proclamation recognizing the deportation and the suffering it caused "would entail a measurable increase in the risk of legal action against the Crown by the heirs and descendants of the Acadians." Anyone who wanted to sue for compensation or launch a class-action suit would be freed from the burden of proving, to the satisfaction of a court of law, that the historical allegations were true. The lawyers were adamant that the government should refuse to acknowledge that the deportation occurred during "a time of peace" because "aggression seems less legitimate during peacetime than wartime."

Even without such precautions, the government's best legal minds were of the opinion that any lawsuits that might be filed were unlikely to succeed in court. The government could protect itself by inserting a clause making it clear that the proclamation was not an acknowledgment of legal responsibility. Lawyers also pointed out that the deportation occurred long before United Nations covenants on human rights and Canada's Charter of Rights and Freedoms, "neither of which can be applied retroactively."

Early drafts of the proclamation show that the government was toying with a watered-down document that was silent on the scope of the tragedy. One version recognized the deportation as "part of Canada's history with its tragedies as well as its triumphs" and praised the Acadians as "a model [of] strength, resolve and perseverance." The Société nationale de l'Acadie submitted a draft proclamation in October 2003 stating that thousands of Acadians had perished of disease, in shipwrecks, or while confined to prisoner-of-war camps in Nova Scotia and England. The SNA also wanted to insert a clause recognizing that the deportation had "catastrophic socio-economic repercussions" for all Acadians. This was undeniably true, but government lawyers strongly advised against an explicit admission that Acadians and their descendants had been harmed. "Any official recognition of this sad chapter of Acadian history ... [as] a cause of 'catastrophic socio-economic repercussions' as stated in the proclamation," they warned, "could be used by lawyers representing this community in the event of future lawsuits."

The cabinet memorandum recommended that the government incorporate the SNA's description of the hardships and deaths the deportation caused and also adopt the organization's request to have July 28, the day Lawrence and his council issued the deportation order, declared "A Day of Commemoration of the Great Upheaval." The government recently had backed a motion put forward by Gerald Comeau, an Acadian senator from Nova Scotia, and given official recognition to the Acadian national day, August 15. Designating a day to remember the deportation, the memo noted, "costs nothing and brings Canadians together from coast to coast."

The final proclamation reads as though it was drafted by a committee of high-priced lawyers, which it was. Set in ornate Gothic type and rendered in both English and French, it acknowledges a raft of historical facts, but offers no apology. The proclamation applauds Acadians for making "a remarkable contribution to Canadian society" over the past four centuries "through the vitality of their community." Then it gets down to business, stating that on July 28, 1755 "the Crown, in the course of administering the affairs of the British colony of Nova Scotia, made the decision to deport the Acadian people." There's no concession that the decision of Lawrence and his council to deport the Acadians was wrong, unjustified, or even ill advised. Next, the proclamation states that deportations continued until 1763 "and had tragic consequences, including the deaths of many thousands of Acadians from disease, in ship-wrecks, in their places of refuge and in prison camps in Nova Scotia and England as well as in the British colonies in America." Those are the SNA's words and a bitter pill to swallow for the nation that championed the rule of law. "We acknowledge these historical facts and the trials and suffering experienced by Acadian people during the Great Upheaval," the proclamation continues. "We hope that the Acadian people can turn the page on this dark chapter of their history."

That's as far as the admissions go. The balance of the document explains how the authority of the British Crown is now vested in the government of Canada. The queen makes it perfectly clear that her proclamation "does not, under any circumstances, constitute a recognition of legal or financial responsibility" on the part of the governments of Canada and its provinces, or affect the rights or obligations of any group or individual. In other words, no one whose ancestors were stripped of their land can use these admissions as the basis for a legal claim for compensation. The proclamation ends with the declaration of July 28 as a day of commemoration of the deportation, to be marked for the first time in 2005.

The queen's representative in Canada, Governor-General Adrienne Clarkson, signed the proclamation in Ottawa on December 9, 2003. "We are turning the page on one of the darkest moments of our collective history," Heritage Minister Sheila Copps said at a ceremony marking the event. "We cannot erase the errors of the past, but we can create a better Canada by understanding them and passing them along to our children." It was the last official act of the Liberal government of Jean Chrétien, whose retirement became effective the following day. The president of the Société nationale de l'Acadie described the proclamation as "a big victory" and a "gesture of respect" for Acadians. "This is important because it makes historic records a fact, and the Crown is admitting it caused irreparable damages to the Acadian people," said Euclide Chiasson, whose ancestors took to the woods to escape deportation. "It is symbolic ... much like a flag for a country."

Media reaction was for the most part favorable, although some pundits made note of the absence of an outright apology. "It declares closed the centuries-old debate over whether the deportation was justified or not," Ralph Surette, a journalist of Acadian descent, wrote in *The Halifax Herald*. "It is now finally and totally admitted that it was not." A leading naysayer was Colby Cosh, an Alberta-based columnist for the *National Post* who was loose with the facts. Expressing relief that the proclamation "stops short of apologizing for a decision taken in wartime," Cosh echoed the nineteenth-century apologists' view that the deportation was the logical outcome of the Acadians' stubborn resistance to Nova Scotia's military authorities. The proclamation, Cosh groused, had rewritten history in an effort to turn Lawrence into "a cardboard Darth Vader" and transform "a legitimate tragedy" into "a cheap little robbery." A man whose mother was Acadian, and who described himself as "pretty tired hearing about this," fired off a cranky letter to the editor of a New Brunswick newspaper asking why anyone would apologize for something that happened so long ago.

The answer is, no one apologized for anything. The proclamation falls far short of the detailed apology Perrin demanded in 1990. The draft version he prepared used terms like "profound regret" and "apologizes unreservedly," and would have acknowledged that the Acadians "were treated cruelly, unjustly and in bad faith." It also declared that the deportation was unlawful, a violation of basic human rights, and "a designed effort to end the Acadian culture and community"—in other words, an act of genocide. None of those admissions appear in the final proclamation. Still, Perrin considers it "a clear repudiation of the wrongs committed during the Acadian deportation." At the very least, he insists, it is a symbolic apology. "History, as it now stands, incorrectly judged the Acadians as a corrupt people who refused to cooperate and honor their oath," he argues. "The reconciliation should restore the good name of the Acadian people."

August 9, 2004: Louisiana Day at Grand-Pré, a homecoming for the Cajuns who have come north for the family reunions at the heart of the third Congrès mondial acadien. A copy of the Royal Proclamation has taken its place among the displays in Grand-Pré's Memorial Church, and Perrin is here to reflect on its significance. Close to 300 people have gathered under a large tent for his keynote address. He has just completed a book, *Acadian Redemption*, that chronicles Beausoleil Broussard's struggle against the British and his own fourteen-year-long fight with the queen.

Perrin begins with some thoughts about his illustrious ancestor, who has become a folk hero in Louisiana. Broussard, he says, was a ruthless militant who waged a guerrilla campaign against the British. "He engaged in acts of terrorism that most of the world would condemn today," he concedes. "But we know that when imperial powers invade homelands, as the British did, that people react to that pressure in certain ways." No one knows what Beausoleil looked like, but the face of a determined-looking young man stares out from Perrin's T-shirt and the cover of his book. The illustrator, at Perrin's request, modeled Beausoleil after modern-day revolutionary Che Guevara. Beausoleil should be remembered as "a cultural icon who had many foibles, an imperfect man who ended up accomplishing much more than he ever imagined, " Perrin believes. "He didn't start out to save the Acadian culture in Louisiana, but ultimately that's what he accomplished."

After recounting Beausoleil's tumultuous life, Perrin turns to the deporta- tion and the proclamation. Like Antonine Maillet, he dislikes the term *le grand dérangement*. "That was a British-coined term to make it seem like it was a rearrangement of sorts," he says. "They make it seem like people didn't die during the deportation. They were taken care of, they were put on ships. Yeah," he adds with disdain, "cattle ships." He prefers the word "deportation," even though it too falls short of capturing the enormity of what happened. "One-third of the Acadians died. One-third of the Jewish population died in World War Two," he says. "The Acadian deportation was our holocaust, pure and simple."

Despite the harsh words, Perrin praises the British for atoning, at long last, for the mistreatment of the Acadians. "By the Royal Proclamation, Queen Elizabeth II takes the moral high ground. She recognizes wrongs occurred. She reaffirms the Commonwealth's commitment to protecting human rights," he argues. "I think that's something we should all celebrate." He hopes the proclamation will be seen as a model for how countries deal with one another—and send a message to his own country, which has invaded and occupied the sovereign nation of Iraq in the pursuit of the war on terrorism. The proclamation, Perrin hopes, will set a moral standard and deter countries bent on "imperialistic actions, by occupying other countries or by occupying other people, or destroying other ethnicities." Such brutality did not start with the Acadians and ethnic cleansing continues even as he speaks, in the deserts of Sudan. As his fellow Cajuns stand and applaud, Perrin pumps his right fist skyward in a defiant salute worthy of his ancestor.

Does the proclamation put the deportation to rest? Dale Broussard, one of Beausoleil Broussard's many Louisiana descendants, thinks the acknowledgment is overdue. "We were thrown out of this country and we had to survive," he says after listening to Perrin, a distant cousin. "You get the impression from everything you read that the British enjoyed doing this." The proclamation gives him "a deep satisfaction of knowing that they recognize that they made a mistake .... You can't go back and undo what has been done, but with that in mind it [proclamation] makes you feel just a little bit better."

Lafayette newspaper columnist and raconteur John Bradshaw says the proclamation barely caused a ripple in Louisiana. Whenever he catches a mid-winter weather report from Canada, he feels like scribbling a thank-you note to Buckingham Palace before hitting the golf course. "I guess there's some symbolism to it, it's kind of like finally burying the hatchet," he allows, "but I think that's long past."

Alan Melanson, who strives to be fair to both sides as he recounts Acadie's troubled history to tourists visiting Annapolis Royal, does not need an apology from the queen to make him proud of his heritage. "I feel sorry for the people like my ancestors who ended up dying in Quebec. But you've got to gain strength from what happened in the past and go toward the future, and try to do the best you can for yourself and your family and your community today," he says. "I like presenting the past, but I also like living in the present."

Later in the day, after shaking many hands and signing the first fifty copies of his book, Perrin pauses in front of the statue of Evangeline to reflect on what he has accomplished. He did not get everything he wanted when he launched his quest, but the queen has acknowledged that the Acadian people suffered terribly as the result of acts carried out in the name of the Crown. There seems to be a tacit admission that the deportation violated the law of the day—there is no attempt to justify the "tragic consequences" of the decision made "in the course of administering the affairs" of Nova Scotia. Senator Gerald Comeau continues to push for an inquiry to identify the long-dead officials responsible, but history already has condemned Lawrence and the other culprits. The demand to formally lift the deportation order that has hung over the heads of Acadians ever since, at least in a technical sense, was "a symbolic thing," Perrin says. He has no fear that British soldiers are going to spring out from behind Grand-Pré's manicured hedges to seize him or the thousands of other Acadians who live in Nova Scotia or have returned for the *congrès*. The British policy of allowing Acadians to resettle in Nova Scotia after 1763, he conceded in his speech, was tantamount to an annulment of the deportation order.

"It's like being a child on Christmas morning, and the polite and respectful thing to do is not to ask for more toys for next Christmas, but to be thankful and appreciate the toys you got this Christmas," he says. "When I started this, neither the Crown nor the British government had apologized or even issued any regrets for anything in their colonial past. And I was told by most people that it wasn't about to start." He thinks back to those early, frustrating days of negotiation and stonewalling, when it often took three months to simply get a reply to a letter. "I'm very satisfied and grateful that we've gotten so much, frankly, so quickly." One of the turning points, he believes, was the support of the Société nationale de l'Acadie and a shifting in the fight from legal channels in the United States to political ones in Canada.

His timing was also good. The end of the Cold War ushered in a period of peace and stability that lasted until the 9–11 terror attacks plunged the world into an era of fear and conflict. "We had a decade of real good introspection, where governments were not afraid to re-examine their past. And I think we benefited from that." But much of the credit lies with Perrin's Cajun stubbornness. "I think we've been pretty patient, and I think that works in our favor. But there's a determination there also—I wasn't going to go away, this was not going to end—I mean, I was going to do what it took .... And we just took it to different levels, but we kept it positive. I think that was the secret, too. We always tried to give the Crown and the British respect, and assure them they would gain as much as we would gain."

Also on his original wish list was the erection of a monument to mark the end of what Longfellow called the "exile without end." The day of commemoration offered in its place will be observed for the first time on July 28, 2005 and the queen, who will be touring western Canada, has been invited to visit Grand-Pré to formally read out the proclamation. It would be a powerful gesture—the monarch journeying to the deportation's epicenter to acknowledge the injustice committed on the watch of her predecessor, George II. Regardless of whether Her Majesty obliges, Perrin prefers a day of commemoration to building a monument that could be overlooked or forgotten. "I think a day is a bigger way of remembering it; you're exposing more people to it," he says. "Who's going to visit a statue? I think this is a wonderful alternative."

There's irony in Perrin's words, for as he speaks a group of Louisiana visitors patiently await their turn to have their photo taken at the base of Evangeline's statue. There's no shortage of interest in this particular monument. But Longfellow's wistful heroine, long the symbol of a people's resilience, remains a creature of fiction. As Perrin points out in his book, "our only shrine was based on a myth ... there was a need for a tangible symbol of the Acadians' history which all Acadians could respect." It has taken a real-life character, a man as committed and patriotic as his ancestor, Beausoleil Broussard, to give Acadians a new day—and a new reason—to celebrate their cultural survival.

At first glance, it looks as if a landscaper-gone-mad has attacked the grounds to one side of Grand-Pré's Memorial Church. A gaping hole has been dug next door to the church. Smaller pits, each a half-yard square, have been cut into the sod in a checkerboard pattern along either side of a gravel path. On this July afternoon in 2004, one or two university-age students crouch over each hole, gingerly scraping away the soil with trowels and dustpans. A white-marble bust of Longfellow gazes toward the statue of his creation, Evangeline, oblivious to the archeological work being carried out around it.

If the deportation was an act of genocide, Grand-Pré was the scene of the crime. And that makes Jonathan Fowler as much a crime-scene investigator as an archeologist. For four summers Fowler, who teaches archeology and history at Saint Mary's University in Halifax, has led a team of field-school students in search of an elusive quarry—the remains of the church of Saint-Charles-des-Mines, where Lieutenant-Colonel John Winslow imprisoned the area's men and boys and read out the deportation order. The church is the Holy Grail of Acadian archeology, the building at the center of the deportation and a tangible link to the horrors that followed. "It's symbolic of what happened here and the survival of the Acadian people," Fowler says as he checks out the dig's progress. "Take a look at it this way: Winslow & Company wiped all this out, right? So this can be interpreted not only as an assault on the people to whom he did this, but an assault on their posterity in a sense. It's like cross-generational abuse—he's robbed them of their past, in a sense. Nobody can identify this site."

"Historical genocide," offers Mike Gibson, a bespectacled archeology graduate from Halifax, looking up from his patch of excavated ground.

"Yeah," says Fowler. "And so, hopefully, we get to give it back."

Saint-Charles-des-Mines is supposed to lie under the Memorial Church built in 1922—that, after all, was the whole point of building the replacement where it stands today. John Frederic Herbin, who preserved and poked around this site a century ago, was convinced he had found the church's foundations on that site. But the scientist in Fowler wanted hard evidence, not supposition or wishful thinking. A lot of things do not add up. For starters, eighteenth-century churches were generally built on an east-west axis. The Memorial Church faces south, ensuring that tourists alighting from trains in the early years would be treated to the Kodak-moment sight of Evangeline's statue framed by the church behind it. "The more we began looking," Fowler says, "the less we learned because there was no really strong body of evidence confirming that it was the church site."

Back in 2001 his students uncovered a stone foundation just a few yards away from the church. The small basement yielded hundreds of artifacts as well as two layers of charred wood and melted window glass, proving the building above had burned down twice. The second fire could have occurred during the deportation and certainly happened after 1734 because a British halfpenny bearing that date, the kind of conclusive artefact archeologists dream of unearthing, was found in the top layer of charcoal. While the foundation was a tantalizing find, its walls were not thick enough or long enough to support a building large enough to become a prison for more than 400 people.

After poring over Winslow's journal, old maps, and descriptions of the "Land of Evangeline" lifted from early travel books, Fowler became convinced the church was located dozens of yards farther east, beside the cemetery where Winslow's troops pitched their tents in an in-your-face gesture to the locals. There's no doubt the cross honoring Herbin stands on the cemetery—excavations conducted when it was repaired in the 1980s located four grave shafts and nails standing in neat rows, the only remnants of the coffins they once held together. Fowler knows from Winslow's journal that the church was located to the west of the cemetery, with the priest's house, commandeered as Winslow's headquarters, separating the two. Both buildings and the cemetery were enclosed within a long wooden palisade. With those parameters in mind, Fowler has concentrated this summer's efforts on an area to the east of the Memorial Church, keeping a respectful distance from the cemetery.

He has opened a pattern of test holes at 13-foot intervals in hopes of finding evidence of the church's foundation or postholes from the surrounding palisade. He likens the process to "looking into a room through a pinhole," but if they luck out and hit something interesting, the pinhole in the earth will be expanded. A magnetic scan of the area detected a concentration of stones and other debris within a yard of the surface, not enough to indicate a structure but too much to be of natural origin. New England planters farmed this field for generations before Herbin came along, and Fowler suspects the ruins of the buildings were smashed up with plows or carted away as fill. But some evidence should remain, and his students have unearthed plenty of clues—rusted nails, brick fragments, shards of window glass, roofing slates, gobs of hardened clay that the Acadians used to fill gaps in walls, flagstones that may have served as a walkway to the church.

Fowler, who could pass for a young Tom Hanks with his boyish looks and quick one-liners, conducts his rounds to find out what has turned up. One student, his nostrils pierced with a silver ring big enough to be classified as an artefact in its own right, has found an iron shard that looks like the side of a kettle. Marble-sized musket balls, the lead aged to a whitish patina, have been found throughout the area, no doubt left behind by Winslow's soldiers. Gibson has uncovered a blackened area about the size of a dinner plate, surrounded by orange clay that stands out from the surrounding soil. Given the evidence of burning and the unnatural presence of clay, Fowler asks him to expand the excavation to one square yard. Within minutes, Gibson is brushing dirt from a hefty fragment of dark-green glass, the bottom of an onion-shaped wine bottle. Rob Ferguson, a Parks Canada archeologist assisting in the dig, takes a look and declares it to be English-made, dating from the eighteenth century. Visitors strolling by on the path that connects today's church to the Herbin cross stop to find out what the team is up to, amazed that artifacts are hidden only inches below their feet. A group of tourists from Quebec are pleasantly surprised when Ferguson hands over the chunk of the wine bottle and invites them to pass it around.

Flannery Surette has found a green glass bead as tiny and dainty as she is. A native of the Boston area with the accent to prove it, she has a knack for finding small items that would pass through the quarter-inch mesh of the screens used to sift the excavated soil. She's heading into the final year of an honors degree in religious studies and anthropology at Saint Mary's, and one of two students on the dig who has Acadian roots. She's fuzzy on the details, but her ancestors were deported and returned to southwestern Nova Scotia, which remains a Surette stronghold. But in the early 1900s, after a number of Surette men drowned in a storm that swamped their fishing boats, her great-grandmother moved from Yarmouth to Malden, Massachusetts. Her Acadian connection is a coincidence—low tuition fees, not ancestry, attracted Flannery to Nova Scotia. While she would rather be exploring some ancient site along the Mediterranean coast, this is her fourth summer on the Grand-Pré dig and the experience has brought her closer to her roots. "I'm interested in the past as a whole, and for me, archeology is a means to hand people back their past," she says, peering out from under an oversized Red Sox cap. "And it's kind of interesting having my own past handed back to me."

Fowler and his team have collected and cataloged thousands of artifacts. His goal is to display photos of them on a web site, and some will likely find a place in Grand-Pré's new interpretative center. "It has always bothered me that we never interpreted the Acadian story here," notes Ferguson, who has excavated Port-la-Joye and other Acadian sites on Prince Edward Island. Most pre-deportation sites across the Maritimes have never been pinpointed, let alone excavated, and many have been lost forever under farms, towns, highways, and shopping malls. The significant finds at Grand-Pré—the well, the cemetery, the purported ruins of the church—were all made in the 1880s by treasure hunters and antiquarians like Herbin. Their methods were as destructive as they were unscientific, and they left no field notes to guide late-comers like Fowler. A team from Acadia University in Wolfville explored a couple of Acadian cellars near the church in the 1950s and Parks Canada excavated two more houses in the 1970s, and that's about it for exploration under Grand-Pré. Most archeological work on the French regime in Nova Scotia has centered on Louisbourg, where a major reconstruction of the fortress was undertaken in the 1960s. Acadian homesteads at Belleisle, upriver from Annapolis Royal, were excavated in the 1980s and students from l'Université Sainte-Anne began follow-up work there in the summer of 2003. Meanwhile, treasure hunting continues despite heritage-protection laws. Bale seals, musket balls, and other items described as coming "from French/Acadian" sites pop up for auction on eBay from time to time, fetching a few dollars each.

Fowler has a wish list of sites he would like to check out. He has done some preliminary work at Fort Vieux Logis near Grand-Pré, a ramshackle fort the British built in 1749 to protect Halifax. He has only scratched the surface at Mission Sainte-Anne, a base for Abbé Le Loutre's Mi'kmaq raiding parties, which lies under a cornfield on the Shubenacadie River. Fowler esti-mates the remains of as many as thirty villages are scattered along the Gaspereau, Cornwallis, Canard, and Habitant Rivers, destroyed by Winslow's soldiers. "Ninety-nine percent of that material has not been even touched archeologically, not even properly surveyed," he notes, but for now, there's still plenty of work to be done in Grand-Pré. Fowler points to the ridge just south of the historic site, where local farmers have filled in a half-dozen cellars. Pre-deportation accounts describe a continuous line of farms stretching more than a mile and a half in each direction. Somewhere up there is the foundation of the house where Colonel Noble died in 1747. Remnants of the stone house that sat next door to Noble's quarters, Fowler suspects, may have found their way into the foundations of Grand-Pré's older homes. Off to the left, under an orchard, there should be a mass grave containing the bodies of the dozens of soldiers killed in the battle.

Fowler was completing an education degree at Acadia in 1996 when he happened upon a nineteenth-century reprint of Winslow's journal in the university library. When he read Winslow's vivid descriptions of places and events, he was hooked. Dammit, he remembers thinking, where is this stuff? After a side trip to England to complete a master's degree in landscape archeology, he pursued Acadian history with a vengeance. He has come to appreciate the Acadians as a sophisticated people with modern sensibilities. "The Acadians were punished for their modernity .... They were democratic and revolutionary by the standards of their day," Fowler says as he looks south to the fields dotted with the unexplored cellars of Acadian homes. "They wanted the same things that any modern person would want. They wanted the same things that became revolutionary causes later in the eighteenth century—freedom from arbitrary abuse by your government. 'Leave us alone. Let us farm. We don't want to be pressed into your military.'

"Their crime," he adds, "was that they were modern in their thinking."

Survival is on the minds of those gathered under the old French willows behind Grand-Pré's rebuilt church a couple of weeks later, as Louisiana Day winds down. Warren Perrin and about 100 others form a circle around a couple of young fiddlers from Louisiana, Blake Miller, and Brandon Moreau, who play a lament so mournful their instruments seem to weep with sadness. The late afternoon sun casts long shadows and a stiff breeze kicks up as they play, as if on cue, scattering some yellowed leaves over the listeners. Cows graze on the marsh behind them and, in the distance, Blomidon keeps its stoic vigil over Grand-Pré. The program bills the gathering as "If the Willows Could Talk," and it is a chance for people to share their thoughts and feelings about being here, or simply about being Acadian or Cajun.

When the song ends, Brenda Comeaux Trahan, from the Acadian Memorial in St. Martinville, steps forward. "*Vive l'Acadie*," someone shouts, sparking applause that is drowned out as a tractor rumbles along a marsh road behind the church. "If the willows could speak, what would they say? What would they tell us?" she asks. "Could it be that, during the times before the deportation, the Acadians may have been here partying together, playing music, eating together, saying that this was a good life, a life that they loved and appreciated? I feel the identity of Acadians, and Cajuns, is stronger than ever now, because the *congrès* brings us together. And we know that the more numbers we have, the more strength we will have in continuing our identity and getting to know who we really are."

A straw poll is taken to find out how far people have come to take part in the *congrès*. The responses are a roll call of the diaspora—Louisiana, of course, but also Texas, Massachusetts, Quebec, New Brunswick, Cape Breton, even Idaho. Shirley Thibodeaux LeBlanc, the Thibodeau family genealogist, is the first to step forward. She has been in Nova Scotia for two weeks and, in the eyes and features of the relatives she has encountered, she has seen her father, her grandfather, and herself. She noticed how the wind picked up as the fiddlers played. For her, it was "a sigh of relief from our ancestors, our forefathers. We are home. We are here. We are one. A circle has been completed today."

A man from New Brunswick moves to the center of the circle and complains about having to pay five bucks to park at the historic site. "I could have been raised here ... I had to pay to visit land that might have been mine." Another New Brunswicker invites everyone to attend the next *congrès* and hopes to see "lots more people speaking French" when Acadians and Cajuns assemble in his province, at Caraquet, in 2009. A Jewish woman from New York, whose long braids and peasant dress would blend in at any folk festival, says she's here with her partner, an Acadian. Her ancestors were from Lithuania and Poland, and many of them were lost in the Holocaust. "My people were not wanted either," she notes. "This is very beautiful."

Several speakers suggest that something is missing from this reunion. The Mi'kmaq helped the Acadians before and after the deportation and many Acadians have Native blood in their veins. Likewise, the Natives and Blacks helped the exiles who assembled in Louisiana to adapt to their new land. "They're not here today," one woman notes. "Maybe next time," she adds in French as the group applauds to signal its approval. The desire for reconciliation even extends to the English-speaking farmers who now work the fields around Grand-Pré. The final speaker tells how his son gave him a jar before he left Louisiana and asked him to bring back some earth from the land their family farmed before the deportation. It was at Starr's Point, just across the Cornwallis River from Grand-Pré. "There's an Englishman there with a large farm, but he has respect for the Acadians and he has left a little path that you can drive through, between his farmhouse and the river," the man notes. He was able to get to the area along the river where his ancestors once lived and scoop up some soil as a souvenir.

"That," he adds in a soft voice, "was a great thing for me."

EPILOGUE:
FINDING RECONCILIATION

This is a story about a landscape shared by two families with a
very unique connection to the land—and, by extension, to each
other—for more than 300 years.

—Sara Beanlands, presentation to Thibodeau family reunion,
Grand-Pré, August 1, 2004

As he stood at the crest of the hill and looked down on the river valley, Dick
Thibodeau knew the search that had consumed so many of his summer vaca-
tions was over. The sharp bend in the river matched the snaky lines on the old
surveyor's map he held in his hands. The map was drawn in 1756, a year after
Alexis Thibodeau and his family were shipped from the Piziquid area to
Philadelphia. According to the map, a cluster of five dots on the north side of
the river was the site of Village Thibodeau, with each dot representing the location of a house. The bend in the river on the map pointed directly at the dots.
The bend in the St. Croix River as it brushed past the village of Poplar Grove
was pointing directly at Dick Thibodeau. He knew he was standing on the site
of one of those dots, one of the houses of his ancestors.

Thibodeau went back to Massachusetts, back to his job as a serviceman for
a natural-gas company. He was elated at his discovery. A genealogy buff, he had
traced his family's roots from Quebec to Pennsylvania and finally to Alexis
Thibodeau in Nova Scotia. Alexis, his wife, Anna Blanchard, and their two
young sons—Simon, five, and Etienne, just three—were among the 454 people
deported to Pennsylvania. Acadians endured some of the worst conditions of

the exile there: disease, starvation, a hostile colonial government. Anna died, but no one knows when or how. Alexis then married Catherine LeBlanc, a widow with four children, in Philadelphia in 1762. Their son, Joseph, was born there in 1763. Dick Thibodeau knew all this, but what he had wanted more than anything else was to walk the land his family had farmed in Nova Scotia. In the summer of 1985, after several trips to the province in search of clues, Thibodeau stood on a hilltop within sight of the town of Windsor and the weathered blockhouse at Fort Edward, double-checked his map, and declared the mystery solved.

Eighteen years passed. Thibodeau's son was putting together material for a web site and asked his father to write something about the family's history. By this time Thibodeau was retired, living in Maine in the summer and wintering in Florida. Digging out his genealogical research rekindled his interest in Village Thibodeau. He remembered the moving experience of standing where his ancestors had stood. "A spiritual thing," he would later say as he struggled to put the feeling into words, as if his entire family history was coursing through his veins. Allen Shaw, whose family had farmed the land for seven generations, had been kind enough to show Thibodeau around back in 1985. Thibodeau looked up Shaw's phone number and gave him a call at the beginning of 2003. It was the first time they had spoken since Thibodeau's visit. They chatted for a while, but Thibodeau knew nothing more about the village and neither did Shaw. Not long afterwards, Shaw sat down to a family dinner with his sister, Hope, her husband, Gordon Beanlands, and their daughter, Sara. He happened to mention the call and recounted the story of the stranger from the States who had turned up one day searching for his ancestors' village.

Sara Beanlands was astounded. A slim brunette in her early thirties with a wide smile and enthusiasm to spare, she was the unofficial Shaw family historian and about to embark on graduate studies in history. She had spent summers on the farm as a child, and had heard stories of the French coins her grandfather sometimes turned up with his plow. The dikes along the river, she knew, had been built by the Acadians. Everyone called the winding dirt road that crossed the farm the Old French Road and, according to family tradition, it was there when their Planter ancestor, Arnold Shaw, arrived from

Rhode Island in 1760. Even the name of the 200-acre spread, Willow Brook Farm, paid homage to the Acadian willows that the earliest Shaws found on the property. But Beanlands was barely a teenager when Dick Thibodeau dropped in, and this was the first she had heard of his visit or his map of Village Thibodeau. This man, she realized, could shed light on the history of the farm before the Shaws arrived. She wrote to Thibodeau the next day, he phoned back, and they began to cobble together the 300-year history of a single farm that unites two families and two cultures.

After collaborating by phone and e-mail for more than a year, they were ready to present their findings. The Thibodeau family reunion, held at Grand-Pré as part of Congrès mondial acadien 2004, was the perfect venue. Dick Thibodeau, short and stout with a crewcut of thick gray hair, stood before more than 200 Thibodeau descendants gathered from across North America. He could barely contain his delight as he described his discovery of the village that Pierre Thibodeau and his wife, Anne Bourg, founded in 1690.

Then Beanlands, who had met Thibodeau in person only a couple of days earlier, took the stage. She stumbled at first as she worked out the glitches in her first PowerPoint presentation. She was a bit nervous, unsure how the Thibodeaus would react to having a Planter descendant lecture them on their family history. Beanlands presented slides of old maps and aerial photographs of the Shaw farm to show the exact spot where Village Thibodeau had stood. Archeologist Jonathan Fowler and his team conducted a dig on Dick Thibodeau's hilltop and found pre-deportation artifacts. Beanlands displayed photos of a clay pipe, shards of stoneware, hinges, sewing needles, and clumps of the telltale clay used to insulate Acadian homes. Then a slide of a blue-shuttered, Cape Cod–style house flashed onto the screen. It is the home of her uncle and aunt, David and Joanne Shaw, who farm half the land with her uncle Allen. According to family tradition, the house was standing when the Shaws arrived five years after the deportation. Its wide floorboards, thick stone foundation, and simple architecture were consistent with those of Acadian houses. There is strong evidence, she said, that the house escaped destruction in 1755, which would make it the only known pre-deportation Acadian house in Nova Scotia. She ended with an invitation to all the Thibodeaus to tour the farm and see the house.

Beanlands was besieged with well-wishers after her talk, and the next morning about 150 Thibodeaus showed up at the Shaw farm. They walked the Old French Road and checked out mounds flanking a brook that may be traces of a gristmill. "I feel like I'm walking on the land that my ancestors walked on," said Betty Fontenot of Opelousas, Louisiana. They descended into the basement of the Shaw house to touch the hand-hewn beams overhead and an exposed stone wall in the furnace room. They surveyed the bend in the river from the hilltop where Dick Thibodeau stood in 1985. They took photos and scooped soil into plastic bags as souvenirs. Marcel Thibodeau of Meteghan River on the French Shore had lived his whole life in Nova Scotia and never knew about the site. "They had a good life here. This was good for us to see," he told journalist Ron Thibodeaux, a descendant of Pierre Thibodeau, who wrote a heartfelt account of the reunion for his newspaper, the New Orleans *Times-Picayune*.

The family tree of every Acadian clan is a testament to the upheaval of the deportation and its tragic legacy of wasted lives. Ancestors who can be traced through church registers and other surviving records turn up in places far from Acadie. Time after time, the trail ends with a premature death. The saga of a single branch of the Thibodeaus tells the tale of death, separation, and loss that befell every family.

Marie Thibodeau married Antoine Landry in Grand-Pré about 1681. Their oldest son, Antoine, and his wife, Marie Blanche LeBlanc, were about seventy years of age when they were deported from the Chignecto area. Both died in Boston sometime after 1755. One of the couple's sons, Jean-Baptiste, ended up in France. Another son, Pierre, was sent to Philadelphia. Five of Marie Thibodeau and Antoine Landry's other children—Anne, Francois, Francoise, Germain, and Jean—made their way to Quebec, where they lived out their lives. Their youngest son, Joseph, was deported to Maryland with his wife and five young children. Joseph died sometime before 1769, likely in Louisiana. His widow, Marie, died in Louisiana's Ascension Parish in 1792. The fate of two of Marie Thibodeau's other grandchildren is also known.

Charles Hebert ended up in France, where his first wife, Marguerite LeBlanc, died in the late 1750s while still in her forties. Another grandson, Basile Landry, was in his late twenties at the time of the deportation and reached St. Martinville, Louisiana, by 1786, likely by way of France.

A nephew, Joseph LeJeune, and his wife, Cecile, were on their way to France when they died at sea in December 1758. The couple was among the thousands deported from Île Saint-Jean and had the misfortune to be on either the *Violet* or the *Duke William*, the transports that sank off the coast of England with 700 aboard. He was fifty-four, she was fifty. Another nephew, Augustine Robichaud, was in his mid-sixties when he died in March 1759 in a hospital in St. Malo, one of the many who survived that crossing but succumbed to disease once in France. Augustine's younger brother, Francois, died two months later, also in France. Another of Marie Thibodeau's nephews, Germain Thibodeau, was sent to Virginia and re-deported to England, where he died in Falmouth in 1756 while still in his late forties. Two of her nieces, Agnes and Marguerite Thibodeau, married Acadian resistance leaders Beausoleil and Alexandre Broussard. They accompanied their husbands to Louisiana, where the Broussard brothers and Marguerite Thibodeau died of yellow fever in 1765. About a dozen of Marie Thibodeau's other nephews and nieces are known to have died in Quebec, France, or Louisiana. Many more of these third-generation Thibodeaus died in exile sometime before the Treaty of Paris was signed in 1763. How, when, and where remain a mystery.

The Thibodeaus survived and thrived despite the scourge of the deportation. The descendants of the Pierre Thibodeau who founded Village Thibodeau now number in the tens of thousands. And the family has even made its peace with the descendants of the family of one of the soldiers who played a pivotal role in the deportation. Page Thibodeaux, a retired accountant from Orinda, California, came to the family reunion at Grand-Pré with a fascinating story of chance and coincidence. His great-grandfather fled Louisiana after the Civil War and his family tried to shake off its Acadian roots. They were reborn as Frenchmen from New Orleans and when Page married Ginnie Cobb fifty years ago, neither of them knew much about their ancestry. "Had we done our genealogy ahead of time," he joked, "maybe we would not have been married." They named their son Page Winslow Thibodeaux, finding the middle name in Ginnie's family tree—her great-grandmother was a Winslow—and thinking it sounded better than Cobb. Years later, they discovered that one of Ginnie's ancestors was the brother of John Winslow, who deported so many of Page's ancestors in 1755.

The rediscovered Village Thibodeau is as good a place as any to speculate about what might have been. What if the events that hurtled toward Lawrence's July 28, 1755 expulsion order had veered in another direction, and the Acadians had remained on their lands? There are any number of points in the Acadian saga where a single decision or event could have dramatically altered the outcome. A stronger British show of force after the conquest of 1710 may well have won over the Acadians by degrees—that was the belief of Mascarene and other officers on the ground at Annapolis Royal. Consider the implications for the region if London had supplied the 600 redcoats Philipps sought in 1720, or founded Halifax decades earlier. The Mi'kmaq threat within Nova Scotia and the French threat on the borders could have been kept in check and, at the very least, it would have been clear that the British meant business. The Acadians would have been forced to choose between swearing allegiance or emigrating, as provided under the terms of the Treaty of Utrecht. For that matter, what if Philipps had not duped the Acadians as well as his superiors a decade later when he extracted the oath exempting the Acadians from military service? The Lords of Trade believed the issue had been settled, and the Acadians were under the impression their claim of neutrality would be respected. Philipps's deceit lulled both sides into a false sense of security until war broke out in the 1740s. The attacks on Fort Anne, the massacre of Noble's troops at Grand-Pré, and Acadian collusion, real and imagined, meant there was no going back. The treason of a few Acadians branded the entire population as untrustworthy and potential fifth columnists.

Even the founding of Halifax in 1749 did not seal the Acadians' fate. The challenges were the same as after the conquest—securing the colony and asserting that British rule was here to stay. Once again, London dropped the ball. Cornwallis did not have enough troops to secure the borders and guard Halifax, let alone to protect the Acadians from Native reprisals if they swore allegiance. But the British were unwilling to budge on the demand for an unconditional oath, leaving no room for negotiation with an Acadian population that had embraced surprisingly modern processes of consultation and negotiation; a nation governed by committee faced an empire that recognized only loyalty and obedience. But the impasse over the oath did not make deportation inevitable. While Lawrence and his cheerleader Belcher manipulated the threat of war to make it look inevitable, there was simply no need, strategic or otherwise, to press for unconditional allegiance in 1755. An oath would not have made the colony suddenly more secure, nor would it have enabled the British to sleep better at night. The fall of Beauséjour put the French on the run and left Nova Scotia more secure than it had been in years. What the British really needed was Acadian neutrality and, if they had been able to see beyond their own prejudices and distrust, they would have realized the vast majority of Acadians had been true to that pledge.

To say so is not to fall into the trap of imposing modern values on an earlier era. It is a matter of reducing a complex situation to its essential elements. Pose the question this way: if Mascarene had been in charge, would he have deported the Acadians without London's explicit authorization? Would Cornwallis or Hopson, for that matter? Only Lawrence possessed the toxic mixture of ambition, inflexibility, cruelty, and arrogance needed to conceive and execute such a plan of his own volition. The accidents of history put him in charge at a pivotal moment. Would the Acadians have been deported if Lawrence had died on the battlefield at Fontenoy? If Hopson's health had improved and he had remained governor? Even with Lawrence in office, the expulsion was not inevitable. If Vergor and his garrison had held Beauséjour for a few more weeks, even until the end of June, it might have been too late for Lawrence or anyone else to entertain thoughts of a full-scale deportation in 1755. As it was, the operation was barely completed before winter set in. The deportation became possible only when Lawrence emerged as a governor determined to achieve a final solution to the Acadian problem, regardless of the cost. It became inevitable only when the swift capitulation of Beauséjour gave Lawrence the soldiers, ships, and time required to undertake the massive operation. The defeat also handed him the pretext he needed—hundreds of Acadian collaborators—to sell his plan to his council, the visiting admirals, and, ultimately, to the Lords of Trade.

Imagine, then, Nova Scotia in the spring of 1756 with the Thibodeaus of Village Thibodeau and all the other Acadian families still on their farms, gearing up for spring planting. Britain and France are at war, but Chignecto is in British hands, much of the Bay of Fundy has been secured, and Louisbourg is cut off from a major source of provisions. While Boishébert and the Broussards wage a campaign from their base in southern New Brunswick, their forays do not pose a serious threat to the colony's security. Since there has been no deportation, there are few Acadians bitter enough and desperate enough to join Boishébert's resistance force. The British have backed down on demands for an oath of allegiance for the time being, and their restraint has been rewarded with continued Acadian neutrality. A few hotheads defect now and then to the French territories or help the French and Mi'kmaq marauders. A new war tugs at old loyalties and strains new ones, but the overwhelming majority of Acadians cling to the middle ground and choose peace. With the French on their heels, some Acadians may even feel secure enough to stand up to the insurgents in order to bring peace to their villages. Louisbourg and Île Saint-Jean would have fallen in 1758, followed by Quebec in 1759 and all of New France the following year. The victories, historian John Reid has argued, made the Acadians' presence in Nova Scotia "irrelevant" from a military standpoint. Acadian communities were destroyed "in the interests of a military strategy which was already questionable when implemented and which ceased to matter at all within five years." It is, perhaps, unrealistic to expect a military man like Lawrence to envision Nova Scotia as a joint British–Acadian colonial enterprise. As he mused a year before the deportation, it was better "that they were away." To his mind, deportation was the only solution, and as soon as he had the chance he pursued that goal with ruthless efficiency.

Had there been no deportation, the map of Canada and the United States would have been redrawn and history rewritten. The Acadians were in a majority position in 1755 and, had it not been for the deportation, they were destined to become the predominant ethnic group on Canada's East Coast.

One needs only to do the math: if the population had continued to double every twenty-five years, demographers estimated there would have been more than 7.5 million Acadians by 1975. That figure would have doubled again, to some 15 million, by the year 2000. While such calculations fail to make allowances for wars, epidemics, and declining birthrates, Acadian descendants would number several times the 3 million now scattered around the globe. Even after allowing for the North American trend of westward migration in search of land and jobs, French-speaking Canadians would now enjoy majority status in all provinces east of Ontario, with the exception of Newfoundland.

Canada would have emerged as a country split down the middle, predominantly French in the east and English in the west. The Atlantic provinces might have developed much like Quebec, where British administrators were forced to accommodate a French-speaking Catholic majority after the conquest. The challenges would have been daunting, as they were in Quebec, but the experiment could have worked on the Atlantic coast as it did along the banks of the St. Lawrence River. Nova Scotia's two founding peoples would have been forced to accommodate their religious and language differences in a bilingual society much like the one that evolved in New Brunswick, but strike gumbo and jambalaya from the menus of the world and edit the term *laissez les bons temps rouler* from the tourist guides. The Cajuns would not exist and neither would the half-million Americans who trace their ancestry to the Acadian exiles. The southern Louisiana of today would still be a melting pot of French, Spanish, and African cultures, but without its distinctive Cajun twist.

That was what might have been. The clash of empires and the ruthlessness of Charles Lawrence dictated a more brutal and tragic fate. But deportation and exile could not destroy the Acadians. They fought back with the only weapons they had—strong faith and even stronger family ties, tenacity, and a powerful sense of themselves as a nation and as a people. One year shy of the 250th anniversary of the deportation, on a summer morning on Willow Brook Farm, two families—one English, one Acadian and Cajun—came together on the land that nurtured them both. As the Shaws showed the Thibodeaus around, two seven-year-old boys ran along the Old French Road. Austin Shaw had found a new playmate—Page Ryan Thibodeaux, the grandson of Page and Ginnie

Thibodeaux of California and a flesh-and-blood reconciliation between the Thibodeaus and the Winslows. As she watched them laugh and toss pebbles at one another, something dawned on Sara Beanlands. After all the pain, under the weight of so much history, who could have imagined this? A little Thibodeau boy and a little Shaw boy playing together. The laughter of children once again rippling across the fields of Piziquid, just as it did before that dark summer of 1755.

NOTES ON SOURCES AND SUGGESTIONS FOR FURTHER READING

It is impossible to visit Nova Scotia—or to grow up here, as I did—without being acutely aware of the deportation of the Acadians. This province was built on the ruins of the Acadie that Charles Lawrence tried so hard to eradicate. Highway signs for places like Grand-Pré and Belleisle are silent reminders of the province's Acadian past; communities like Chéticamp, Pubnico, and the French Shore are proof of its continued, vibrant presence.

My real introduction to the deportation and exile of the Acadians, though, began in the late 1970s when I was an undergraduate student in Canadian history at Mount Allison University in Sackville, New Brunswick. Sackville is one of the many English communities that rose from the ashes of Acadie, and the town and campus lie at the northern edge of the Chignecto marshes, within sight of Fort Beauséjour. By then, I knew the basic facts of what happened in 1755—thousands were deported, an appalling number succumbed to disease and shipwreck, and many exiles returned to found new communities. But I did not fully appreciate the nightmare the Acadians endured, or the remarkable story of their survival as a people, until I dug beneath the surface to write a paper on their years in exile for a Mount Allison history course.

My starting point then, and for this book, was the insightful work of historian Naomi Griffiths. Her book *The Acadians: Creation of a People* (Toronto: McGraw-Hill Ryerson Ltd., 1973) remains perhaps the best introduction to Acadian history. Griffiths argues persuasively that the Acadians evolved into a distinct people before 1755, giving them a sense of community that was strong enough to survive the disruption of exile. Her essay "The Acadians" in the *Dictionary of Canadian Biography*, vol. 4, 1771–1800 (Toronto: University of Toronto Press, 1979), pp. xvii–xxxi, fleshes out her argument and the details of Acadian history. Lectures that Griffiths delivered while a visiting professor at Mount Allison were published in 1992 as *The Contexts of Acadian History, 1686–1784* (Montreal and Kingston: McGill–Queen's University Press). As the title suggests, the book fits the Acadian story into the context of colonial and imperial history.

The American historian Francis Parkman produced some of the first scholarly accounts of the deportation, but readers must be wary of his pro-English bias. *Montcalm and Wolfe* (New York, Collier Books, 1962), originally published in 1884, argues that French meddling and Acadian stubbornness forced Lawrence to order the expulsion. I also consulted Parkman's article "The Acadian Tragedy," which appeared in 1884 in *Harper's New Monthly Magazine*, vol. 64, no. 414, pp. 877–886. A New Brunswick writer, James Hannay, argued the deportation was justified in *The History of Acadia, 1605–1763* (Saint John: J. & A. McMillan), published in 1879. Adams G. Archibald, a retired Nova Scotia politician, weighed in with a rebuttal to Henry Wadsworth Longfellow's poem *Evangeline: A Tale of Acadie* in an address to the Nova Scotia Historical Society. His paper, "The Expulsion of the Acadians," was published in the *Collections of the Nova Scotia Historical Society*, vol. V, 1886–1887, pp. 11–95. These portrayals of the Acadians as the authors of their own misfortune came under fire in 1895 from Edouard Richard, whose two-volume work *Acadia: Missing Links of a Lost Chapter in American History* (New York: Home Book Company) is a passionate reassessment of events from an Acadian viewpoint. Archivist and historian Arthur G. Doughty took an objective approach in *The Acadian Exiles: A Chronicle of the Land of Evangeline* (Toronto: Glasgow, Brook & Company, 1921). Doughty's account is worth consulting even though it is dated and, at times, unreliable—

he failed to detect, for instance, that Governor Richard Philipps misled his superiors about the oath of allegiance the Acadians swore in 1730. Charles D. Mahaffie Jr.'s *A Land of Discord Always: Acadia from Its Beginning to the Expulsion of Its People, 1604–1755* (Camden: Down East Books, 1995) offers the general reader an even-handed account of events leading up to the deportation. Clarence-J. d'Entremont, a priest who moonlighted as a writer and historian, published 100 articles on Acadian history in the Yarmouth weekly newspaper *The Vanguard*, in 1989 and 1990. They are available on the web site of the Acadian Museum and Archives in West Pubnico: http://www.museeacadien.ca/english/archives/articles/index.htm.

Many contemporary records relating to the deportation and exile have been published, including the minutes of the Nova Scotia council and letters the Lords of Trade and Plantations exchanged with Lawrence and other governors. T.B. Akins, *Selections from the Public Documents of the Province of Nova Scotia* (Halifax: Charles Annand, 1869), was compiled to challenge the fictional liberties Longfellow took when he published *Evangeline* in 1847. Even though Akins was a prominent apologist for Lawrence, a surprising amount of incriminating material, including letters proving that the Lords of Trade advised against the deportation, survived his heavy-handed editing. In any event, the full minutes of the council's dealing with the Acadians under British rule, from 1710 until the 1760s, have been preserved. Minutes of pre-1749 sessions can be accessed through the web site of Nova Scotia Archives and Records Management: http://www.gov.ns.ca/nsarm/Acadian.asp.

The Public Archives of Canada (now known as the National Archives of Canada) compiled hundreds of Acadian records drawn from archives in Canada, the United States, and France in *Report Concerning Canadian Archives for the Year 1905*, vol. 2 (Ottawa: Public Archives of Canada, 1906). The collection includes documents missing from Akins, chief among them Jonathan Belcher's legal opinion supporting the deportation and William Shirley's 1747 proclamation reassuring Acadians they were safe from expulsion if they remained loyal. The report also reproduces letters and petitions that capture, in vivid detail, how the exiles were treated in Massachusetts. Naomi Griffiths edited a collection of accounts of the deportation, *The Acadian Deportation: Deliberate Perfidy or Cruel Necessity?* (Toronto: Copp Clark Publishing, 1969), which combines excerpts from contemporary records with the assessments of later writers and historians, both French and English.

Historian John G. Reid examined the troubled history of Acadie before the conquest in *Acadia, Maine and New Scotland: Marginal Colonies in the Seventeenth Century* (Toronto: University of Toronto Press, 1981). Reid shows how infighting and imperial neglect hindered the development of Acadie during the colony's first century. M.A. MacDonald's *Fortune and La Tour: The Civil War in Acadia* (Halifax: Nimbus Publishing, 2000), originally published in 1983, offers a popular account of the destructive rivalry between La Tour and d'Aulnay. *Champlain: The Life of Fortitude* by Morris Bishop (Toronto: McClelland & Stewart, 1963), was originally published in 1948 but remains a good overview of the early years of French colonization and life at the Port-Royal Habitation. Griffiths has produced the best overview of life in Acadie before the deportation. Her article "The Golden Age: Acadian Life, 1713–1748," appeared in the journal *Histoire sociale—Social History*, vol. 17, no. 33 (mai–May 1984), pp. 21–34. Brenda Dunn, a retired Parks Canada historian, brings Acadie's oldest community to life in *A History of Port-Royal/Annapolis Royal, 1605–1800* (Halifax: Nimbus, 2004). Gisa Hynes, "Some Aspects of the Demography of Port Royal, 1650–1755," *Acadiensis: The Journal of the History of the Atlantic Region*, vol. 3, no. 1 (Autumn 1973), pp. 3–17, examines life and family structure in the community. To understand how the Acadians farmed, built dikes, and expanded their settlements along the Bay of Fundy, see Andrew Hill Clark, *Acadia: The Geography of Early Nova Scotia to 1760* (Madison: The University of Wisconsin Press, 1968). The Société Promotion Grand-Pré published *Dykes and Aboiteaux: The Acadians Turned Salt Marshes into Fertile Meadows*, a 2002 booklet in which writer Sally Ross explains how the Acadians reclaimed the Fundy marshes. Another of the société's booklets, Susan Surette-Draper's *Return to Acadie: A Self-Guided Memory Walk of the Annapolis Valley*, published in 2004, pinpoints the locations of Acadie's lost villages. A translation of Sieur de Dièreville's *Relation of the Voyage to Port Royal in Acadia or New France*—offering his insights into Acadian life, circa 1700—was published by the Toronto-based Champlain Society in 1933. For an overview of Acadian settlement on Île Saint-Jean, see Rob Ferguson, "The Search for Port La Joye: Archaeology at Île Saint-Jean's

First French Settlement," *The Island Magazine*, no. 27 (Spring/Summer 1990), pp. 3–8.

The most detailed contemporary account of the fall of Port-Royal is the "Journal of Colonel Nicholson at the Capture of Annapolis, 1710," which appeared in the *Collections of the Nova Scotia Historical Society*, vol. I (1878), pp. 59–104. For insights into the Annapolis Royal regime's struggle to win the hearts and minds of the Acadians, see Thomas Garden Barnes, "'The Dayly Cry for Justice': The Juridical Failure of the Annapolis Royal Regime, 1713–1749," published in Philip Girard and Jim Phillips, eds., *Essays in the History of Canadian Law: Volume III, Nova Scotia* (Toronto: The Osgoode Society, 1990), pp. 10–41. Columbia University historian John Bartlet Brebner's *New England's Outpost: Acadia before the Conquest of Canada* (New York: Columbia University Press, 1927) remains the definitive account of Acadie under British rule. It should be read in tandem with George A. Rawlyk's *Nova Scotia's Massachusetts: A Study of Massachusetts–Nova Scotia Relations, 1630–1784* (Montreal and London: McGill–Queen's University Press, 1973), which challenges Brebner's assertions about New England's hegemony over Nova Scotia and Governor Shirley's duplicity in the deportation. For a recent reassessment of the British takeover and the influence wielded by the Mi'kmaq, see John G. Reid, Maurice Basque, Elizabeth Mancke, Barry Moody, Geoffrey Plank, and William Wicken, *The "Conquest" of Acadia, 1710: Imperial, Colonial, and Aboriginal Constructions* (Toronto: University of Toronto Press, 2004).

Rawlyk and Brebner examine the pivotal decade of the 1740s when the War of the Austrian Succession tested Acadian loyalty—and both the British and the French found it wanting. The North American military campaigns are also recounted in George F.G. Stanley, *New France: The Last Phase, 1744–1760* (Toronto: McClelland & Stewart, 1968), and in W.J. Eccles, *France in America* (New York: Harper & Row, 1972). Brebner and Rawlyk did not always see eye to eye, but Rawlyk saw fit to include Brebner's sympathetic profile of Paul Mascarene when he edited *Historical Essays on the Atlantic Provinces* (Toronto: McClelland & Stewart, 1967); Brebner's article, "Paul Mascarene of Annapolis Royal," appears on pp. 17–32. Barnes produced an insightful account of how Mascarene and Shirley dealt with Acadian collaborators: "'Twelve Apostles' or a Dozen Traitors? Acadian Collaborators During King George's War, 1744–8," published in F. Murray Greenwood and Barry Wright, eds., *Canadian State Trials, Volume I: Law, Politics, and Security Measures, 1608–1837* (Toronto: University of Toronto Press, 1997), pp. 98–113. Parkman's *A Half-Century of Conflict* (New York: Collier Books, 1962), originally published 1892, contains a blow-by-blow account of the battle of Grand-Pré in 1747. Norman McLeod Rogers, "The Abbé Le Loutre," *Canadian Historical Review*, vol. XI, no. 2 (June 1930), pp. 105–128, provides one of the few objective treatments of the reviled "black priest" who terrorized the Acadians and the British.

The founding of Halifax is recounted in Akins, "History of Halifax City," published in the *Collections of the Nova Scotia Historical Society*, vol. VIII (1892–1894), pp. 3–317. While Akins describes Belcher's elaborate swearing-in as chief justice, see as well the account in Beamish Murdoch's *A History of Nova Scotia, or Acadie* (Halifax: James Barnes, 1865), vol. 2, pp. 250–251. Belcher's tenure as chief justice and lieutenant governor are examined in Barry Cahill and Jim Phillips, "The Supreme Court of Nova Scotia: Origins to Confederation," which appears in Philip Girard, Phillips and Cahill, eds., *The Supreme Court of Nova Scotia 1754–2004: From Imperial Bastion to Provincial Oracle* (Toronto: University of Toronto Press, 2004), pp. 53–139. The same collection contains an article by Phillips and James Muir, "Michaelmas Term 1754: The Supreme Court's First Session," pp. 259–293, which records Belcher's courtroom tirade demanding blind loyalty to the British Crown. There are several first-person accounts of the capture of Fort Beauséjour, the battle that sealed the fate of the Acadians. John Clarence Webster, a former curator of the museum at the site, edited *The Siege of Beauséjour in 1755: A Journal of the Attack on Beauséjour, Written by Jacau de Fiedmont* (Saint John: The New Brunswick Museum, 1936). Webster also oversaw the publication of *Journals of Beauséjour: Diary of John Thomas, Journal of Louis de Courville* (Halifax: Public Archives of Nova Scotia, 1937). Thomas's diary was first published in *Collections of the Nova Scotia Historical Society*, vol. I (1879), pp. 119–140. Transcripts of Commandant Vergor's court martial—filled with evidence of the Acadians' reluctance to fight—were published in "Papers re: Bigot, Vergor and Villeray," *Report Concerning Canadian Archives for the Year 1904* (Ottawa: Public Archives of Canada, 1905), Appendix G, pp. 303–321.

Lieutenant Colonel John Winslow, an unwilling conscript in the war against the Acadians, left a detailed and sensitive account of the deportation. His diary recording events at Grand-Pré, Piziquid, and Chignecto was published in the *Collections of the Nova Scotia Historical Society*, vol. III (1882–1883), pp. 71–196, and vol. IV (1884), pp. 113–246. See also *Lt. Col. John Winslow's List of the Acadians in the Grand-Pré Area in 1755* (Société Promotion Grand-Pré, 2002). Webster edited the *Journal of Abijah Willard 1755*, which records Willard's role in the deportation and was reprinted from the *Collections of the New Brunswick Historical Society*, no. 13 (1952). The story of Charles Belliveau's mutiny on the *Pembroke* is retold in Placide Gaudet, "Charles Belliveau et les siens durant la Déportation et après: Prises de bateau anglais par les Acadiens (1)," *Cahiers*, La Société Historique Acadienne 30, vol. 3, no. 10 (1971), pp. 388–397. Earle Lockerby's "The Deportation of the Acadians from Ile St.-Jean, 1758," *Acadiensis*, vol. 27, no. 2 (Spring 1998), pp. 45–94, corrects many misconceptions about this replay of the original expulsion. Unfortunately, he fails to question the callousness of British commanders who gambled with the lives of 3,000 civilians sent across the Atlantic at the most hazardous time of the year. George Winslow Barrington, "Remarkable Voyages & Shipwrecks: Loss of the *Duke William* on the Atlantic Ocean," was reprinted in *Cahiers*, La Société Historique Acadienne 18, vol. 2, no. 8 (Jan.–Feb.–Mar. 1968), pp. 286–299. The loss of 700 Acadians aboard the *Violet* and *Duke William* is also recounted in "A Remarkable Circumstance Respecting the French Neutrals of the Island of St. John, Related by Capt. Pile of the Ship 'Achilles'," *Collections of the Nova Scotia Historical Society*, vol. II (1881), pp. 148–149.

The experiences of the exiles on three continents are recorded in Carl A. Brasseaux, *"Scattered to the Wind": Dispersal and Wanderings of the Acadians, 1755–1809*, Louisiana Life Series, no. 6. (Lafayette: The Center for Louisiana Studies, 1991). Robert G. LeBlanc's "The Acadian Migrations," *Canadian Geographical Journal*, vol. 81, no. 1 (July 1970), pp. 10–19, provides an overview of their destinations. Bona Arsenault's *History of the Acadians* (Quebec: L'Action Sociale Ltée, 1966) recounts the experiences of the exiles at each destination. Griffiths's article "Petitions of Acadian Exiles, 1755–1785: A Neglected Resource," *Histoire sociale–Social History*, vol. 11, no. 21 (Mai-May 1978), pp. 215–223, provides insights into the Acadians' reaction to their plight. Evidence of how the exiles kept in touch with far-flung family and friends is produced in Brasseaux's "Phantom Letters: Acadian Correspondence, 1766–1784," *Acadiensis*, vol. 23, no. 2 (Spring 1994), pp. 124–133. The shabby treatment of the deportees in Pennsylvania is described in William B. Reed, *The Acadians Exiles, or French Neutrals, in Pennsylvania* (Philadelphia: J.B. Lippincott & Co., 1858). Descriptions of the American colonies at the time of the deportation were drawn from the following sources: Paul S. Boyer, ed., *The Oxford Companion to United States History* (New York: Oxford University Press, 2001); Louis B. Wright, *The Cultural Life of the American Colonies, 1607–1763* (New York: Harper & Brothers, 1957); H.W. Brands, *The First American: The Life and Times of Benjamin Franklin* (New York: Anchor Books, 2000). Two scholarly articles examine the Acadians' detention in England: Naomi Griffiths, "Acadians in Exile: the Experiences of the Acadians in the British Seaports," *Acadiensis*, vol. 4, no. 1 (Autumn 1974), pp. 67–84, and Dorothy Vinter, "The Acadian Exiles in England 1756–1763," *Dalhousie Review*, vol. 36, no. 4 (Winter 1957), pp. 344–353. Oscar Winzerling's *Acadian Odyssey* (Baton Rouge: Louisiana State University Press, 1955) tells the story of the exiles who endured poverty in France before setting out for Louisiana in 1785. Griffiths, "The Acadians Who Had a Problem in France," *Canadian Geographic*, vol. 101, no. 4 (August/September 1981), pp. 40–45, describes the failed attempt to resettle exiles on Belle-Île-en-Mer.

Details of the guerrilla war fought after the deportation and the plight of escapees were gleaned from several sources. For an early account grounded in contemporary documents, see Will R. Bird, *A Century at Chignecto: The Key to Old Acadia* (Toronto: The Ryerson Press, 1928). W.O. Raymond's *History of the River St. John* (Saint John: 1905) recounts the *Pembroke* mutiny, the 1759 massacre at St. Ann's, and the appalling conditions of the refugee camp on the Miramichi River. Dianne Marshall, *Georges Island: The Keep of Halifax Harbour* (Halifax: Nimbus Publishing, 2003), offers details of the detention of the Broussards and other resistance leaders who surrendered after the fall of New France. Accounts of the follow-up deportations of Acadians from Nova Scotia's south coast are found in J.S. Martell, "The Second Expulsion of the Acadians," *Dalhousie Review*, vol. 13, no. 3 (October 1933), pp. 359–371, and

"Major Morris Report: His Raid from Pubnico to Chegoggin—1758." *Cahiers*, La Société Historique Acadienne 17, vol. 2, no. 7 (December 1967), pp. 259–272. The death and funeral of Lawrence and Belcher's stormy tenure as lieutenant governor are described in Brebner's *The Neutral Yankees of Nova Scotia: A Marginal Colony During the Revolutionary Years* (Toronto: McClelland & Stewart, 1969), originally published in 1937.

The *Neutral Yankees* also tackles Montagu Wilmot's tenure as governor and the return of the exiles in the 1760s. The full story of the establishment of Clare, Pubnico, Chéticamp, and other new Acadian communities is told in Sally Ross and Alphonse Deveau, *The Acadians of Nova Scotia: Past and Present* (Halifax: Nimbus Publishing, 1992). Journalist Merilyn Simonds offers a thumbnail sketch of the history of Clare in her article "The French Shore," published in *Canadian Geographic*, vol. 117, no. 1 (January/February 1997), pp. 40–48. "Église Saint-Bernard/Saint Bernard Church," an undated pamphlet printed by Sentinel Printing Ltd. of Yarmouth, tells the story of the thirty-two-year effort to build the stone cathedral that stands as a monument to Acadian perseverence. *The Acadians of the Maritimes: Thematic Studies* (Moncton: Centre d'études acadiennes, 1982), edited by Jean Daigle, is a collection of essays on the resurgence of the Acadians in Nova Scotia, New Brunswick, and Prince Edward Island. Daigle covers much of the same ground in succinct fashion in "The Acadians: A People in Search of a Country," which appeared in Raymond Breton and Pierre Savard, eds., *The Quebec and Acadian Diaspora in North America* (Toronto: The Multicultural History Society of Ontario, 1982). Griffiths offers her insights into the cultural revival of the Acadians in "Acadian Identity: The Creation and Re-creation of Community," *Dalhousie Review*, vol. 73, no. 3 (Fall 1993), pp. 325–349. The story of how the Acadians adopted their flag, anthem, and patron saint is found in Perry Biddiscombe, "'Le Tricolore et l'étoile': The Origin of the Acadian National Flag, 1867–1912," *Acadiensis*, vol. 20, no. 1 (Autumn 1990), pp. 120–147. How an American writer's fictional heroine became an enduring symbol of Acadian pride is explained in Griffiths's article "Longfellow's *Evangeline*: The Birth and Acceptance of a Legend," *Acadiensis*, vol. 11, no. 2 (Spring 1982), pp. 28–41. Barbara Le Blanc tackles the same topic in greater detail in *Postcards from Acadie: Grand-Pré, Evangeline & The Acadian Identity* (Kentville: Gaspereau

Press, 2003). There are hundreds of editions of the rambling poem that introduced millions of people around the world to the Acadian story, or at least Longfellow's embellished version. I relied on a souvenir edition that includes a useful introduction written by Nova Scotia archivist C. Bruce Fergusson (Halifax: H.H. Marshall, 1956).

Perhaps no aspect of Acadian history is more clouded in mythology than the migrations to Louisiana from the American colonies and France. Carl Brasseaux separated fact from fiction in *The Founding of New Acadia: The Beginnings of Acadian Life in Louisiana, 1765–1803* (Baton Rouge and London: Louisiana State University Press, 1987). A condensed version of his findings was published in the article "A New Acadia: The Acadian Migrations to South Louisiana, 1764–1803," *Acadiensis*, vol. 15, no. 1 (Autumn 1985), pp. 123–132. Brasseaux examined how the exiles adapted to their new surroundings in *Acadian to Cajun: Transformation of a People, 1803–1877* (Jackson and London: University of Mississippi Press, 1992). Lafayette journalist Jim Bradshaw popularized Cajun history in *Our Acadiana: A Pictorial History of South Louisiana* (Lafayette: Thomson South Louisiana Publishing, 1999). Another journalist, William Faulkner Rushton, tackled Cajun history and culture in *The Cajuns: From Acadia to Louisiana* (New York: Farrar Straus Giroux, 1979). Shane K. Bernard's insightful and meticulous *The Cajuns: Americanization of a People* (Jackson: University of Mississippi Press, 2003) examines the assimilation of the Cajuns into mainstream American life after the Second World War. Griffin Smith Jr.'s article "The Cajuns: Still Loving Life," *National Geographic*, vol. 178, no. 4 (October 1990), pp. 40–65, celebrates the resilience of Cajun culture. In "Culture at a Crossroads: Cajuns Strive to Preserve Their Way of Life," a three-part series published in the New Orleans *Times-Picayune* on July 15–17, 2001, staff writers Ron Thibodeaux and Angela Rozas paint a less optimistic picture of the prospects for the survival of Cajun culture in the new millennium. Warren Perrin describes his fourteen-year battle to win the Royal Proclamation in *Acadian Redemption: From Beausoleil Broussard to the Queen's Royal Proclamation* (Erath: Acadian Heritage and Cultural Foundation, 2004). For the full text of the petition, Perrin's legal brief, and media accounts of his campaign, consult his web site: http://www.acadianmuseum.com/petition.html. I obtained the

Canadian government's file on the petition and the proclamation, complete with legal opinions and cabinet briefing notes, through an application under the Access to Information Act.

The best source of biographical information on the people caught up in the deportation, heroes and villains alike, is the multi-volume *Dictionary of Canadian Biography*, a massive work in progress first published by the University of Toronto Press in 1966. A fully searchable on-line edition is available at http://www.biographi.ca/EN/. *The Macmillan Dictionary of Canadian Biography*, 3rd ed., edited by W. Stewart Wallace (Toronto: Macmillan of Canada, 1973), provides snapshots of many of the historians who have written about the Acadians. For more information about the village that symbolizes the expulsion, see A.J.B. Johnston and W.P. Kerr, *Grand-Pré: Heart of Acadie* (Halifax: Nimbus Publishing/Société Promotion Grand-Pré, 2004). A French travel writer, George Nestler Tricoche, provides an entertaining account of a Depression-era trip through the Land of Evangeline in *Rambles through the Maritime Provinces of Canada: A Neglected Part of the British Empire* (London: Arthur H. Stockwell, Ltd., c.1930). John Frederic Herbin's *The History of Grand-Pré: The Home of Longfellow's Evangeline*, first published in 1910, remains in print (Wolfville: Herbin's Jewellers, 2003) and offers insights into the man who preserved the site of the church of Saint-Charles-des-Mines as an Acadian shrine. Genealogies helped trace the stories of Acadian families and individuals, among them Margaret C. Melanson, *The Melanson Story: Acadian Family, Acadian Times* (Toronto: 2003); William D. Gerrior's five-volume *Acadian Awakenings* series (Brookside: Port Royal Publishing, 2003); and Shirley Thibodeaux LeBlanc's genealogy of the descendants of Pierre Thibodeau, published on CD-ROM. There is no shortage of examples of school textbooks and popular histories that perpetuated the image of the Acadians as ignorant peasants. I consulted three: I. Gammell, *History of Canada* (Toronto: W.J. Gage & Company, Ltd., 1923); John B. Calkin's *A Brief History of Canada: Nova Scotia Edition* (Halifax: A. & W. Mackinlay, Ltd., 1907); and James Bingay's *A History of Canada for High Schools* (Toronto: Thomas Nelson and Sons, Ltd., 1934).

INDEX